War has traditionally been studied as a problem deriving from the relations between states. Strategic doctrines, arms control agreements, and the foundations of international organizations such as the United Nations, are designed to prevent wars between states. Since 1945, however, the incidence of interstate war has actually been declining rapidly, while the incidence of internal wars has been increasing. The author argues that in order to understand this significant change in historical patterns, we should jettison many of the analytical devices derived from international relations studies and shift attention to the problems of "weak" states: those states unable to sustain domestic legitimacy and peace. This book surveys some of the foundations of state legitimacy and demonstrates why many weak states will be the locales of war in the future. Finally, the author asks what the United Nations can do about the problems of weak and failed states.

CAMBRIDGE STUDIES IN INTERNATIONAL RELATIONS: 51

The state, war, and the state of war

CAMBRIDGE STUDIES IN INTERNATIONAL RELATIONS

Series list continues after index

The state, war,
and the state of war

K. J. Holsti

Department of Political Science
University of British Columbia

Published by the Press Syndicate of the University of Cambridge
The Pitt Building, Trumpington Street, Cambridge CB2 1RP
40 West 20th Street, New York, NY 10011–4211, USA
10 Stamford Road, Oakleigh, Melbourne 3166, Australia

© Kalevi J. Holsti 1996

First published 1996

Printed in Great Britain at the University Press, Cambridge

A catalogue record for this book is available from the British Library

Library of Congress cataloguing in publication data
Holsti, K. J. (Kalevi Jaakko), 1935–
The state, war, and the state of war/by K. J. Holsti.
        p.   cm. – (Cambridge studies in international relations: 51)
Includes bibliographical references.
ISBN 0 521 57113 8. – ISBN 0 521 57790 X (pbk.)
1. War.   2. Legitimacy of governments.   3. Political stability.
4. Civil war.   5. Military history, Modern.   I. Title.   II. Series.
U21.2.H62723   1997
355.02–dc20   96–3881   CIP

ISBN 0 521 57113 8 hardback
ISBN 0 521 57790 X paperback

CE

Contents

vii

Preface

War has been the major focus of international relations studies for the past three centuries. As the immense and growing literature on the subject attests, it is a problem of continuing interest. Claims of a "new world order" notwithstanding, wars continue to make headlines and become inscribed on the agenda of the United Nations and regional organizations. The moral, legal, human, and strategic character of these conflicts command no less attention today than previously. Yet, our understanding of contemporary wars is not well served by older analytical approaches. War today is not the same phenomenon it was in the eighteenth century, or even in the 1930s. It has different sources and takes on significantly different characteristics.

My previous study, *Peace and war: armed conflict and international order, 1648–1989* (1991) looked backward to examine the sources of war in the modern states system. It also explored the various devices and contrivances diplomats and statesmen organized to reduce the incidence and destruction of violent interstate conflicts. The present study, in contrast, inquires into contemporary and future wars: their sources and essential characteristics.

Wars today are less a problem of the relations between states than a problem within states. But it is not chronic to all states. New and weak states are the primary locale of present and future wars. Thus, war as a problem that commanded the attention of experts in strategy and international relations is now becoming a problem better addressed by students of the state creation and sustenance processes.

We can understand contemporary wars best if we explore the birth of states and how they have come to be governed. The problem of legitimacy is particularly acute. The Rwandas, Sri Lankas, and Somalias of today and tomorrow – and there will be many tomorrow – are caused fundamentally by a lack of political legitimacy between rulers and the communities over whom they rule. In today's world, as throughout history, there are competing principles of legitimacy. Heroic acts, once a primary source of legitimacy, are passing from the scene despite the efforts of Hitler, Mao Tse-tung, Kim Il-Sung, Fidel Castro, and others to base their rule on them. The legitimizing principle of proletarian revolution has also disappeared since 1989. Three main principles remain today: popular sovereignty – what I call the "civic state" – religion, and "natural" community, often rendered as ethnicity. War arises primarily in states based on the latter two principles because they are exclusive. They seek to establish rule over single communities of believers or communities of blood, language and religion, whereas most states today are comprised of multiple communities. The contradiction between exclusive principles of legitimacy and the demographic and social constitution of most post-colonial and post-Soviet societies creates weak states and, ultimately, war.

One solution that emerges from the analysis is the strengthening of states. This will not be good news to many contemporary analysts who believe that it is the state itself which is the source of so many of our current problems. In an age of economic interdependence, erosion of sovereignty, and "globalism," the idea that political organizations that artificially divide the human community should be sustained and strengthened runs counter to much conventional wisdom. Ideas – and clichés – like "spaceship earth," the "world community," "the endangered planet," and "globalism" are much more popular than the idea of the state. Yet, in many areas of the world where weak states are on the threshold of civil war, or have collapsed, we see little evidence of globalism and a world community. The alternative to the state may not be a harmonious universal society, but fragmentation into warlordism, rule by gangs, communal massacres, and "ethnic cleansing." Those who have been fortunate enough to survive the wars and collapse of Lebanon, Liberia, Rwanda, Yugoslavia, Somalia, and many other countries would probably prefer to have a strong state than no state. Who today would exchange Iceland, Denmark, or Japan for Myanmar or Sudan?

This is not to argue that the strong state based on secure foundations of legitimacy is the only solution to the problem of war. It is not. Alternative configurations of state-like political units are at least imaginable, and may become necessary in an age when "identity," ethnicity, and religious community seldom correspond with state frontiers. But that is a matter for another book and for far-sighted politicians, activists, and economic organizations. In the meantime, strong states are an essential ingredient to peace within and between societies. This is the gist of the argument. The evidence is contained in the pages that follow.

The relationship between war and the state is a subject of continuing controversy. At the turn of the last century, a debate raged among anthropologists, philosophers, and political analysts around the question: is war essential to the creation and sustenance of states? Social Darwinists, among others, argued that it is. Liberals vehemently disagreed. My father, Rudolph Holsti, engaged in this debate on the latter side. His doctoral dissertation at the University of Helsinki entitled "War and the Origins of the State" (1913), based on an exhaustive examination of ethnographic evidence, concluded that many societies emerge, develop, and thrive without the institution of war. By accident, I find that the argument that follows fits into the genre but with the difference that it links war to certain *kinds* of states rather than to the state itself. It relies on evidence from post-1945 states rather than on the entire record of human history.

Some of the ideas of the analysis that follows were introduced in pioneering work by Barry Buzan (1983 and 1991). I acknowledge my intellectual debt to him. The idea of the weak state, though dubbed "negative sovereignty," also comes from the fertile mind of my colleague, Robert Jackson (1990). I gladly record my debt to Pentti Sadeniemi (1995) for an essay on principles of legitimacy that stimulated a considerable part of the discussion in chapters 5 and 6.

Funding for this enterprise was provided by a research grant from the Social Sciences and Humanities Research Council of Canada. I am most grateful to this organization which has provided me with numerous opportunities to engage in research and writing. Brian Job of the Institute of International Relations at the University of British Columbia offered support and encouragement, particularly by organizing a conference in 1992 where some of the ideas developed here were first introduced (Holsti, 1992). I was twice a visiting professor at the International University of Japan while this work was under way. This institution offered me both library resources and an excellent environment for research and writing. I am grateful to Professors Chihiro Hosoya and Bruce Stronach who made those visits possible. Professors Mark Brawley and T. V. Paul of McGill University, Montreal, invited me to give a seminar in the spring of 1993 where early versions of the main ideas were first presented for outside consumption, criticism, and comment. That presentation led to a summary argument presented at the 1994 Berlin meetings of the International Political Science Association and subsequently published in the *International Political Science Review* (1995).

Five students at the University of British Columbia served as research assistants. Each excelled in the work. My sincere thanks to Rosemary Bird, Peter Chalk, Ronald Deibert, Karen Guttieri, and Darryl Jarvis, all of whom demonstrated their research skills and helped in many other ways.

Several colleagues were kind enough to read and make numerous helpful suggestions on individual chapters. I am particularly grateful to Arie Kacowicz of the Hebrew University of Jerusalem, Scott Pegg and Darryl Jarvis of the University of British Columbia, and Paulo Wrobel of the Catolica Universidad Pontifica do Rio de Janeiro. Professor Wrobel also helped in many ways to organize my interview trip through South America in the spring of 1994. My friend and colleague, Robert Jackson, read the entire text of an earlier draft and made numerous helpful suggestions. An anonymous reviewer for Cambridge University Press offered an insightful critique that encouraged me to make changes to strengthen the argument. I express my gratitude to these persons for their assistance; none is responsible for my interpretations and arguments.

1 Thinking about war in international politics

When thinking about war, we usually conjure up the image of two countries arraying their military forces against each other, followed by combat between distinctively designated, organized, and marked armed forces. The purpose of fighting is to destroy the adversary's capacity to resist and then to impose both military and political terms on the defeated party. This was the pattern in the 1991 Gulf War, World War II, and World War I, to mention several of the most famous wars of this century. Diplomatic practitioners, military leaders, and academic experts on international politics typically regard war as a contest between states. This characterization of war is also found in the Charter of the United Nations, in hundreds of bilateral and multilateral treaties between states, in government defense ministries, and in standard textbooks on international politics and security studies.

War defined as a contest of arms between sovereign states derives from the post-1648 European experience, as well as from the Cold War. It is historically and culturally based. In other historical and geographical contexts, wars have been better characterized as contests of honor (duels), marauding, piracy, searches for glory, and pillaging forays. Armies, navies, gangs, and hordes battled, sometimes in quick but massive battles, at other times in decades-long campaigns. They represented clans, tribes, feudal barons, city states, empires, and religious orders such as the Templars and Hospitallers. For many, such as Genghis Khan's hordes, war was at once a style of life, an economic system, and an instrument of the Khan's temper to punish those who offended him. It was largely devoid of political purpose because it did not result in the rearrangement of political units, the creation of empires, or the alteration of a state's territories. Wars in Europe until the seventeenth century reflected medieval, not modern, objectives.

The numerous wars of the first half of the fifteenth century, for
example, were fought to assert or defend personal rights of property or
succession, to enforce obedience among vassals, to defend or extend
Christendom against the Muslims, or to protect Church interests
against heresy. The first category predominated. Most wars consisted
of personal quarrels between kings, queens, and princes over rights of
inheritance; they were not "in any sense conflicts between states, let
alone nations, over what they perceived to be their interests" (Howard
1976: 20). As late as 1536 Charles V, the Holy Roman Emperor,
challenged his rival, Francis I of France, to a duel to resolve their
quarrels.

War as an instrument of state policy is a relatively new form of
organized violence.[1] While predation, plunder, and glory might rank
among its by-products, the main purpose of the use of force in Europe
for the past 350 years has been primarily to advance and/or to protect
the interests of the state. War has been political. This is the Clausewitzian conception of war, summarized in his famous definition "war is a
continuation of politics by other means." While the dynamics of armed
combat may cause a decline into uncontrolled total violence ("war is
an act of violence pushed to its utmost bounds"), the purpose of armed
forces is to sustain and advance the diplomatic interests of the state.
Those purposes might range from territorial defense, through claims
for a crown or gaining control of colonies, to constructing an expanding empire. Military force has purposes which the governments of
states in a system of states define, defend, and promote.

If the purposes of two or more states are incompatible, then war is
also an instrument of conflict resolution. It is undertaken when
diplomats are unable to negotiate conflicting claims and objectives. The
contest of arms produces an outcome, which is then set down in a
peace treaty that defines a new set of rights, obligations, and resource
allocations between the combatants. Territories may be annexed or
exchanged, states may be created, partitioned, or extinguished, navigation rights may be denied or established, or the claim to a throne may

[1] Wars in other civilizations have taken numerous forms, in some cases in the service of
state-like entities. In many respects, however, the European territorial state is historically unique. Features such as fixed and formal lineal frontiers, the interests of the
"state" (as opposed to the personal interests of the ruler(s)), the concepts of sovereignty and legal equality, and the longevity of the state format are seldom to be found
elsewhere. For a discussion of forms of warfare in Europe that are not distinctly
related to the modern territorial state, see Howard (1976: chs. 2–3).

2

be honored or rejected. War is thus a rational if not always desirable activity, a means to a known end defined in terms of state or national interests.

Following the mayhem and slaughters of the Thirty Years War (1618–48) that depopulated a large part of central Europe, the Clausewitzian view of war reflected dynastic and Enlightenment politics and etiquette. Centralizing monarchies by the eighteenth century had slowly gained a monopoly of force within their own territories and could get on with the task of state-making with less concern from military challenges within their realms. Their problem now was to define the state more precisely in its external dimensions and how to finance the wars that were necessary to strengthen the state. To do this, they laid claims to old titles and crowns, sought lineal and defensible borders against external threats – which often meant dispossessing others of their own territories – and competed for colonies and their resources. The result was that as states became more established in their sovereignty, they became greater threats to their neighbors. Their rulers demanded that others recognize their status as sovereigns, but they did not always reciprocate the favor, for some aspired to reorganize the states system under principles different than that of sovereign equality of independent states. They thought in terms of hierarchies and domination. Dreams of empire and hegemony did not die out with Charles V and the Treaties of Westphalia. Louis XIV, Napoleon, the Germans in 1914 and again in the 1930s sought to establish clear paramountcy on the continent, a condition that posed mortal threats to the other states.

Until the wars of the French Revolution, professional and mercenary armies led by noble officers, and not infrequently by kings and princes themselves, pursued a variety of dynastic and state objectives. Charles XII of Sweden, Peter the Great, and Frederick the Great were battlefield warriors as well as monarchs. War in the seventeenth and eighteenth centuries reflected the dynastic (and later, Enlightenment) ethos of reason, moderation, and calculation. It was highly regulated and institutionalized in the form of strict etiquette, standardized tactics, uniforms, and informal "rules of the game." War was also a *legitimate* instrument of dynastic diplomacy. The concept of sovereignty, buttressed by the doctrine of the divine origins of dynastic rule, allowed a sovereign to advance or protect his or her interests (dynastic and state interests were often the same) through the use of armed force against other states. While wars of these centuries cost the taxpayers dearly

3

(leading Immanuel Kant to formulate his famous proposition that if the "people" ruled, there would be no wars), they were not commonly seen as a great problem that required regulation. The unlimited right to wage war was reflected in international law until the twentieth century. As late as 1880, the eminent international lawyer W. E. Hall could write that "both parties to every war are regarded as being in an identical legal position, and consequently as possessed of equal rights" (quoted in Keegan 1993: 383).

Napoleon's assaults on Europe changed public views of war, although not the central concept of war as basically a political contest between two or more states. While Napoleon did not introduce fundamentally new technologies to war, his political purposes went far beyond those of the preceding century's dynasts. His military tactics changed war from a limited exercise into great campaigns of annihilation against enemies. The Napoleonic wars were the most costly in lives and resources since the Thirty Years War. But more important, their purpose was to destroy the European states system and to replace it with a Paris-centered, hierarchical empire. Born of the French Revolution, these wars also had the purpose of changing the domestic orders of the defeated: these were the first wars of "national liberation." The goal was to bring ideological and political orthodoxy to the continent (under French tutelage), a gross deviation from the principles of the Treaties of Westphalia (1648), whose purpose was to sanctify political and religious heterogeneity rather than conformity in Europe.

By 1815, then, war had become a problem of public policy. Something had to be done to prevent a replay of the two decades of revolutionary–Napoleonic war. The Treaty of Paris and declarations of the Congress of Vienna were the first modern attempts to control the use of armed force between states. Sovereigns were henceforth – in theory at least – to use force only with the consent of the great powers (the Concert). This limitation applied to the great powers themselves (Holsti 1992b). If war was to become increasingly unlimited, as it had in the 1791–1815 period, then the society of states had the right and obligation to impose restrictions on its use.

World War I (the "Great War") shattered a century of relative peace in Europe. The war was unprecedented in the scale of destruction and lives lost, if not in its futility. By the late nineteenth century, public peace movements had become increasingly vocal as transnational interest groups. The Great War helped to create a massive groundswell of opinion to impose even greater constraints on the use of force. The

Covenant of the League of Nations restricted the legitimate use of force to only three possibilities: (1) for self-defense; (2) to enforce League-sponsored sanctions; and (3) to resolve a conflict – after a ninety-day waiting period – when the League could not fashion a solution. Once the unlimited right of sovereigns, armed force was now viewed as an *ultimate* instrument of policy, to be used only in circumstances generally approved by the international community.

Not content with the remaining loopholes in the League Covenant, the 1928 General Treaty for the Renunciation of War (Kellogg–Briand Pact) formally outlawed war as an instrument of policy and compelled signatories to resolve their conflicts by peaceful means. States that violated the new universal norm were to be guilty of "crimes against humanity."

The Tokyo and Nuremberg war trials after World War II established individual responsibility for both waging aggressive war and violations of the laws of war, including "crimes against humanity." These trials further eroded the Clausewitzian conception of war as simply a continuation of politics by violent means. Once the unlimited right of a sovereign, the new doctrine characterized aggressive war as a criminal activity. Thus, today, under the Charter of the United Nations, states can use armed force only in two circumstances: (1) individual or collective self-defense, and (2) enforcement of collective sanctions. The Korean, Suez, and Gulf Wars were significant test cases: in each, aggressors were condemned, and in Korea and the Gulf the Security Council sanctioned the collective use of armed force to repel invaders and to liberate conquered territories. There were, of course, other wars. Most of them were "wars of national liberation" justified on the basis of the anti-colonial sentiments of a majority of United Nations members. As argued during the 1950s and 1960s, these were to be regarded not as wars between states – the combats which the United Nations was designed to prevent – but as uprisings of populations exercising their right to self-determination.

The United Nations was created to provide "international peace and security," which in 1945 meant the prevention of war *between* states. It had many other purposes as well, but the prominence devoted to the problem of international peace and security emphasized that in government and public circles, war remains *the* problem of international politics. Virtually all members of the United Nations nevertheless continue to maintain military forces and to develop strategies and deployments to deal with potential or actual military threats from

5

external sources. No member has been willing to rely exclusively upon the organization for its own security. Hence, although the use of force has been highly circumscribed in terms of norms, it remains a constant possibility in the relations between states. Defense policies are designed to cope with external threats, and "national security" is a condition in which those threats are successfully deterred or contained, or vulnerabilities reduced. In brief, the Clausewitzian concept of war as a means of serving state interests continues to form the intellectual and conceptual foundation for international organizations, national military institutions, the practices of diplomacy, and the academy. The ultimate problem for all of them remains war between states.

The end of the Cold War has not fundamentally changed either practitioners' or academics' views about war. After 1991, a blizzard of proposals suggested a new "security architecture" for Europe, meaning the creation of new institutional capacities for the Organization on Security and Cooperation in Europe (OSCE) and NATO to deal with the age-old problem of war between states. Despite a few novel ideas, such as Samuel Huntington's concept (1993) of a "clash of civilizations," diplomats and strategists continue to concentrate on Clausewitzian-type wars and the problems that nuclear proliferation would create for regional and universal security. The academic study of international politics similarly continues to be motivated by and concerned with the two faces of Janus: war and peace between states.

The theoretical analysis of war

Since the eighteenth century, philosophers, historians, and experts on international affairs have sought to locate the "causes of war" – meaning organized and politically directed violence between the armed forces of two or more states. They have indulged in a variety of diagnostic exercises from which prescriptions and solutions have flowed. Leading politicians have frequently been influenced by these analyses. This is not the place to develop a full historical survey of systematic thinking on the causes of war and the conditions of peace, order, and stability. A few intellectual highlights are appropriate, however, for they demonstrate the continuing significance of Clausewitzian conceptions of war in the analysis of the problem, and the ways that statesmen and strategists base their policies on academic diagnoses and prescriptions.

At the time that Jean-Jacques Rousseau was developing his thoughts about the causes of war and the conditions of peace in the middle of the eighteenth century, war was a regular feature of the European diplomatic landscape. Between the Treaties of Westphalia and the French Revolution, Europe's dynasts fought forty-eight bilateral and multilateral wars. Some monarchs earned temporary glory for their victories (primarily Louis XIV, Charles XII, Peter the Great, and his fellow great, Frederick), but most drained treasuries, bankrupted the state, and motivated peasants to organize tax rebellions. If not commonly perceived as a social problem requiring remedies, at least there were many who opposed these many wars because of their economic costs. For Rousseau and Kant, however, war was more than a cost-ineffective pastime of princes. Their critiques of war were founded primarily on their republicanism. For Kant, at least, republican virtue could replace the prevailing dynastic warrior culture.

I concentrate on Rousseau because he was the first to propose a fundamental explanation for the persistence of Clausewitz-style war between states, an explanation that continues to inform theoretical scholarship in international politics. He developed, though not in a systematic or consistent manner, a generic theory of war. It does not explain the origins of any particular armed combat, but demonstrates why war is a necessary feature or outcome in a system of independent states. Such a system is called an *anarchy*. Anarchy does not mean chaos. It is, rather, the literal Greek meaning of the *lack of governance*. States are sovereign and, by definition, no authority resides above them. Only states make laws for their citizens and subjects, and ultimately states must rely only on themselves for their defense. States are legally equal, and thus there are no hierarchies of formal command and obedience, as one would find in a feudal system.

Rousseau used a parable to illustrate why war is inevitable in anarchic state systems. I will embellish his simple story to amplify main points and to underline the systemic or structural character of the explanation.

Five primitive hunters meet by accident. They do not know each other, nor can they communicate for lack of a common language. They have a common purpose, however. It is to kill a stag seen in the neighborhood. Each hunter is armed with only a spear. Each makes the calculation that if he cooperates with the others to encircle the stag, he will increase the probability of making the kill. Put in quantitative terms, a hunter by himself has only a 10 percent chance of killing the stag; but if he succeeds, he gets 100 percent of the kill. If the hunters collaborate to encircle the game, the chances of a kill increase to, say, 80 percent. However, in the event of success and assuming an equality of effort, each hunter will receive only 20 percent of the kill. By a simple calculation each hunter sees the greater payoff in collaboration: 100 percent of 10 is only 10, whereas 20 percent of 80 is 16. Assuming hunters to be value maximizers, Rousseau shows why cooperation brings greater gains to all. Even for egotists – those motivated solely by self-interest – it is rational to cooperate.

And so it should be in international relations. Everyone gains through peaceful contacts, including trade. If there were less threat of war between states, a great deal of money could be saved for more constructive purposes. The argument has a very modern ring: how much more could the developing and industrialized countries gain by investing in health, education, and the arts, for example, rather than in weapons and preparations for war?

Why, then, don't governments make these rational choices? Why do they consistently forgo important gains available through cooperation and trade for the destructive activities of preparation for war and fighting? To Rousseau, the explanation lies in the situation rather than in the caprices of human sentiment or the attributes of the states themselves.

One hunter finds a hare close by. It is a certain kill for him. He must then make a new calculation. "Should I kill the hare? It is much smaller than the stag, but my 100 percent certainty of food tonight is better than the 80 percent probability attached to the stag." In killing the hare, however, the hunter makes noise that scares the stag, which then flees. Our rational hunter has gone for the short-term and certain gain that ruins the prospects of his fellows.

This would not necessarily preclude future cooperation, but in international politics, *every* hunter (state) knows that the other hunters may have a hare nearby. In other words, mistrust pervades the relations between hunters (states). In this environment, each hunter is compelled to go for the short-term gain because if he does not, another one might and then the rest go home hungry.

This is the predicament of states. It is a necessary feature of all anarchical systems and is based on the fundamental situation, not on the predispositions of individual rulers or states. This is a powerful structural explanation of war, one that remains the centerpiece of neo-realist theories of international politics.

Rousseau went beyond this analysis to show also why the defensive policies of any state necessarily cause distrust among neighbors. The stag hunt parable explains defection, or war. The concept of the *security dilemma* explains the mistrust that lies behind it. States create armaments and deploy them for a variety of reasons. Since they cannot rely on others for their own security, they must have the insurance of arms for self-defense. But when the defensive-minded state arms, its buildup creates suspicion among its neighbors. They cannot always accept the peaceful pretensions of the first state, and thus must obtain insurance for themselves. Competitive arming is the result. As Rousseau and others put it, the means that states develop for their survival constitute a threat to their neighbors. The price of domestic sovereignty (a monopoly over the use of force within a defined territory and the status of supreme lawmaker over a community) is external insecurity and war. If you want a system of sovereign states, the price is permanent insecurity and occasional war.

It is not necessary to question some of the assumptions of the stag parable (for example, the assumption of the non-sociability of the hunters: how many states today are completely isolated and unable to communicate with others?) to see that it is a powerful theoretical explanation for the persistence of war between states. Such wars remain a central concern of statesmen and scholars of international politics despite numerous charters, covenants, treaties, balances of power, arms control measures, and nuclear deterrents. The logic of anarchy overrides all efforts to control the use of armed force.

Rousseau's analysis did not sweep the academic and diplomatic communities, however. Both have continued trying to find paths to lasting peace in the anarchical system of states. The discipline called international relations developed in the United States and the United Kingdom shortly before and immediately after World War I. Its purpose was both diagnostic and prescriptive. Few academics in this era adopted Rousseau's pessimistic perspective on war. Their diagnoses presented an array of non-systemic causes of interstate war, including the human psyche, imperialism, militarism, nationalism, and racism (cf. Sharp and Kirk 1941).

Yet other observers, including leaders such as Woodrow Wilson and Vladimir Lenin, focused their diagnoses of the war problem at the level of states. It is not so much the system of states that is the fountain of conflict and war, but the nature of the individual states. To Lenin, it was capitalist states that became imperialist and thus drove war. For Wilson, militarism and autocracy were the culprits. Democracies, in his view, are fundamentally pacific. In his early version of the League of Nations, Wilson wanted the organization to restrict membership to democracies; only a covenant between peace-loving democracies could guarantee peace.

Theoretical solutions to war

Under the influence of Rousseauian realism, Wilsonian liberalism, and Marxist revolutionism, government leaders and academics developed a full roster of prescriptions and solutions to the problem of interstate war: disarmament, judicial settlement of disputes, democratization of states, peace education, international organizations and institutions, world federalism, and world revolution – all ideas that remain current in one form or another. But none helped to prevent the serial aggressions of Hitler, Mussolini, Stalin, and the Japanese in Asia during the 1930s.

World War II resulted in a resurgence of realist thought, personified best in the work of Hans J. Morgenthau (1948). Unlike Rousseau, who saw the source of war in the nature of the states system, Morgenthau explained the perennial struggle for power among states by reference to an immutable human personality. Man (generically speaking) always seeks power. There can be a "struggle for peace," based on skillful diplomacy and balances of power, but at best these offer only temporary respites from the perennial problem of war driven by the human being's search for power. Solutions in the sense of a permanent end to war are therefore utopian. There can only be eras of more or less peace generated by skillful and prudent statesmen and diplomats with a design to create and sustain a global balance of power.

Rousseau's analysis remains currently in the guise of "neo-realism," the idea that the basic structural properties of the international system cause conflicts. The solution to the problem, as in Morgenthau – but for entirely different reasons – is a bipolar balance of power (Waltz 1979). Wilson's ideas, whose genealogy go back to early nineteenth-century British liberals, live on in the OSCE Charter of Paris (1990), which emphasizes the connection between democracy within states to peace between them, while Lenin's vision, if not its substance, finds heirs among those who would destroy states and replace them with localisms of various kinds.

Whether emphasizing human nature, the characteristics of states, or the structure of the states system, all these theoretical diagnoses of war as well as their derivative prescriptions use the same conception of the state. It is the sovereign territorial state of seventeenth-century European origins. The premier problem of international relations is interstate war as it had been experienced since the Treaties of Westphalia. Whether caused by the personal lust for power, imperialism, aggressive militarism, or international anarchy the problem that must be dealt with is essentially a problem of the relations between states. It follows that if war is seen in the Clausewitzian sense as an instrument to support state interests, then solutions to the problem have to be fashioned in the relations between states.

Rousseau could not develop a solution to the problem. If you want states, he argued, then the price is insecurity and war. Other realists emphasized balances of power. It does not solve the problem of war, for war may be used to sustain or create a balance. But at least it helps provide security for the individual states. Those of the Wilsonian persuasion argued for the progressive democratization of individual states, or for democratization of their mutual relations through devices such as open diplomacy, arbitration of disputes, and publicizing treaties and other understandings. Whatever the solution, it depends upon improving the patterns of bilateral and multilateral diplomacy and international institutions. Only Lenin prescribed a solution that was not state-centered: world revolution in which individual states would be cast away and new forms of governance would emerge under the dictatorship of the proletariat. Classes, not states, were to be the actors of the future. And since working classes cannot have any contradictions between them, the problem of war would be solved.

The Cold War changed few of these proposed – and often popular – solutions to the problem of war. There was one major exception, however. For the majority of both civilian and military strategists, the ultimate solution to the problem of war is nuclear deterrence. This idea represented a revolution in thinking. The atomic bombs dropped in Hiroshima and Nagasaki in 1945 ushered in a new military age, according to most observers. Henceforth, the purpose of armed force is not to fight wars for offensive or defensive reasons, but to prevent them. The traditional cost-benefit analysis underlying any decision to use force is obsolete in the nuclear age. The costs of nuclear war are so horrendous that the old Clausewitzian conception of war as a means of supporting state claims no longer makes sense. What country could conceivably use nuclear weapons to advance its interests if in so doing it would bring massive retaliation resulting in its obliteration as a recognizable state? Or worse, the end of mankind?

The fundamental dilemma of nuclear deterrence, of course, is that it has to be based on a credible threat of retaliation. But if nuclear retaliation guarantees nuclear war, how can any threat to retaliate be credible? And how can governments extend deterrence to allies and friends? Would the United States destroy itself to save France? Or more pertinent to the pattern of war since 1945, can you threaten to use nuclear weapons to prevent or terminate a guerrilla war in a distant Third World country? Nuclear deterrence as a solution to the problem of war is inherently non-credible when any rational calculation of costs and benefits is made. Even the attempt to impose a Clausewitzian rationality onto nuclear war by proposing it be confined to the exchange of tactical weapons lacks credibility. A "limited nuclear war" is one of the great oxymorons of modern strategic studies. It is also non-credible when wars of a non-Clausewitzian type are at issue. Of what relevance are nuclear weapons in Bosnia or Somalia? Despite these unsolvable intellectual and practical contradictions, strategic studies as an academic subfield of international relations focused for forty years on the problem of creating effective deterrents.

Cold War era peace movements were also consumed with the problem of nuclear war. Their leaders could not abide the deterrence theorists because they saw the problem of nuclear weapons in fundamentally different ways. For the strategic community, nuclear doctrine and deployment were the avenues to peace; for the peace groups, they are guaranteed paths to Armageddon. The two communities were united, however, in their adherence to the old idea that the problem of war is essentially a problem of the relations between states. The context of war and peace is the competition and general incompatibility of purpose between the two superpowers and their respective alliance systems. The two communities also shared the realization that nuclear war could result from human error, fanaticism, or technical malfunction. Deterrence may be a rational means of preventing war but, going beyond Clausewitz, it could also lead to colossal mistakes. The solution to this problem is negotiated, verifiable arms control and disarmament agreements between the nuclear powers.

Analysts of the problem of war, from Rousseau to deterrence theorists, have examined primarily the behavior of the great powers. This was natural because between the Thirty Years War and World War II, most wars were precipitated by or eventually involved the great powers (Levy 1983). Diagnosticians of international relations and war therefore insisted that the field of study should also focus on great-power activity. According to Kenneth Waltz (1979: 72), a premier theorist of international politics during the second half of the twentieth century, "the story of international politics is written in terms of the great powers of our era." Statesmen have concurred and insisted that the major powers hold special responsibilities for maintaining international peace and security. This idea was enshrined in the Concert of Europe, in the League of Nations Covenant, and continues in the Charter of the United Nations.

What recent analysts and practitioners have largely overlooked is that most of the war and killing since 1945 has occurred far away from the central battlefields of the Cold War in Europe and Pacific Asia. The initiators of the many post-1945 wars have not been the traditional great powers, but relatively new and weak states. Most of these wars have been noted, but to the extent that they were analyzed seriously, it was usually from a Cold War perspective (Korany 1986). The developing countries – the Vietnams, Afghanistans, Ethiopias and Somalias – were simply the arenas in which great-power competition was taking place. Their security problems were a reflection of Cold War politics. Academics and professional strategic thinkers characterized many wars of "national liberation" as combats between "freedom" and "communism." The history of these areas was essentially the events and personalities that eased or thwarted the aspirations of the United States, the Soviet Union, or communist China. In Washington, "states" like South Vietnam, Lebanon, Afghanistan, Burma, Angola, and Somalia were threatened by Soviet and/or Chinese "subversion." In Moscow, "states" like North Vietnam, Laos, Cambodia, and North Korea were threatened by "imperialism." Naives like Ronald Reagan or the leaders of many communist parties in Europe thought that once the problems of communist subversion or imperialism had been resolved, perpetual peace would reign between states. Simple diagnoses paved the way for simple solutions.

The relevance of old concepts to new environments

Our ideas about war – its sources, nature, and solutions – come from the European and Cold War experiences. When we think of it either as a practice or as the object of study, Clausewitzian conceptions of armed combat to support or extend state interests remain in our minds. Our explanations of the phenomenon derive largely from Rousseau's compelling analysis, from human-nature-based theories (including biological theories), or from theories about the attributes of states.

Largely hidden in all this thinking about the causes of and solutions to interstate war is the experience of Europeans in their numerous imperial wars and campaigns, to say nothing of the theory and practice of war in non-European societies (cf. Keegan 1993). Yet it is these types of war that are the precursors to many of the post-1945 and contemporary wars. The Clausewitzian conception of war as organized combat between the military forces of two or more states fits our mental maps naturally because it reflects the predominant forms of great-power warfare within modern (post-1648) European civilization at least until World War II. This is the model of war enshrined in the Charter of the United Nations, in collective defense organizations like NATO, and in definitions of war and aggression in international law.

Key analytical concepts such as balances of power, hegemony, alliances, deterrence, power projection, and a whole range of geopolitical ideas also derive from the European and Cold War experiences. Their relevance to most post-1945 wars is highly problematic.

The problem is that the Clausewitzian image of war, as well as its theoretical accoutrements, has become increasingly divorced from the characteristics and sources of most armed conflicts since 1945. The key question is: given that most wars since 1945 have been *within* states, of what intellectual and policy relevance are concepts and practices derived from the European and Cold War experiences that diagnosed or prescribed solutions for the problem of war *between* states? Are we to understand the Somalias, Rwandas, Myanmars, and Azerbaijans of the world in classical European terms? Do we find balances of power, alliances, and wars to promote state interests in Africa, South America, South Asia and other regions of the world, as we saw them in eighteenth-century Europe? Are we to assume that the ideas and practices that drove interstate wars between Prussian, Saxon, Austrian, and French dynasts in the eighteenth century must repeat themselves in twenty-first-century Africa? Are the rationalist calculations of balance of power or deterrence theory applicable to ethnic, religious, and/or language communities bent upon destroying each other? Should we continue to regard the security problems of post-1945 states as merely the reflections of great-power interests? Do not various regions of the world have their own unique set of security problems and dynamics? Is the United Nations, an organization created by the victors of World War II to resolve conflicts between European-type states and European-style wars, and to sustain the Westphalian principles of sovereign independence, particularly well suited to handle the types of conflicts that comprise the current diplomatic landscape? Should the academic study of international relations continue to employ concepts and organizing devices derived from the European and Cold War milieux?

Many have argued that the concept of national security should be broadened to include threats such as environmental pollution, depletion of the ozone layer, earth warming, and massive migrations of unwanted refugees (cf. Waever *et al.* 1993). Pleas by strategists for conceptual innovation are understandable since the prospects of conventional war between industrial countries have declined precipitously. If new threats are not identified, strategic planners may become redundant. To remain relevant, some have begun to focus on "low intensity conflict" but this is done from the perspectives of American foreign policy interests rather than as a serious exercise to understand the etiology of such conflicts. The assumption is that Americans should better understand such forms of warfare if they wish to intervene effectively to protect their interests, however those might be defined. Overall, however, strategic studies continue to be seriously divorced from the practices of war as we have seen them in the West Bank, Bosnia, Somalia, Liberia, and elsewhere (Cf., Rice 1994). Most fundamentally, the assumption that the problem of war is primarily a problem of the relations *between* states has to be seriously questioned. The argument of this chapter is that security *between* states in the Third World, among some of the former republics of the Soviet Union, and elsewhere has become increasingly dependent upon security *within* those states. The classical formula was: international peace and security provide an environment in which domestic politics can unfold untroubled by external disturbances. The equation is now becoming reversed. The problem of contemporary and future international politics, it turns out, is essentially a problem of domestic politics. The source of the problem is found in the nature of the new states.

On what foundations can we make this claim? The next chapter provides the evidence. Although there has not been a clear break between the era of wars between states and the era of wars within states, 1945 serves as a convenient breakpoint. The trend is clear: the threat of war between countries is receding, while the incidence of violence within states is on an upward curve. Saddam Hussein's short-lived conquest of Kuwait in 1990 may prove to be among the last classical-style military aggressions.

John Mueller's (1989) argument that man will learn to avoid "major" war (war between the major powers) just as he learned to eliminate other social institutions such as slavery and dueling may be correct. The reasons for such a dramatic breakthrough lie in part in the massive change in cost-benefit calculations arising from the possession of nuclear weapons. I will argue, however, that they have more to do with the nature of the state in industrial societies: these states, after more than 500 years of development, have become "strong" in the sense that for the first time in history, they enjoy popular legitimacy. There has been no war in Western Europe or North America for more than a half-century, in part because of nuclear balances and ideological compatibilities, but more importantly because there has been peace *within* the states of these regions.

Does the end of major war also reflect the "end of history," the universal victory of liberalism (Fukuyama 1989)? This interesting argument has received notoriety for its optimism. Many would like to agree with Fukuyama, but unfortunately his concept of ideology is limited. Fascism and communism have indeed been discredited, but there are other forms of "ideology" than those Fukuyama acknowledges. Some forms of religious fundamentalism are not very compatible with liberal democracy, for example. But, more important, Fukuyama fails to consider that an issue more important than ideology is the nature of *community*. That issue was more or less settled in many industrial societies before 1945, although it is still expressed in the separatist impulses in Scotland, Wales, Quebec, and elsewhere. It has not been settled in most new states.

The processes of state formation in Europe during the last half-millennium were attended by wars, revolutions, rebellions, and massacres. The process is not yet universally complete. Five centuries ago, the world's population was organized in an amazingly heterogeneous array of political units: empires (of which there were many varieties), city-states, independent religious communities, kingdoms, dukedoms, republics, nomadic and sedentary tribes, gangs, and others. That heterogeneity reflected not only different forms of military power, religion, and culture, but also different concepts of community. Some, like the Knights of Malta or the Templars, defined themselves as religious communities and they took on the attributes of a state in order to promote religious preoccupations. Others reflected the dynastic principle, with the king or emperor as the "father" of a community of loyal subjects. Communities, such as the Hansa cities, were defined primarily in terms of economic interests and practices. And reflecting the oldest basis of community, the clans, lineages, and tribes were based on blood relations.

This heterogeneity of political forms remains with us, but the range of possibilities is dwindling. The Soviet Union and Ethiopia were perhaps the last empires (some would say that China is). Monaco and Liechtenstein represent the leftovers of feudal princedoms. Andorra and San Marino are the only remaining free cities. The Catholic Church remains an important diplomatic agent with most of the attributes of statehood except territory and armed forces. All survive with the tolerance of the world's states. A few communities, such as the transnational drug cartels, pose the same kind of challenges to states that pirates did for many centuries.

Despite these remaining anomalies, the state format has become nearly universal. Heterogeneity of political forms has been replaced by homogeneity. Only states can make treaties under international law; only states can join the United Nations; only states can have (legitimate) armies; and unless one wants to be shunted around from refugee camp to refugee camp, all individuals must have an identity defined in terms of statehood. A woman, child, or man without a passport is trapped within his or her country. The state, then, has become universalized.

The problem is that, in many areas of the world, the state is not the same as the community. In so far as many communities have adopted the mystique of statehood as the ultimate and final political format, then states based on other principles will lack legitimacy. This whole problem has not yet been sorted out. More fundamental than the future hypothesized "clash of civilizations" (Huntington 1993) is the clash over different conceptions of community and how those conceptions should be reflected in political arrangements and organizations. Regrettably, those clashes are not likely to be resolved by debates, votes, plebiscites, or other peaceful means. They will be settled – if settlement is even an appropriate term – by the force of arms, by terrorism, and by ethnic cleansing and massacres. The problem of the early years of the next millennium, then, will not be war between states, but wars about and within states. Internal wars may escalate or invite external intervention, but their primary if not exclusive etiology resides in the fundamental quarrels about the nature of communities and the processes and problems of state-building. Most fundamentally, the question is whether the European concept of the state can be transported to non-European environments. Is the state infinitely reproducible, no matter what the context? Recent wars certainly raise questions about an appropriate answer.

Wars within and between communities are not the same as wars between states. The latter throughout modern European history were highly institutionalized and formalized. That is why, when we think of war, we also think of uniforms, chains of command, sophisticated weapons systems, campaigns, honors and decorations, regimental regalia, the laws of war, and peace treaties. Few of these are relevant to wars about communities and states. These wars are not institutionalized. And there seems to be little one can do about them. The French, British, Americans, Russians, Portuguese, and others found out that conventional means of waging war against non-state-sponsored adversaries just don't work. "The cold, brutal fact," writes Martin Van Creveld (1991: 27), "is that much present-day military power is simply irrelevant as an instrument for extending or defending political interests over most of the globe; by this criterion, indeed, it scarcely amounts to 'military power' at all." And if major military powers cannot prevail or help settle quarrels about community and statehood, can the United Nations? Perhaps it can succeed where others have failed, but a fundamental flaw in the organization has to be corrected. An organization designed to prevent or help settle wars between states faces fundamentally different types of problems in wars about and within states. The difficulties faced in Somalia and most poignantly in the former Yugoslavia reflect the conceptual flaws of the organization. But this is anticipating the analysis. First, we must supply the evidence to support the assertion that wars of the recent past and the future have been and will continue to be fundamentally different from those of the European and Cold War experiences. We are concerned with wars of a "third kind."

2 Wars of the third kind

In 1740, using a trumped-up claim to territorial title, Frederick the Great invaded Austrian Empress Maria Theresa's domains in Silesia. The war lasted two years, which was typical of the times. The Seven Years War (1756–63) earned that title because combat lasted substantially longer than the norm of the eighteenth century. In the first half of the twentieth century, most wars were fought by the organized armed forces of two or more states, and decisive victories were usually achieved within two years of the inauguration of hostilities. The Russo-Japanese War (1904–5), the Italian campaign in Libya in 1911, the Balkan Wars of 1912–13, the Soviet–Polish War of 1920–2, and the Soviet war against Finland, 1939–40, among others, lasted less than two years, some only several months. Wars during the eighteenth century on average lasted only one year (Levy 1983; Tilly 1990: 72).[1]

Wars were not only relatively brief. Reflecting the Clausewitzian concept of war, they had a regular sequence from beginning to end. There was an initial crisis where diplomatic negotiations could not reconcile the incompatible foreign policy or defense requirements of the states concerned. An ultimatum or an incident – often staged by the aggressor – then led to a formal declaration of war. We know the exact dates that eighteenth-, nineteenth-, and early twentieth-century wars commenced. Following the declarations of war, armed combat led either to stalemate or, more often, to a decisive military defeat in a single battle or a short series of battles. The defeated party then agreed to a formal armistice and sued for peace. Both parties negotiated a preliminary peace, which usually included the terms of military with-

---

[1] Levy's figure is based on great-power wars only. The average war listed in my previous study (Holsti 1991: 85–7) lasted four years.

drawal and general principles that would guide the negotiation of a
final peace. The final peace would then be concluded within a year or
two after the armistice or preliminary peace. In the eighteenth and
nineteenth centuries, final peace treaties would often be dispatched for
review by other interested governments that might make their own
claims and recommend amendments. The Congress of Berlin (1878),
for example, incorporated a number of changes to the Treaty of San
Stefano that had been negotiated bilaterally between the Russian
victors over the Ottomans in 1876. The final peace treaty established a
new set of rights, responsibilities, and territorial adjustments that were
to become part of established international law. Violations of those
new arrangements legally justified armed reprisals or other forms of
punishment. Wars were the middle stage of clearly demarcated
sequences of international conflicts and their permanent settlement.
We know that something has changed when these sequences and
stages become blurred or fail to develop.

A typical war since 1945 has a very different profile. No single crisis
precipitates them, and they typically do not start at a particular date.
There are no declarations of war, there are no seasons for campaigning,
and few end with peace treaties. Decisive battles are few. Attrition,
terror, psychology, and actions against civilians highlight "combat."
Rather than highly organized armed forces based on a strict command
hierarchy, wars are fought by loosely knit groups of regulars, irregu-
lars, cells, and not infrequently by locally-based warlords under little
or no central authority.

Wars of the late twentieth century typically last for decades. The
Vietminh took up arms after Japanese evacuation of Indochina in 1945.
They achieved victory thirty years later. Eritreans began a rebellion
within the Ethiopian empire in 1961. They more or less fought –
sometimes against each other – for thirty years until the Mengistu
regime in Addis Ababa collapsed in 1991 from a rebellion of its own
people. Kashmiris have been fighting on and off, either for independence or for annexation to Pakistan, since 1948. Minorities in Myanmar
have sustained armed resistance against the central government since
the early 1960s. The East Timorese have resisted their incorporation
into Indonesia since 1975. Ulster was in a state of war between 1961
and 1995. Even when victorious, as was the case of the Vietnamese and
Eritreans, no peace treaty is negotiated. (The Vietnamese negotiated
peace accords in Paris in 1973, but immediately broke their main
provisions and completed the military rout of South Vietnamese and

American forces.) Most frequently, one set of governors replaces another, so no new rights, responsibilities, or allocations between states are made. The prize is not territory, resources, a crown, or navigation rights. It is the establishment and control of a particular kind of state. The wars are not about foreign policy, security, honor, or status; they are about statehood, governance, and the role and status of nations and communities within states.

Tables 2.1 and 2.2 summarize the profile of war since 1945. The figures are based on standard sources. They include several armed conflicts with fewer than 1,000 annual fatalities. (The 1,000 figure is a standard cutoff point in most data collections. See, for example, Small and Singer 1982.) Lowering the cutoff point is necessary in order to capture the irregular character of warfare since 1945. The list of wars, reproduced in the appendix, errs if anything on the side of caution. It does not include some limited armed interventions. What is important from these figures is not the precision of details, but the broad pattern that emerges. If we were to add or delete a few more cases, the percentages would not change significantly.

The tables are categorized according to types and location of 164 wars. There are three types, the categories based on types of actors and/or objectives: (1) standard state versus state wars (e.g., China and India in 1962) and armed interventions involving significant loss of life (the United States in Vietnam, the Soviet Union in Afghanistan); (2) state-nation wars including armed resistance by ethnic, language and/ or religious groups, often with the purpose of secession or separation from the state (e.g., the Tamils in Sri Lanka, the Ibos in Nigeria); and (3) internal wars based on ideological goals. Examples include the Sendero Luminoso in Peru and the Monteneros in Uruguay (cf. Ekwe-Ekwe 1990; Chubin 1991; Djalili 1991). Nineteen de-colonizing wars of "national liberation" are not included.

Regions are defined according to standard criteria or common usage. South America is distinct from Central America/the Caribbean for reasons discussed in chapter 8. The Middle East includes Arab North Africa. The Balkans do not include Greece, which is designated as part of Europe. Turkey is placed in the Middle East category.

When we look at the types of war, the claim raised in the last chapter that since 1945 most wars have been within and about states is confirmed. Almost 77 percent of the 164 wars were internal, where armed combat was not against another state but against the authorities within the state or between armed communities. This figure is

Table 2.1 *Armed conflicts by type and region, 1945–1995*[a]

Type	Africa	Middle East	South Asia	Southeast Asia	East Asia	South America	Cent.Am. Carib.	Balkans/ E. Eur.	Former USSR	Western Europe	Total
State vs. state/ Intervention	7	11	4	5	3	1	4	3	–	–	38
Secesssion/ resistance	21	12	10	11	1	–	–	2	5	2	64
Ideological/ factional	16	10	4	9	2	8	10	–	2	1	62
TOTAL	**44**	**33**	**18**	**25**	**6**	**9**	**14**	**5**	**7**	**3**	**164**
Of which internal	37	22	14	20	3	8	10	2	7	3	126
Percent internal	84%	66%	78%	80%	50%	89%	71%	40%	100%	100%	77%
In which external armed intervention	8	9	4	7	2	–	6	–	2	–	38
Percent with external intervention	22%	41%	29%	35%	67%	–	60%	–	29%	–	30%

Note: [a] based on data in the appendix. Anti-colonial wars of national liberation are not included in the tables.

supported by other studies using somewhat different data (cf. Nietschmann 1987; Copson 1994). The figure would be even higher if we
acknowledge that most external armed interventions, classified here in
the same category as interstate wars, were actually the result of internal
rebellions and wars. Soviet interventions in Hungary and Afghanistan,
and American intervention in Vietnam are examples. In fact, the list in
the appendix includes only thirty purely state versus state wars in fifty
years. This is just 18 percent of the total. When we adjust for the large
number of states in the system since 1945 the incidence of interstate
war has plummeted compared to pre-1945 eras. As Table 2.2 indicates,
there have been on average only 0.005 interstate wars and armed
interventions per state per year since the end of World War II. This
figure contrasts to the 0.019 wars per state annually in the European
states system of the eighteenth century, 0.014 in the nineteenth century,
and 0.036 in the 1919–39 period.

Data are not available for internal ethnic/ideological wars for
previous centuries, but a cursory review of history would suggest a
significantly lower incidence of these types of wars. Where the eras do
show similarity is that a high proportion of the relatively fewer internal
wars of previous centuries were also wars of secession. They were
fundamentally about the creation of states. The American, Greek, and
Irish wars of liberation are examples.

The tables also reveal interesting patterns when we break down the
overall figures into warfare by region. Two anomalies are immediately
apparent: no interstate war in Western Europe, and only one (Falk-
lands/Malvinas) in South America. That one, as we will see in chapter
8, can be eliminated because it was fought outside the continent
against an extra-continental adversary. Other than this marginal case,
there has been no international war south of Panama since 1941. A
third fact, but not listed in the tables, is the absence of both interstate
and domestic war in North America since the American armed intervention in Mexico in 1913. Since there are only three states in the
region, the figure is somewhat less compelling than its counterpart in
Western Europe and South America. Overall, then, we have had three
no-war zones in the world since 1945 (since 1941 in the case of South
America). Other areas of the world have been scenes of more or less
chronic warfare and armed intervention, particularly war within states.
But there are significant gradations between areas, as Table 2.3 shows,
when we normalize for the number of states in the region.

The Middle East has had a high incidence per state of both interstate

The state, war, and the state of war

Table 2.2 *The decline of interstate wars, 1715–1995*

Period	Avg. no. states in central system[a]	No. central system interstate wars[b]	Interstate wars/ state per year
1715–1814	19	36	0.019
1815–1914	21	29	0.014
1918–1941	30	25	0.036
1945–1995	140	38	0.005

Note: [a] average number of central state system members for the period.
[b] excludes imperial wars, wars among or against non-members of the central state system of the time (e.g., Boxer rebellion, South American wars in nineteenth century), and wars of "national liberation" since 1945. Interstate wars include armed interventions involving significant loss of life.
Source: Holsti (1991), data from pp. 85–7, 140–2, and 214–16. Data for the post-1945 period are from the appendix.

Table 2.3 *Armed conflicts per state by region, 1945–1995*

Region	Number of states	Interstate interventions	Internal wars
Africa	43	0.16	0.86
Middle East	18	0.61	1.22
South Asia	7	0.57	2.00
Southeast Asia	11	0.45	1.82
East Asia	6	0.50	0.50
South America	12	0.08	0.67
Central America/Caribbean	20	0.20	0.50
Balkans/East Europe	8	0.38	0.25
Former USSR	15	–	0.47
West Europe	18	–	0.16
Average	–	**0.30**	**0.85**

and domestic wars, although South Asia has the highest figure for armed combat of domestic origins. The figures that best support the argument of this chapter are the averages at the bottom of Table 2.3: in all the regions of the world, not including North America, there has been an average of 0.85 internal wars per state since 1945, compared to only 0.30 interstate wars per state, or a ratio of 2.9 domestic wars for every interstate war and armed intervention.[2] In 1990, a reasonably

[2] The figures may be distorted by the number of states per region. It is as of 1995, whereas many of the wars were fought when there were fewer states. This is

24

typical year for the post-war period, there were thirty-one armed conflicts in progress, only one of which was an interstate war. In 1993, there were forty-seven armed conflicts, none of which was between states (Wallensteen and Axell 1994). The trend of declining interstate wars and increasing internal wars is gaining momentum.

Three major conclusions emerge from these figures. First, classical interstate wars have declined dramatically compared to previous historical periods, and constitute only about 18 percent of all wars since 1945. The main problem of war since 1945 has been within and about states, not between states. Second, the realist and neo-realist prediction that in any system of anarchy, including its component regions, wars must occur with some regularity is not borne out by the data. Three regions have been free of interstate war for more than a half-century and two regions – Europe and North America – have been relatively free of *all* kinds of war during the same period.

Finally, perhaps the most remarkable datum about war since 1945 is that there has been no great power war. The problem of war in the theoretical and practical literatures on international relations has been characterized as essentially a great-power phenomenon; great powers are both the sources of war and the authors of means of alleviating or resolving the problem (cf. Waltz 1979; Bull 1977: ch. 9). Although there have been numerous American, Soviet, British, and French armed interventions since 1945, almost all of them were occasioned by wars and rebellions within states in the Third World, in the communist bloc, or among the post-communist states. The cast of war-launching characters has fundamentally changed in the last one-half of the twentieth century. It is no longer the great powers, but the Israels, Egypts, Indias, Croatias, and Iraqs of the world. Interstate war, to the extent that it still exists, has become primarily a small- or medium-power activity.

These trends and patterns cannot be explained by the standard theoretical devices of international politics, particularly by neo-realist analysis. Rousseau would have been surprised that in some areas of the world his hunters seem to collaborate regularly and none suffers from a security dilemma in his backyard. He could not have predicted the end of great-power war, nor the rise of wars within states.

If such a large proportion of wars have domestic origins, then the

particularly the case in Africa. It is unlikely, however, that a calculation based on an annual ratio of wars per state would produce an overall pattern significantly different from the one in table 2.3.

place to pursue explanations is not in the character of relations between states, but in the character of the states themselves. We are particularly interested in how they were born and how they have fared in creating coherent civil societies and tolerable links between governments and those societies. We move into the area of state creation and state morphology (and sometimes, state pathology) rather than international politics. This is not to exclude all international influences on security problems within states. These will be addressed in chapter 7.

But to pursue the argument, we have to establish that there is more to the problem than mere location of war. Why did people take up arms? What ideas, conditions, and aspirations drove them to the point of rebellion and war? Though the wars listed in the appendix had many issues being contested, the majority dealt with the question of political community. Since 1945, many wars have taken the form of "national liberation." These are wars which have the purpose of ending what is broadly considered to be illegitimate rule over a more or less well-defined community. In the nineteenth century, they were predominantly rebellions of ethnically and/or religiously defined communities against Russian, Austrian, and Ottoman imperial rule. Since 1945, they have been wars of de-colonization, primarily but not exclusively fought against Dutch, French, British, Spanish, Soviet, and Portuguese rule. In each case, the purpose was to transform a colony or satellite into a prototype of a European state.

In addition to wars of "national liberation," there are wars of "national unification." Their purpose is to re-unify some community, real or imagined, that has been torn apart or divided by the great powers in the aftermath of world wars. Vietnam, Korea (also ideological struggles), and the Indian incorporation of Goa are included in this category. Internal faction and ideological wars, ostensibly fought for universal principles such as democracy or socialism, often mask ethnic and other social cleavages within the war zone.[3]

Finally, there are the numerous secession wars fought by communities in post-1945 states: communities that have not been successfully integrated into that larger community that sought independence from colonial rule. The Biafra armed secession, Eritrea, the Tamils in Sri Lanka, the Sikhs in the Punjab, the several lengthy armed resistance movements by the Karen, Chin, Mon, and other groups in Myanmar,

---

[3] For example, the Sendero Luminoso armed uprising during the 1980s and 1990s was based largely among disaffected groups of Indians in Peru.

the Christian and animist population's struggle to tear away from Muslim Sudan, Bougainville's secession fight against the central authorities of Papua New Guinea, and an independence movement within Senegal are just some of the many examples. Although of later origin, many of these conflicts are similar to wars of "national liberation" because they are driven by a community that seeks to create its own state. They involve resistance by various peoples against domination, exclusion, persecution, or dispossession of lands and resources, by the post-colonial state. We can term these state-nation wars.

These kinds of war concern, ultimately, the question of statehood and the nature of community within states. They are very different from the kinds of issues that drove most wars in eighteenth- and nineteenth-century Europe. While many of them have become inter-nationalized through foreign intervention, questions about statehood and state-nation relations, and not Cold War strategic competition, centrally define them. Since these are wars about states rather than about international politics, and since most have been fought in what used to be called the Third World, we might also expect that the European-based norms and styles of warfare would not be duplicated. This is indeed the case. If eighteenth- and nineteenth-century European wars were characterized by etiquette, rules, and formal sequences (crisis, war declaration, military defeat, followed by a negotiated peace), wars about states have had very different characteristics. War since 1945 has become de-institutionalized. We are debating, then, not only a very different geography and typology of armed conflict, but also very different forms of war.

Before exploring the etiology of wars about states, we need to show how wars have changed in strategy, tactics, and rules. Wars of the "third kind" (Rice 1988) bear little relationship to the European wars of the eighteenth and nineteenth centuries or to the total wars of the first half of the twentieth century. The main criteria for distinguishing forms of war are: (1) the purposes of war; (2) the role of civilians during wartime; and (3) the institutions of war. The duration and phases of war, as the opening paragraphs of this chapter demonstrated, are also fundamentally different. When two or more of these criteria change fundamentally, we can say that there has been a transformation of war. Typical wars of the late twentieth and early twenty-first centuries bear about as much relationship to their eighteenth-century predecessors as Louis XIV's wars related to the marauding mercenary

27

bands that constituted the "armed forces" of the Hundred Years War (1373–1453). Indeed, if we look at contemporary Afghanistan or Somalia, the wars there have more in common with the thirteenth century than they do with the Crimean War. Fernand Braudel's (1990: 159–60) description suggests the comparison:

> The Hundred Years' War was nothing like modern conflicts of course. It would be more appropriate to call it "a hundred years of hostilities rather than a hundred-year-war." The battles – sociological and anarchical as much as political – were intermittent, punctuated by truces and negotiations. On average, there was perhaps one year of actual fighting in five. But the countryside was laid waste, either by pillaging troops, who invariably lived off the land, or by scorched earth tactics . . . Whenever they could, the peasants who had taken refuge behind city walls, returned to their land as soon as the danger had passed.

Since 1648, war has been of three essentially different forms. We can call them "institutionalized war," "total war," and wars of the third kind, sometimes called "peoples' wars." The discussion below is not based on the three types of wars since 1945, defined in terms of actors and/or objectives. Rather, it looks at the *forms* of war and how the major organizational, operational, and legal principles surrounding combat have changed over the last 350 years.

Institutionalized war

The Thirty Years War devastated large swaths of Central Europe. Marauding mercenary armies lived off the land and regularly pillaged, burned, raped, and sequestered the peasants' means of living. Religious differences helped the butchery: whole towns of Catholics and Protestants were put to the torch and their inhabitants slaughtered. The war ended through attrition and financial exhaustion rather than through decisive battles. According to Michael Howard (1976: 37), the period of the Thirty Years War (1618–48) was one in which "warfare seemed to escape from rational control; to cease indeed to be 'war' in the sense of politically-motivated use of force by generally recognized authorities, and to degenerate instead into universal, anarchic, and self-perpetuating violence."

Late seventeenth- and eighteenth-century dynasts were concerned about such war. For one thing, temporary mercenary armies were not politically reliable; for another, they could be hired by local dukes and

barons and then used to challenge central state authority. The Habs-
burg emperor had his chief of staff, Wallenstein, murdered because he
feared the marshal's independent mercenary army: it could be used to
establish an independent state for the military leader (Van Creveld
1991: 50). The organization for war between 1648 and 1789 thus came
to reflect the dynasts' political interests in establishing a monopoly of
force within the state. War-making and state-making became organically linked. By the late seventeenth century European wars were
fought by centrally controlled, permanent, full-time professional
armed forces in the service of the state. The development of state
centralization and power made such forces possible. But, in a dialec-
tical fashion, these professional forces also helped centralize the state
by providing the means for securing financial and other resources for
the state treasury. Armed forces that could encourage reluctant Estates
into voting subsidies and coerce peasants and burghers to pay taxes
were also a crucial institution for citizen surveillance and agents for
disarming and policing those who might challenge state authority by
armed force (cf. Howard 1976: 55).

The effort to establish central control over the conduct of war also
helped to manage its worse excesses. The conduct of battle reflected
the culture of moderation that came to be known as the Enlightenment.
Historians have characterized the age as one of "limited war,"
primarily because there were deliberate efforts to impose strict codes of
conduct for soldiers and their leaders and because the highest form of
the art of war was to maneuver the adversary into an untenable
defensive position rather than to annihilate him. It was also limited
because unwritten codes made a clear separation between soldiers and
civilians. Diplomatic goals were to be achieved by military victories
over an adversary's armed forces, not by waging war against civilians.

Permanent professional armies cost much more than "hire for fire"
temporary mercenary forces. Peasants paid the price, but sometimes
only after rebellion. The high costs of professional forces nevertheless
brought an immediate advantage to dynasts. A monarch with access to
the national treasury was the sole person capable of funding a standing
army. The day of the nobles with their own armies was now at an end.

Financial considerations also dominated strategy and tactics. Permanent armies and fleets represented an immense investment that could
not be squandered in orgies of uncontrolled violence. Infantry and
their equipment were valuable assets that could not be gambled away.
Students of dynastic warfare point out that it took on average six years

29

to train a soldier to perform adequately in battle. Constant drills were used to suppress the natural reflexes of turning and running when confronted by ranks of firing soldiers within a stone's throw. Troops had to be trained to march, maneuver, fire in unison, and maintain formation during the exchange of volleys (Childs 1982: 105). A battle was not in the offing unless one or both commanding officers were fairly certain they could win with a relatively low cost in lives.

Battles were carefully choreographed patterns of ranks engaged in march, deployment, volley firing, wheeling, and enveloping. There was no room for individual movement or soldierly initiative. Battle "was not a question of running, flying, bursting in, nor was it a question of speeding up the process ... System was necessary, caution, even slowness sometimes. Teamwork and discipline were always required" (Quimby 1957: 262). Strategy and tactics were highly standardized. Military establishments copied each others' procedures so that the elements of surprise and innovation in war were few. An appropriate metaphor for interstate wars of the late seventeenth and eighteenth centuries – what I have called "institutionalized wars" – was a duel or lethal minuet (Holsti 1991: ch. 5).

The lethal minuet corps was well dressed, symbolizing the gentlemanly ethos of court life extended to the battlefield.[4] The same uniforms that were worn in battle were also worn at the interminable ceremonial displays and parades, all to honor the local dynast. Childs (1982: 73) describes the uniforms of a Württemberg infantry battalion:

> Every infantryman had to sport a black moustache complete with well-waxed pointed ends, and if a man had facial hair of the wrong colour or little or no beard, he adopted the theatrical expedient of gluing on false bristles. Above this he wore a white, heavily powdered wig adorned with up to six curls on each side. The grenadiers' uniform culminated with the shako, which was so heavy that it had to be held in place by a metal chinstrap that compelled the men to walk with their heads bent forward, eyes staring at their shoes ... The gaiters were lined with two pieces of stiff cardboard which gave the soldiers a fine, shapely leg but tensed the calf muscle to such an extent that he could scarcely sit down.

War was limited, finally, by the lack of political motivation among troops and leadership. Military service was a job filled by the none-too-

---

[4] Mercenary soldiers that populated the armed forces during the Thirty Years War wore no distinctive garb, hence contributing to the weak distinction between civilians and soldiers.

well-off strata of society, in fact, frequently by its "scum," to use a popular term of the times. There was no sense of duty to the monarch nor to the country; high desertion rates were the result. Among the nobility, good careers could be made in the service of any king or queen. Nationality was irrelevant. What united the dynast and his military leaders was not nationalism, but personal loyalty and the common interest in fighting at an advantage in order to lose as few men as possible and to subsist comfortably at the enemy's expense (Childs 1982: 103).

War as an instrument of state policy meant that hostilities were a contest of wile, tactics, and precision maneuvering of formations. The purpose of combat was to force the surrender of the adversary. Rules determined when an honorable surrender could be made. A certain breakthrough, such as a two-meter wide breach of a walled fort or town, symbolized victory. It was neither necessary nor good form to annihilate the enemy or visit depredations upon civilians. Hatred was not normally a part of the soldier's or officer's mentality. Both were doing a job, not fighting a cause or seeking revenge for some previous butchery. That job was a contest, and personal feelings beyond group solidarity rarely intruded. Officers of adversary armies routinely socialized with each other. Rothenberg (1978: 91) describes how "junior officers of warring armies [in Spain during the Napoleonic wars] met to exchange small tokens, trade cognac for rum, discuss their past exploits, boast a bit, and arrange for letters to be forwarded to a fellow officer prisoner in France." Prisoners were on the whole treated well, due perhaps less to humanitarian sentiments than to the recognition that they could replace soldiers captured or killed by the enemy.

A number of tactical "rules of the game" guided the fighting. It was not considered good form to fire at individual leaders, especially generals, messengers, and flag bearers. Troops had to wear proper identification and weapons had to be carried openly. Most important, war was to be a self-contained activity separate from civilian life. Civilians in the path of marching armies often faced forced requisitions, theft, and occasional looting, but honorable leaders did not target civilians in any way. Trade, commerce, travel, and other forms of contact between societies remained quite normal during wartime. According to Frederick II, the ideal war was one where civilians were unaware that it even existed.

The duel or ballet analogy extends to the role of outsiders. They

31

were onlookers, an audience, and in no way involved in the action. The laws of neutrality were developed to make a clear legal distinction between combatants – a declaration of war was always against another specified state – and those who were not to be involved. These rules established the rights and restrictions on forms of aid available from non-combatants. The clear distinction between soldiers and civilians and their virtual separation in war carried beyond to other states. They could trade with the belligerents and had the right of naval passage but they could not sell arms and *matériel* nor allow troops of the belligerents to pass through their territories. All these conventions, "rules of the game," and laws of warfare demonstrated that it was highly institutionalized.

This portrait of limited war is not meant to idealize it. There were plenty of brutalities. Discipline was often cruel and deserters were usually hanged. There were frequent depredations against civilians in the paths of marching armies and the troops suffered high mortality rates, due more to disease than to armed combat. Yet, the actual conduct of war was suffused with rules, norms, and etiquette. It was stylized in preparation and commission. Military service was a life-long career (at least for the nobility) based on rigorous training and study (the first military academies date from the seventeenth century: Keegan 1993: 344). Finally, wars reflected the fairly limited political purposes of dynasts: a province, a crown, more defensible frontiers, a cut of colonial trade, or domination of particular waterways. Dynasts had no interest in re-making foreign societies in their own image, militarily intervening in foreign court intrigues, or "liberating" their own or foreign peoples. Compared to what was to happen in the next two centuries, we can look back with a certain nostalgia at eighteenth-century war. Perhaps Ferrero summed it up best: "Restricted warfare was one of the loftiest achievements of the eighteenth century. It belongs to a class of hot-house plants which can only thrive in an aristocratic and qualitative civilization. We are no longer capable of it" (quoted in Dyer 1985: 75).

The descent to total war

The story of war transformation in the twentieth century is familiar and needs no lengthy re-telling here. Only our three criteria will be considered.

Napoleonic war introduced no great new technology. But the manpower and financial limitations of dynastic war were overcome by the 1792 *levée en masse* which symbolically transformed war from an undertaking by professionals to a mighty campaign of a nation-in-arms. With unlimited manpower pools, conscription, national taxation, and armed forces motivated by patriotic zeal and the sentiments of revolutionary equality, many of the eighteenth-century constraints disappeared. Hatred of the enemy replaced equanimity and concern for getting a job done; armies increased vastly in size; the purpose of battle was to annihilate the enemy, not force him to surrender; and the costs of war were to be borne by those who were "liberated." Massive plundering replaced the more genteel treaties of territorial adjustment of the eighteenth century. Most important, the purposes of war became unlimited. They were to "liberate" and re-organize whole societies and to replace the system of dynastic sovereign states with a French-centered empire whose constituent units provided thrones for members of Napoleon's family. Many eighteenth-century "rules of the game" were systematically violated during massive battles.

The peacemakers of 1814–15 recognized the potential disasters to their regimes were French revolutionary–Napoleonic wars to be fought again. The years following the Congress of Vienna saw the restoration of the military as a professional and socially distinct instrument of the state. Napoleon's innovations, except at the tactical level, were rejected in favor of a more restrained form of warfare.

Codification of the rules of war began to replace the unofficial "rules of the game" that had developed in the eighteenth century. After the 1791–1815 interlude, the eighteenth-century ground rules of war were strengthened. States continued to insist that they had a monopoly over the use of force (privateering was terminated); soldiers had to wear proper identifying marks; they could not conceal weapons. The massive German warbook of the late nineteenth century contains reams of regulations that describe proper war conduct. The primary conceptual emphases of the warbook reflected clear distinctions between war and peace, soldier and civilian, belligerent and neutral.

Codification was also the result of international negotiations. The Geneva Convention (1864) dealt with the treatment of prisoners, sick, and wounded. The two Hague Conferences (1899 and 1907) reviewed all and amended some laws and customs of war and outlawed certain munitions. The St. Petersburg Conventions announced the classical Clausewitzian edict that "le seul but légitime de la guerre est l'affaiblissement des forces militaires." Civilians were not a proper target of military action. In the years prior to the Great War, most people could still believe that war was a reasonably civilized means of advancing or sustaining foreign policy purposes.

This was not the case, however, when European armies operated outside the continent. Laws and conventions of war did not apply to "barbarians" and "savages." Resistance to the colonial endeavor was met with harsh reprisals. "In the colonies," writes Van Creveld (1991: 41), "European troops often acted as if what they were waging was not war but safari. They slaughtered the natives like beasts, scarcely stopping to distinguish between chiefs, warriors, women, and children."

There is an oil painting, *Sturmangriff* ("Offensive Storm") by Carl Strathann in the Munich city gallery. It depicts close up a packed group of German soldiers in field grey, bayonets at the ready, gritting their teeth in unison, angst, fear, hatred, prior to a collective forward charge against the enemy. This image captures, perhaps for the last time, the nineteenth-century view of war: soldiers motivated by nationalist zeal, hatred of the enemy, and trained to operate as a single unit in close formation, centrally directed by the political authorities. The enemy, the viewer can assume, holds a similar posture. War is a contest between clearly identifiable armed forces that have the task of forcing the surrender of the adversary. There is not a civilian in sight and nothing in the painting suggests that civilians have anything to do with what is to follow. Institutionalized war, in Van Creveld's (1991) terms, is "trinitarian." The state, the armed forces, and the civil population are legally, politically, and strategically distinct. Strathann's creation clearly suggests this.

But the Great War took up where Napoleon had left off. Institutionalized war began to unravel. Technology combined with nationalism increasingly threatened the clear distinctions. Two new environments for warfare were opened up: under the sea and in the air. Both led to civilian casualties. As the war – expected in 1914 to last no more than a few months – moved into the stage of attrition, strategic objectives changed from inflicting decisive victories in the field to crippling the adversary's capacity to wage mechanized war. This meant attacking non-military targets. Unrestricted submarine warfare and the Allies' naval blockade of Germany led to mounting civilian casualties. If it was a "nation" going to war, then a "nation" would have to bear the burden. Frederick the Great's ideal war was a thing of the past.

To mount a lengthy war of attrition, the whole population had to be mobilized. This was done in part through extensive government propaganda programs featuring nationalist themes of "us" and demonizing themes about the enemy. New technologies and the need to sustain civilian enthusiasm helped transform war as a contest between armed forces to a contest between nations. "Nobody had started a crusade in 1914, nobody then was out to liberate oppressed nationalities, to make an end of secret diplomacy, or to spread democracy," wrote Raymond Aron.

> The war had not been started in order to bring about the triumph of particular views of life and society; but as the cost of operations mounted these views were felt to be essential to inflate the prospective profits of victory . . . The demand for total victory was not so much the expression of a political philosophy as a reflex reaction to total war.   (Aron 1954: 27)

But except for submarine warfare and the economic blockade between 1914 and 1918, civilians remained mostly the innocent victims of nearby military campaigns featuring long-distance artillery. During World War II, however, civilians became deliberate targets of war. Terror became a component of strategic thinking. To win a war, it was no longer necessary only to inflict defeats on armed forces. Civilian morale had to be destroyed as well. This was to be done primarily by massive bombing raids against population centers, whether or not those areas had any military significance (Allied bombing raids on Hamburg, July 1943, with 39,000 dead; the 1945 raid on Dresden, with over 100,000 dead; German raids on Warsaw, London, Coventry, Antwerp and many others). The Nazis also perfected on-the-ground terror machines against designated groups, primarily Jews, gypsies, and any and all forms of resistance. The Nazis and Japanese systematically violated all norms and legal obligations with respect to the treatment of war prisoners. Prisoners were turned into slave labor and usually worked to death. Of the approximately five million Soviet prisoners in Nazi captivity, more than three million died of mistreatment and privation (Keegan 1993: 373).

The list of war horrors between 1937 and 1945 is well known so we need not elaborate in more detail. The reader can realize easily enough that eighteenth- and twentieth-century European wars share little in common. Most legal and political constraints no longer operated. The end result of war also changed. Negotiated peace treaties were replaced by doctrines of unconditional surrender. War in the twentieth century was total not only in its destructive capacity and deliberate targeting of civilians, but also in its purposes: the Nazis and Japanese turned their conquests into large slave labor and resource-exploitation zones. The victorious Allies reconstructed their conquests into duplicates of their own societies, the long-range consequences of which have been happy.

From total war to wars of the third kind

Brutal occupation generates resistance. Resistance against highly organized intelligence and terror systems cannot be organized along traditional military lines. The weak must remain hidden. They must be indistinguishable from the general population. Engagements must be sporadic, their perpetrators unobserved and unidentifiable. To the extent that resistance is organized at all, it relies upon a sympathetic civilian population for food, communications, hideaways, and other services.

These practices, observed in Nazi- and Japanese-occupied territories, became immortalized in the revolutionary theories of "peoples' wars" of Mao Tse-tung, Vo Nguen Giap, Che Guevara, and others. Peoples' war is at once a war of resistance and a campaign to politicize the masses whose loyalty and enthusiasm must sustain a post-war regime. While there are many debates about best tactics, the forms of revolutionary propaganda, and the most appropriate location to launch the wars (city versus country, for example), from our perspective the critical issues are the ways in which all of these ideas and debates have de-institutionalized war. Martin Van Creveld (1991) is among the first to recognize that the Clausewitzian eighteenth- and nineteenth-century concept of war – which I have called "institutionalized war" – is not only fast fading, but is inappropriate as both an analytical and policy guide to those who must think and respond to violence that concerns ideology and/or the nature of communities, rather than state interests. The symbolic manifestations of war transformation are clear: in wars of the "third kind" there are no fronts, no campaigns, no bases, no uniforms, no publicly displayed honors, no *points d'appui*, and no respect for the territorial limits of states (Van Creveld 1991: 206). There are no set strategies and tactics. Innovation, surprise, and unpredictability are necessities and virtues. The weak must rely on guile, and often crime, to raise funds for the bombings, assassinations, and massacres. Prisoners are used as hostages to extract political gains;

terrorist incidents are designed to make publicity, not to defeat an enemy armed force. Terror is also used to cow the timid, the "collaborators," and the indifferent. The clear distinction between the state, the armed forces, and the society that is the hallmark of institutionalized war dissolves in "peoples' war."

Casualty figures are a grim indicator of the transformation of armed conflict represented by wars of the "third kind." In the decade of the 1970s, there were 921,000 deaths through armed combat. Of these, almost 90 percent (820,000) died in civil wars (Small and Singer 1982: 134, 263). Of the 90 percent, another 90 percent, approximately, were civilian casualties. Civilian casualties of wars in Africa have been particularly high. The five wars in Sudan, Ethiopia, Angola, Mozambique, and Uganda produced between 100,000 in Angola and reportedly more than one million deaths in Sudan. In these large wars, the overwhelming majority of victims were civilians. One estimate is that between two and three million African civilians died in wars during the 1980s (Copson 1991b: 23). Gurr (1991: 153) estimates that between one-half million and 1.7 million Africans died from government policies of genocide or "politicide" in the 1980s. The figures for the 1990s, which include vast numbers of civilian casualties in Liberia and Rwanda and the continuation of the war in Sudan, will probably not be significantly lower. A report by Africa Watch, *Thirty Years of War and Famine in Ethiopia*, emphasized in its conclusions that in the Eritrean war between 1961 and 1991 "the most characteristic feature ... was the indiscriminate use of violence against civilians by the Ethiopian army and police. The number of innocent people killed during the war undoubtedly exceeds 150,000." The description of both Eritrean and Ethiopian atrocities against civilians makes depressing reading. Bosnian Serb and Croatian "ethnic cleansing" received far more attention in the international media than its predecessors in many other parts of the world. But numerically it was less significant.

In wars of the third kind, just as the civilian/soldier distinction disappears, the role of outsiders becomes fuzzy. The laws of neutrality no longer apply because those who are militarily weak rely on outsiders for arms, logistical support, and sanctuary. The North Vietnamese received massive quantities of aid from China and the Soviet Union, while the Mujahideen in Afghanistan were funded, housed, and armed by a disparate set of sponsors including Pakistan, Saudi Arabia, and the United States. Arms merchants, drug cartels, and a bevy of foreign sympathizers organized into "support groups" transform the war from a local enterprise into a vast transnational undertaking. Clearly, the duel or ballet analogy has no role in this kind of war.

What else is so different from previous eras? Mostly it is the purposes of armed conflict. War as an instrument of a foreign policy with limited goals is not necessarily the same phenomenon as war fought to preserve or establish a community. Since the early nineteenth century, the community has usually been defined in terms of a state. Wars of "national liberation," unification, and secession are pre-state wars. But their objective is to create a state. For a variety of reasons, most of which do not make economic sense, the goal is to have "my country." In these wars, ordinary cost-benefit analyses that underlie wars as a "continuation of politics by other means" no longer apply:

> Ironic though the fact may be, it is when the stakes are highest and a community strains every sinew in a life-and-death struggle that the ordinary strategic terminology fails. Under such circumstances, to say that war is an "instrument" serving the "policy" of the community that "wages" it is to stretch all three terms to the point of meaninglessness. Where the distinction between ends and means breaks down, even the idea of war fought "for" something is only barely applicable. The difficulty consists precisely in that a war of this type does not constitute a continuation of policy by other means. Instead, it would be more correct to say . . . that it merges with policy, becomes policy, is policy. Such a war cannot be "used" for this purpose or that, nor does it "serve" anything. On the contrary, the outburst of violence is best understood as the supreme manifestation of existence as well as a celebration of it. (Van Creveld 1991: 142–3)

The sacrifices, the extremely high casualty rates, and the endurance of guerrilla-type military formations attests to the psycho-political motivations underlying these forms of combat. American planners during the Vietnam War, as well as their British, French, Israeli, and Soviet counterparts in Cyprus, Algeria, Indochina, the occupied territories, Afghanistan, and dozens of other locales, could never win their "wars" precisely because they operated under a Clausewitzian calculus. Americans asked what possible purpose could the killing of 45,000 fellow citizens serve in terms of United States foreign policy interests? This is not a question the Afghans, Algerians, Karens, or Tamils have asked. No government which is merely pursuing traditional-style interests could possibly mobilize a whole society to conduct a peoples' war for thirty or more years. The Reagan administration withdrew American troops from Lebanon after 238 marines were killed in a Beirut bombing incident; it took only a dozen American fatalities in Somalia to force a withdrawal of American troops from a peacekeeping mission there in 1994. How are these episodes comparable to the 300,000 to one million fatalities among Algerians in their war of independence against France? The use of force in these locales was of a fundamentally different character. Yet, some insist on calling all three episodes the "use of force for political purposes." They have about as much similarity as the Nazi death camps bear to the battle of Blenheim (1704).

Peoples' wars, as the name suggests, also have a fundamentally different nexus between combatants and civilians. For groups and communities, their main strength lies in the civilian population; it is the main source of their manpower, logistical support, and intelligence. But civilians also become targets. Communities are often intermingled so that battle lines cut through cities, towns, and neighborhoods. To the extent that control over territory is a key value, civilian populations are the objects of eviction, rape, massacres, and "ethnic cleansing" (cf. Brown 1993: 16). In wars between communities as opposed to armies, everyone is automatically labeled a combatant merely by virtue of their identity. "They turn everyone," writes John Chipman (1993: 240), "into participants and so give every individual – not only organized groups, parties, factions, or alliances – a personal stake in the outcome. This fact . . . is what makes the resolution of ethnic conflict different from other types of conflict resolution." In eighteenth-century wars, very few had a stake in outcomes. The "sport of princes" was played in far-off fields. In wars of the third kind, the deadly game is played in every home, church, government office, school, highway, and village.

The purposes of such wars is often to politicize the masses, to turn them into good revolutionaries and/or nationalists. Civilians not only become major targets of operations, but their transformation into a new type of individual becomes a major purpose of war. Since the distinction between combatant and civilian is blurred or indistinct, it is not surprising that the brunt of casualties are suffered by the inhabitants of villages, towns, and cities. Even with the genocide machines of World War II, the combatant-to-civilian casualty ratio remained tilted toward the combatant. Peoples' wars are fundamentally about people, not "interests"; it is the people rather than the combatants who pay most of the price. Discipline typical of eighteenth-century armed forces has vanished, and peace is difficult to achieve because instead of interests, identities, psychology, culture, and state creation and survival are involved. "War in our time," writes John Keegan (1993: 56), "has been not merely a means of resolving interstate disputes but also a vehicle through which the embittered, the dispossessed, the naked of the earth, and the hungry masses yearning to breathe free, express their anger, jealousies and pent-up urge to violence." Peoples' wars thus tend to be nasty, brutish, and long (Roberts 1993: 214).

Since these wars of a third kind are fundamentally about people, and involve civilians as both combatants and victims, their main legacy after killing and maiming is the waves of refugees they create. The figures are staggering: 100,000 Hindus escaping the on-and-off war in Kashmir; about the same number of Ossetians fleeing Georgia; one-half million seeking safe haven from the war between Armenia and Azerbaijan; about the same number in Liberia; 200,000 Serbs left Krajina – an area they had inhabited for centuries – after the Croatian invasion of 1995; 600,000 have left the Balkans since the collapse of Yugoslavia, with another three million displaced from their homes but hanging on in the region; two million refugees from the 1994 genocidal slaughter in Rwanda, mostly camped out in neighboring Tanzania and Zaïre; and millions more from the various "wars of national debilitation" (Gelb 1994: 6) continuing in Myanmar, Cambodia, Iraq, Sri Lanka, Sudan, and Tajikistan (Brown 1993: 17). In 1994, according to International Red Cross figures, there were 23 million refugees and 26 million displaced persons, for a total of almost 49 million people uprooted from their homes as a result of wars of the third kind (Centre Québécois des Relations Internationales 1995: 1; Ayoob 1995: 174).

Wars of the third kind have predominated in the international system since 1945. They persist and will continue into the future. Why? Because in many regions of the world the issue of statehood and the relation of the state to its constituent nations, communities, and peoples has not been settled with de-colonization. In particular, weak states – not in the military sense, but in terms of legitimacy and efficacy – are and will be the locales of war. To the extent that those issues might be settled once and for all – a dubious proposition at best – it will often be by armed combat. To understand why this has been and will be the case, it is necessary to examine the birth and nature of modern states. The sources of present and future war lie in the very different European and Third World experiences of state birth and formation.

3   The formation of states before 1945

Wars of the third kind have numerous unique qualities. Their histories vary, as do their outcomes – defeat of insurgents in Malaya, victory in Algeria, stalemate in Kashmir and the Sudan – but they have a common source: the definition of a legitimate political community and the search for statehood. The mystiques of statehood and "nationality" drive today's wars, just as balances of power, successions, searches for hegemony, and rivalry over colonies drove most eighteenth-century wars. The end of the Cold War has not brought a "new world order" because that rivalry was largely irrelevant to a much more fundamental historical process, the definition and determination of legitimate community from imperial to other forms, and the transformation of a heterogeneity of political organizations into a single format, the modern state. To understand why we will continue to have wars of the third kind in future years, we need to have a better understanding, first, of the origins, the drive for, and forms of political community and statehood and, second, of the difficulties facing many new states.

The process of state-formation in Europe has become an area of increased research by historical sociologists and political scientists during the past several decades. We now have a reasonably rich literature that generalizes across many eras and locales and develops a variety of perspectives (cf. Tilly 1990; Hall 1986; Rasler and Thompson 1989; Ruggie 1993). While narratives and explanations by no means agree on details and emphases, there is a general consensus that the development of the state format of political organization was a lengthy process, that it took many forms and trajectories, and that political elites between the fifteenth and twentieth centuries did not have an overall plan or model they were trying to create (cf. Smith 1986: 239; Tilly 1990: 194).

In the year 1200, Europe was carved up into a hotch-potch of political forms, a heterogeneous collection of tributary empires, free cities, ecclesiastical proto-states, dukedoms, hereditary kingdoms, and Arab tribal organizations in parts of Spain. According to Tilly (1990:45), a minimum of 80 distinct political units and a maximum of 500, depending upon how one defines a political organization, dotted the continental landscape. On average, a ruler controlled an area of about 16,000 square kilometers, the size of contemporary El Salvador. By 1900 Europe had been reduced to nineteen units that took only two forms: the modern territorial nation-state and the dynastic multinational empire. Two decades later, the multinational empires had collapsed, leaving only the single format of the territorial state until Lenin and Stalin resurrected a new form of multinational empire in the Soviet Union. Europe moved from extreme heterogeneity of political forms to homogeneity in about five centuries. A few remnants of that heterogeneity remain in the form of non-sovereign entities such as Andorra, Liechtenstein, and Monaco, but they are primarily dependencies and destinations for tourists rather than modern sovereign states.

Authors do not agree on all the conditions that stimulated the development of the modern state format, but among them we can list the relative continental isolation from imperial power centers of the world (although the Ottoman Empire almost succeeded in embracing large parts of east and central Europe in the seventeenth century), a common Christian culture, and the development of print and the replacement of elite Latin by mass vernaculars (cf. Anderson 1983a: 44–7). The development of cities that fostered capital accumulation (Tilly 1990), and the concentration of an ethnic elite core in areas such as the Ile de France, Castile, and England (Smith 1986: 241; Smith 1989) were also critical sources of the territorial state.

The previous chapter emphasized that war also played a major role in the formation of states. As Anthony Giddens (1987: 112) suggests,

> The European state system was not simply the "political environment" in which the absolutist state and nation-state developed. It was the condition, and in substantial degree the very source, of that development. It was war, and preparations for war, that provided the most potent energizing stimulus for the concentration of administrative resources and fiscal reorganization that characterized the rise of absolutism. (cf. Howard 1976: 55)

Indeed, one could make the case that a significant majority of states were born through war and continued to centralize after armed combat. In France, England, Spain, Russia, Germany, and elsewhere, civil wars between centralizing monarchs and local and regional power centers characterized historical development for centuries. French kings subjugated local authorities through a variety of means, both persuasive (bribery of various forms) and coercive. Occasionally, resistance took the form of civil war (the Fronde of the mid-seventeenth century). Peter the Great subdued the *boyars* through military campaigns and mass executions. British kings confronted armed nobles through coercion, bribery, and various forms of armed "pacification." Under the influence of Richelieu and Colbert, French kings systematically destroyed the fortifications of cities and nobles. They were replaced by fortifications on the periphery of France. By the early 1700s, the French population had been effectively disarmed (Tilly 1990: 69) and thus incapable of serious resistance against expanding central authority.

Fixed and delimited territorial boundaries are a relatively recent invention. Throughout most of human history, the territorial base of political jurisdictions was at best fluid. There were vast "grey" areas of overlapping jurisdictions (and thus frequent quarrels) of uncertain domains. Patrimonial realms were not the same as the carefully delimited and defended frontiers of today. Until the late seventeenth century, Europe included vast open spaces where goods, people, and ideas could migrate without reference to citizenship or origins. State core areas were separated from the peripheries by wastelands, forests, or farm areas that were difficult to traverse. Even as late as the 1790s it took eleven days to travel by coach from Paris to Marseilles (Braudel 1990); a trip from Moscow to St. Petersburg was a major undertaking. But the peripheries were also the routes for foreign invasions. To define a realm more precisely – and therefore to be able to defend it better – lineal frontiers were drawn. The move from frontiers to borders, from amorphous zones to mutually agreed upon demarcated lines, did not occur until well into the eighteenth century. The first surveyed lineal boundary in Europe was recorded in a treaty in 1718 (Giddens 1987: 90). As the central authorities began to organize their realms vertically by undermining or destroying local power centers, they also began to organize their horizontal space. By the early nineteenth century, most of the states of Western Europe were well defined in terms of sovereign jurisdiction. The actual delimitation of frontiers was as often as not the result of wars and their resulting peace treaties. A province, duchy, or region was dismembered from one state and annexed to its neighbor. Through the fifteenth to nineteenth centuries, then, uncertainly defined "realms" became specifically located territorial states.

State-making was essentially an internal undertaking (or ordeal, as some monarchs were to learn). But to the extent that it succeeded, it allowed central authorities to extract ever-increasing revenues through taxation of various forms. These revenues were used to further the centralization process by expanding administrative and judicial institutions throughout the realm. They were also used to increase the sovereign's armed might. State-making thus was not a matter solely of domestic concern. Rousseau's concept of the "security dilemma" nicely captures the external consequences of the state-making process: as sovereigns disarmed their populations and lesser power centers, they increased their capacity for maintaining authority within the realm. This was perceived by neighbors as a potential threat. They therefore copied the centralizing practices of their competitors. *Emulation* was critically important to the state-making process (cf. Waltz 1979). As John Hall (1986: 164–5) has put it: empires don't need to copy the barbarians on the peripheries; states must copy each other if they want to survive.[1] Peter the Great's sojourn *incognito* in Amsterdam is just one of the more dramatic tales of emulation. He studied Dutch shipbuilding crafts in order to build a naval fleet capable of holding at bay Russia's enemies in the north and south, Sweden and the Ottoman Empire. His model for the Russian state was France. His Prussian counterpart, Frederick, also saw France as the state upon which to model the disparate and non-contiguous realms of Brandenburg. More than a century later, Japan sent numerous "research commissions" to Europe to copy state institutions and in particular the military institutions of Prussia/Germany. For reasons of prestige, defense, and effective centralization, the state-making process was in a sense a chain reaction.

What is missing from this narrative? Most historical sociologists and political scientists who have studied the state-formation process in Europe are materialists. They emphasize capital and coercion, war, communications, printing, vernacular languages and the slow develop-

---

[1] In some respects, however, empires did copy some of their barbarian adversaries' military tactics and equipment. Cavalry and stirrups were introduced by Mongols and earlier groups who at the time were considered by the major civilizations to be barbarian. I am grateful to the anonymous external examiner of this study for the point.

ment of administrative capacities. They miss the *ideas and myths* that sustain the legitimacy of political orders and the communities on which those orders are based. Historically, leaders of political communities have based their right to rule on combinations of religion (as for example in the doctrine of divine right of monarchy), virtue, inheritance, special achievement (particularly heroism in war), race, lineage, and as in the myths to justify European and American imperialism, the paternalistic ideas inherent in "civilizing missions." Until the late eighteenth century, European princes based their rule on a combination of these, collectively known as the dynastic principle under which hereditary rulers passed on their possessions to offspring with the blessing of the Holy See and other monarchs. The communities over which they ruled were defined as groups of *subjects*, often sub-identified by creed. But under the influence of the Enlightenment, questions began to be raised about both the sources of political authority within the state and the nature of the community over which state rule is exercised. For the next century, two new ideas among a number of older ones became paramount in defining the political community and the right to rule over it: citizenship and nationality.[2]

The community of citizens

We do not need to elaborate on the change of legitimizing myths or principles underlying democratic claims of a right to rule. It is well known: the American and French revolutions substituted the concept of popular sovereignty for divine right and its attending beliefs and doctrines of succession and royal mystique based on warrior and other achievements. What is less understood in terms of its importance for international politics and war, is the change in definitions of political community, that is, the specification of who, precisely, is to be counted as a member of the political order and on what basis.

---

[2] Anthony Smith makes a similar distinction: Western civic and Eastern (German) cultural–national bases of authority. The civic concept contains four elements: (1) a territorial referent ("homeland") as repository of historic memories and associations; (2) the idea of *patria*, a community of laws and institutions; (3) a sense of legal equality; and (4) a measure of common values and traditions. The Eastern concept is based on birth regardless of political context. To define oneself, there is a need for a "pre-historical reality" – a reference to a "people" that existed before the state, as well as culture and ethnicity (Smith 1991: 9ff). I question whether items 1 and 4 are critical in immigrant societies such as Canada and Australia. Legal equality, in my view, is the crucial component of the civic basis of political community.

After the Thirty Years War until the American and French revolutions, the specification of community did not present a problem. The definition of community had been settled in the Treaties of Westphalia on the basis of the religion of the prince. The community was identical with the prince's subjects, whose primary identity was faith. The community was formed historically through wars, successions, and marriages. This was assumed rather than debated. One searches in vain among the writings of Hobbes and Locke for some other specification of community. Curiously, although their metaphor of the state of nature was universal, implying world government, they did not contest the actual limits of territorial jurisdiction of seventeenth- and eighteenth-century Europe. Whether the social contract was between individuals in order to set up a sovereign (Locke), or between individuals and the state-Leviathan (Hobbes), the authors assumed their readers would easily identify the affiliations of these individuals. The "Commonwealth," to use Hobbes's term, was understood to mean the England of the mid-seventeenth century.

In contract theory the state is the creation of individual will, multiplied by the numbers making up the community or commonwealth. There is no reference to groups, associations, or other collectivities based on interest, language, culture, or other attributes. The state is the "executive committee" of the people; it is their creation. If all have as a matter of will made a social contract, it follows that all are equally responsible for the results. There cannot be individuals who make a contract, while others fail to do so, are exempt from it, or who have special privileges.

The individualism of contract theory translates to the concept of the *citizen*. The community, then, is defined in terms of *citizenship* within a territorially bounded realm. Once attained, citizenship provides equal rights and responsibilities for individuals.

The idea of the citizen was developed prior to and during the French revolution. It is often forgotten that the National Assembly drafted the *Declaration of the Rights of Man and the Citizen* (1789). Although in subsequent years the revolutionaries established various qualifications based on wealth ("active" and "passive" citizens) and education, and deliberately excluded servants and women, in theory all citizens were to be equal. But who were they? This was not a matter of debate. It was assumed rather than argued that citizens were to be the former *subjects* of the king.

Residence in the French nation (community), after the age of twenty-one, automatically warranted citizenship. Birth and residence in the nation, rather than privilege mediated through the monarch, became the basis of equal rights (Fitzsimmons 1993: 31). The Revolution destroyed or abolished all subnational jurisdictional boundaries and corporate distinctions. This left the citizen face to face with the state; there were no more buffers (Brubaker 1992: 45). But since, theoretically, it was citizens who now made the laws, buffers were no longer necessary. Most significant, whatever the debates and changes in the formal qualifications of citizenship, they were not based on some concept of nationality, religion, language (very few "Frenchmen" could read the *Declaration of the Rights of Man and the Citizen* in French), or ethnicity. Indeed, in the first version of the citizenship concept, foreigners residing in France were included. The community, then, is defined in terms of citizenship achieved by all people residing within the traditional territorial unit called France, the United States, or whatever.

Humans form all sorts of associations for different purposes, be they economic, religious, familial, political, athletic, or others. In the concept of the citizen, rights and responsibilities transcend such associations. Individuals cannot be put into permanent categories; to do so implies either special privileges or special exclusions. Rights, then, are enjoyed equally regardless of a citizen's location, ethnic origins, language, beliefs, sentiments, or affiliations. A naturalized Canadian of Chinese birth has exactly the same rights and duties as a native-born Canadian. The Canadian-Chinese may be marginalized economically, or discriminated against (illegally) in various associations, but he or she stands in exactly the same relationship to the state as any other Canadian. It is this legal equality that is supposed to provide the glue for society. Questions of "identity," personal association, language, religious practices, and other issues are left to the individual to organize or experience privately. They are beyond the purview of the state.

But not all individuals find citizenship an adequate basis for community. It is individualistic, abstract, and ultimately taken for granted. A second definition of the political community seeks to provide the emotional and sentimental glue that citizenship and popular sovereignty lack.

The community of nationals

The literature on nationalism is vast; the debates are furious and on-going.[3] Definitions abound, as do moral judgments. This is not the place to wade into the thicket. Our concern is to compare the state-formation process in Europe during the past half-millennium with the process in other parts of the world, mostly since 1945, and to see how these differences relate to the incidence of war.

Most contemporary analysts agree that as a sentiment binding members of the state, nationalism is a recent phenomenon. It was expressed first by political elites in the era of the French revolution but did not become a grass-roots sentiment until well into the nineteenth century.

Prior to this time, peasants of eighteenth-century France, Germany, England, Spain, and other European dynastic territories identified themselves primarily as Christians. If there was any political nexus between the peasant and the king, queen, prince, or duke, it was primarily in the form of tax payment. There was a vague sense of being a "subject" of this or that prince or local magnate, or of a distant emperor, but peasants and many townspeople were not conscious of being a member of a "nation" in the modern sense (Pfaff 1993: 61). If there were any secular "identities" that had political impact, they were local. Consider the French case.

France in 1664 was divided by internal customs barriers except inside the area known as the *"cinq grosses fermes"* which had been welded into a customs union by Colbert. That area covered a good portion of northern France, but excluded Brittany and large parts of Picardy. French authorities considered these areas, along with Burgundy and virtually the whole of France south of the Loire, as "foreign." They were legally part of the hereditary territorial realm (except Burgundy), but in fact foreign countries (see the map in Braudel 1988: 68). Braudel (1988: 72) writes of eighteenth-century France:

> Nor shall we find unity where we might have expected in theory to find it – at the level of political power. No structuring force from the political center ever succeeded in imposing unity in a diversity which

---

[3] A useful summary and analysis is in Ole Waever *et al.* (1993: ch. 2). The literature on nationalism is, nevertheless, based heavily on the European and North American experiences. English-language studies of the origins and forms of nationalism else-where are rare (cf. Norbu 1992).

seemed to have ineradicable vitality. No sooner was it disciplined than it broke out again: neither political, social nor cultural order ever contrived to foist more than surface unity on the whole.

He continues when describing the centuries-long efforts of French royalty to bring unity to the realm:

> But what difficulties, obstacles, forces of inertia and counterpowers it had to face! . . . From its long past, it inherited a farrago of disorganization, confusion, downright impotence. French society was by no means under the firm hand of the state, far from it . . . There could be no such thing as an even halfway unified society in France until the French nation had been forged – something that is still so recent that we almost think of it as accomplished within living memory.

Until the late nineteenth century, France was a geographical expression and a territorial state, but not a nation. That key indicator of a nation – a common language – was a creation of the French state between 1536 when Francis I declared it the official language, and today. In between, France was a congeries of local dialects and patois. In a published account in 1707, an English traveler claimed that "it is no less difficult for a peasant from these parts [southern France] to make a speech in French than it would be for a newly-landed Frenchman to speak English in England" (quoted in Braudel 1988: 86). At the time of the French Revolution – often claimed to be the first great manifestation of French nationalism – one-half of France's citizens spoke no French, and only about 12 percent spoke it properly (Hobsbawm 1990: 60). According to Braudel, in the eighteenth century the dialects spoken by the French peasantry generally extended no more than 7 kilometers. Even as late as the mid-nineteenth century, few peasants in Languedoc could speak French. Eugene Weber's (1976) study, *Peasants into Frenchmen: The Modernization of Rural France, 1870–1940*, based on empirical materials, argues that most rural and small-town dwellers in France did not conceive of themselves as members of the French nation until the late nineteenth century.

What Weber has chronicled for France is supported for other European groups by Walker Connor (1990: 92–103). In his study based on American immigrants' self-identification between 1840 and 1950, some startling results appear. Luxemburgers, for example, identified themselves as Germans throughout the nineteenth century. Ukrainians had no idea what *Ukraine* meant; they identified themselves as Rusyns and Ruthenians, and not infrequently as Russians and Poles. Macedonia was non-existent as a social and sentimental community. Immigrants from the Austro-Hungarian empire identified themselves in terms of regions, valleys, and towns, not some "nationality." Writing of Albania, Connor (1990: 96) claims it is not even yet a nation, despite government claims to the contrary:

> [I]t is not at all certain that a single Albanian consciousness has truly welded the highland Gegs and more southerly Tosks. Differences in culture, including social organization, are pronounced . . . Far more consequential are readily perceptible physical differences between the two peoples, a formidable barrier to the inculcation of the myth of common ancestry that the government so assiduously cultivates.

The "nation" as a grass-roots phenomenon, then, is of very recent vintage in most parts of Europe. Its pedigree is of more ancient origins only if we look at elites, for it is the elites that circulated, communicated, and, more often than not, inculcated. They created nations by standardizing education and language policy, by promoting historical myths, and by a variety of policies – including highly coercive ones – designed to assimilate various groups. The European state and various elites created sentiments; they were not primordial and original. Nationalism is a process, not an event or historical fact of a given time and location. Napoleon was as much a creator of French nationalism as an expression of it; so were Swedish kings, Serbian prime ministers, and Czech journalists. Political leaders and movements manipulated symbols, invented doctrines (self-determination, national honor), and drew in grass-roots supporters to sustain their objectives, which ranged from developing concepts of the welfare state to making war (cf. Camilleri and Falk 1992: 27). Bismarck set out to create a German empire. For the inclusiveness of the loose, decentralized Holy Roman Empire, he substituted the exclusiveness of the German state based on the myth of a German "race" (Pfaff 1993: 46).

Not the least of the sources of mass nationalism was war itself. It was chronicled by many during the French revolutionary and Napoleonic wars. These wars were instrumental in breaking down the dynastic regime's deliberate separation of the state, army, and society. The "nation in arms" concept could not have worked in practice without popular sentimental and patriotic mobilization. Military service, conscription, and wartime propaganda all helped develop a sense of national community where only localisms had prevailed previously (cf. Smith 1981).

Nationalism is a set of doctrines as well as expressions of sentiment and identity. But if we know anything about these, it is that they are variable over time and across groups. It is relatively easy to define the political community in terms of citizenship. It is anyone who meets the "admissions" requirements, usually defined in terms of length of residence, place of birth, parent's citizenship, and some minimal knowledge of the community's history. But who, exactly, constitute "nations"? If a sense of nationalism is an important component of the political community, then what about those members of the political community who are not nationalists, or who do not share some of the attributes of the nationalists? Is an Occitanian- or Breton-speaking burgher of France a "Frenchman"? Is "nationality" the only glue for a state, the only or best basis of community? Quite obviously it is not. If it were a necessary condition for statehood, then India, France, the United States, Russia, and many other countries would not exist. In them, the state existed long before a sense of national community emerged. Yet, the idea that there are "natural" communities and that these should form the basis of the state emerged shortly after the French Revolution. Nationalism as an *idea* preceded it as a fact.

Under the influence of Romanticism, particularly in the literary and propaganda work of Johann Gottlieb Fichte, the idea of language as the basis of a "national" political community gained popularity (cf. Kedourie 1966: 66–8). Unlike the concept of citizenship, which is inclusive within the country, the language criterion both includes and excludes. The "nation" is a community whose membership includes only those who communicate via the medium of a unique vernacular. If some do not speak the vernacular, they are "others" – virtual foreigners – who then have a special, and usually inferior, status. If state frontiers separate members of the language community, they are arbitrary and unnatural and must be changed. According to Fichte, the polity must coincide with the community since the community pre-cedes the polity.

While one can sympathize with Fichte's dreams of German unifica-tion, language as the essential criterion for a political community makes no sense given the varied distribution of languages throughout the world as well as the fact that numerous people speak more than one language and that some dialects are virtually different languages. It is estimated, for example, that in 1860 less than 3 percent of Italians spoke Italian for everyday purposes (Hobsbawm 1990: 60), while the vast majority spoke mutually incomprehensible dialects. The historical development of standardized vernaculars is a product of modern means of communication combined with the educational policies of the state. Fichte had it wrong: in most of Europe, states created nations and standardized vernaculars, not the reverse. As an Italian parliamentarian of the 1860s quipped following the unification of his country, "We have created Italy; now we must create Italians" (*The Economist*, Dec. 22, 1990: 43). According to Fichte's ideas, Italy could not have become a nation-state until well into the twentieth century.

By the late nineteenth century, ethnicity, culture, and religion, or some combination of them, joined language as the preferred justification for forming a political community. Elites now emphasized – and often constructed – a genealogical community based on the culture of the "folk." The ethnic nation then seeks to re-create some ancestral *ethnie* which is sufficient grounds for claiming statehood (Smith 1993: 34).

Under the influence of Romanticism and Darwinism, Europeans increasingly came to emphasize differences other than language and religion as the "natural" basis of groups. For the more bizarre and gullible, genetic explanations of "nations" came into play as well, as if anywhere in Europe during the late nineteenth century one could still find "pure" peoples. Whatever the criteria for membership in the community, they all pointed to some idea of a "natural" association upon which the state should rest. Under the influence of Romanticism and Darwinism, Europeans increasingly came to emphasize differences other than language and religion as forming the "natural" basis of groups.

The political doctrine to justify the creation of states based on notions of "natural" community was self-determination. It was used first by Marx in relation to the Polish issue, but became generalized to refer to any "people" who sought liberation from the multinational Russian, Ottoman, Austro-Hungarian, and German empires. These "peoples" had discovered or re-invented their past greatness and glory, rehabilitated their vernaculars, and developed "national" forms of art and literature. Cultural nationalism was transformed into political movements through various forms of oppression and discrimination practiced in the multinational empires, particularly by the crude attempts of Russian rulers under the spell of pan-Slavism forcefully to "russify" various groups within the empire. The diverse communities stretching from the Baltic to the Balkans then sought to upgrade their status from "peoples" to states. By 1914, the idea of "natural" political communities and their preservation through the application of self-determination had become part of the conventional political wisdom of the time.

The problem of state creation in 1919

Self-determination of peoples thus became one of Woodrow Wilson's famous Fourteen Points. In contrast to the Congress of Vienna which carved up "peoples" to create a balance of power – assumed by many a century later to be a major cause of World War I – this time the principle of self-determination would be used to remake post-war Europe. The peace was to be a democratic peace, and what could be more democratic than to give a voice to all the suppressed peoples of Europe? There would be a qualification, however: the principle was to be applied only to the "peoples" of the defeated empires; there would be no discussion in Paris about the "peoples" of the victors – the Irish, for example. Self-determination would also be the principle for re-drawing Europe's map because, Wilson argued, the suppression of nationalities had been a major cause of World War I. Self-determination is not only democratic because it incorporates the idea of popular sovereignty; it is also just. It would be, therefore, a pillar of perpetual peace on the continent.

At Vienna, the diplomats of the great powers relied on the expert advice of demographers and military officials to create a post-war European security architecture based on the concept of a territorial balance of power. In 1919, the experts were linguists, lawyers, historians, and political scientists. They advised the peacemakers how frontiers should be drawn to give every people – the natural community – the right to create their own state. While engaged in this expert exercise, hundreds of spokespersons from dozens of "nationalities" flocked to Paris to get their country recognized. The principle of self-determination let loose a blizzard of appeals from peoples Wilson and his French, British, Italian, and Japanese colleagues had never heard of. Wilson later acknowledged his own ignorance of the practical application of his favorite principle for reorganizing Europe. Testifying to the Senate Foreign Relations Committee on the Versailles Treaty, he declaimed:

> When I gave utterance to those words ["that all nations had a right to self-determination"], I said them without the knowledge that nationalities existed, which are coming to us day after day . . . You do not know and cannot appreciate the anxieties that I have experienced as

53

the result of many millions of people having their hopes raised by what I have said . . . [T]ime after time I raise a question [in Paris] in accordance with these principles and I am met with the statement that Great Britain or France ... have entered into a solemn treaty obligation. I tell them, but it was not in accord with justice and humanity; and they tell me that the breaking of treaties is what has brought on the greater part of the wars that have been waged in the world.   (quoted in Buckheit 1978: 115)

While acknowledging that in the temper of the times there were few politically feasible alternatives to self-determination, the process of designing and engineering a new Europe on the basis of Fichte's and others' notions of "natural" communities at times took on a farcical cast. A member of the American peace delegation described the state-making process in Paris:

We went into the next room where the floor was clear and Wilson spread out a big map . . . on the floor and got down on his hands and knees to show us what had been done; most of us were also on our hands and knees. I was in the front row and felt someone pushing me, and looked around angrily to find that it was Orlando [the Italian Premier] on *his* hands and knees crawling like a bear toward the map. I gave way and he was soon in the front row. I wish that I could have had a picture of the most important men in the world on all fours over this map.   (quoted in Moynihan 1993: 102)

Members of the American and British delegations to Paris were concerned at the way the territorial carve-up of Europe and Asia took place. Harold Nicolson wrote his wife, "darling, it is appalling, those three [Wilson, Lloyd George, and Georges Clemenceau] ignorant and irresponsible men cutting Asia Minor to bits as if they were dividing a cake" (Moynihan 1993: 102).

Self-determination led to some successes. Among these were Finland and Poland, and Czechoslovakia until 1938. But the dismemberment of the multinational empires in accordance with this principle also left more than 30 million people without a state of their own. They were to become the new "minorities." The post-war peace treaties thus did not solve the nationality problem; they merely shifted the locale from the empires to the new successor states. In remaking Europe in this fashion, the seeds of war in the 1920s and 1930s were sown (Holsti 1991: ch. 9). The new states had not only new minorities, but also new causes of *revanche* and irredentism. It seemed that a principle of eminently democratic appearance was to create as many, perhaps more, problems than it solved. The fundamental problem was that the new states that based their theoretical right to rule over a community defined in terms of language or some other "natural" attribute, actually had to rule over populations characterized by ethnic, language, cultural, and religious diversity.

The concept of minority is part of a nationalist agenda that seeks to define "us" against "them." "Minorities" are not some natural phenomenon. Throughout most human history "peoples" have recognized others as basically different. "Delicately shaded identities," according to Fenet (1989: 18), "result from the interaction of the diversities of language, religion, culture and genetic inheritance." They vary over time, but the definition of a minority in legal terms is "an act of power that makes diversity into an inferiority." A group becomes a minority through a political act inscribed in law. To be a member of a "minority" in a modern constitution is to help perpetuate the myth of a permanent "majority." The majority community, supposedly by its largesse, *grants* specific rights to "minorities" as some sort of favor to them. But the logic of an official "minority" status is permanent insecurity because what can be granted can also be taken away.[4] In the Europe of the 1920s and 1930s, with some notable exceptions such as Finland and Czechoslovakia, the "logical implication of trying to create a continent neatly divided into coherent territorial states each inhabited by a separate ethnically and linguistically homogeneous population, was the mass expulsion or extermination of minorities. Such was the murderous *reductio ad absurdum* of nationalism in its territorial version" (Hobsbawm 1990: 133). The statement is as applicable to the Balkans of the 1990s as it was in reference to the interwar period.

In the civic state, there is no permanent majority or minority; rights are not granted to groups but to individuals. They therefore cannot vary in different circumstances except to the extent that they vary for all. Any idea of "minority" automatically indicates some degree of

---

[4] This is not an abstract point. In the early 1990s the Serbs insisted that their kin in Krajina (Croatia) were a "nation" and that under the Tudjman regime many of their rights were taken away – as indeed they were in the Croatian constitutional revisions of 1991. The Krajina Serbs, with full backing from their brethren in Serbia, asserted the right to create their own state. It lasted four years until August 1995, when the Croatian army overran the territory and expelled the Serbian population. When asked about their own treatment of the Albanians in Kosovo, Serbs reply that the Albanians are a "minority," and that under international law they have no right to self-determination. In fact, Albanian rights in Kosovo are highly circumscribed (cf. Newland 1993).

inferiority that can be manipulated according to the whims of the majority (cf. Fenet 1989: 17–18). It can be no other way, since the logic of the *nation* state is basically exclusionary. How can a political community based on supposedly homogeneous physical and/or language attributes remain true to itself if it grants full legal equality to the "other"? It can in fact do so only by resorting to the constitutionalism of the civic state, that is, where it grants not rights but special privileges to people of different attributes.

In 1919 there were basically two solutions to the problems not solved by the principle of self-determination. The first was to grant all citizens in the new country equal rights regardless of language, ethnicity, religion, and other attributes. In the case of languages, they were given equal status, and educational policies were designed to make the entire population bilingual. This was the formula adopted in Finland. The second solution was to guarantee minority rights under international supervision. Austria, Hungary, Bulgaria, and Turkey, all defeated powers, had minority provisions inserted into their various peace treaties. Poland, Czechoslovakia, Yugoslavia, Romania, and Greece, being new or enlarged states, concluded special minority treaties with the victors of World War I. Albania, Lithuania, Latvia, Estonia, and later Iraq, under pressure from the League of Nations, made declarations regarding the treatment of their respective minorities. Germany made a special declaration with regard to the province of Upper Silesia. The Council of the League of Nations was charged with supervision of the provisions aimed at the international protection of national minorities (Claude 1955: 16).

The various instruments contained similar formats: equal civil and political rights and obligations and freedom to practice religion, speak languages, and where the numbers warranted it, a guarantee to allow education in the language of the minority (Sampat-Mehta 1973: 9–10).

The League established procedures for receiving petitions or complaints. It was cumbersome and led mostly to informal procedures for conflict resolution between complaining minority groups and governments. Of a total of 325 petitions taken up by the minorities committees, only 14 reached the agenda of the League Council (Veatch 1983: 375). By the mid-1930s the system had become defunct and, to a large extent, discredited. France and Great Britain would not intervene on behalf of minorities whose rights were violated for fear of upsetting their east and central European allies. Nazi Germany opposed the idea that *any* German should live under foreign rule. In 1934, Poland announced it would no longer be bound by the provisions of its minority treaty (Ryan 1990: 156–7). The signatories complained correctly that they were singled out for special responsibilities towards minorities, while the victors of World War I and new members of the League did not make their own guarantees. A double standard prevailed. A more fundamental problem was the ultimate purpose of the treaty provisions and declarations: were they designed eventually to assimilate minorities, or were they to become permanent restrictions on sovereignty? C. A. MacCartney saw the basic problem which is the contradiction between the idea of a state based on a "natural" community and the special status of "minorities." The treaties and declarations stipulated that all nationals should be equal before the law and enjoy similar civil and political rights. However, the eastern and central European governments at the time desired to make their states instruments of their own national ideals and aspirations. One national character would prevail. In order to grant equality, the majorities would have to sacrifice the idea of national character. The intent of the minority treaties was to encourage a single dominant culture. Most implied that the minorities should not be equal partners in the political sense. This is why majorities required an official language and why minorities received native language training, if at all, only at the primary level. MacCartney concluded that "a 'national' state and 'national minorities' are incompatibles" (MacCartney 1934: 422).

Judgments on the effectiveness of the minority treaties vary (compare Veatch and Claude to MacCartney); certainly matters might have been worse without them and the (weak) international supervision of the treatment of minorities was an important derogation from the sovereignty principle, a derogation that finds many parallels in the United Nations during the past decade (see chapter 9). The fundamental point, however, is that a state based on a mythical "natural" community in the context of many groups within the state's territory will lack a degree of legitimacy that states founded on civic principles enjoy. Minorities either assimilate, as they did mostly in the dynastic states of Europe in the fifteenth through nineteenth centuries, or they agitate to separate. It requires a skillful blend of balancing rewards and political spoils between groups to keep a multinational state intact; few states have succeeded. If minorities are in any way excluded from political participation and/or access to economic resources and entitlements, they challenge the legitimacy of the state, seek secession, and invite responses ranging from repression to genocide. We will return to this theme in chapter 6.

If the principle of self-determination did not settle the issue of the best basis for a political community, it did reveal the extent to which the concept of a "natural" community can be manufactured for political purposes. Two new states were created that fit neither the civic nor "natural" formats of political community: Czechoslovakia and Yugoslavia.

In the light of the collapse of both states since 1990 and "ethnic cleansing" and mass murder in the latter, it is interesting to recall that in 1918–19 the spokesmen of these countries insisted that their communities represented a single "people." "Our race," intoned one official seeking international recognition for the fiction called Yugoslavia, "variously known as Serb, Croat, and Slovene, is nevertheless, in spite of three different names, but one people – the Jugoslavs" (quoted in Connor 1990: 96). It is difficult to imagine a more perfect demonstration of the extent to which a "people" is a variable, a political creation, and not some primordial, fixed, "natural" fact. Virtually all of the states created in 1919 underline John Breuilly's contention (1982) that nationalism is all about access to resources, politics, equality, and rewards and much less about "identity," language, or ethnicity (cf. Newman 1991). A citizen is a constant; a national is a variable. How, then, can you base a permanent territorial unit – a state – on a variable? We return to this problem in chapter 6.

War and the making of states in Europe

War has been a constant companion of the state-making process in European history. Many states, as 1919 demonstrated, have resulted from wars. Dynastic and nationalist regimes conducted virtual or actual warfare in order to establish central authority in historically defined territories. International war was often the by-product or the cause of civil and domestic disturbances. As keen an observer of the society–polity nexus as Fernand Braudel has claimed that virtually every war France fought abroad was an extension of a civil disturbance or war within the country (Braudel 1990). His comment would fit the histories of Russia, Germany, England, and many other countries as well.

But the American and French revolutions, in which the spokesmen of the people "captured" the state, introduced a formula that substantially reduced the probabilities of civil war. That is the formula of the citizen. It did not guarantee domestic peace – the American war of secession was the lengthiest and bloodiest war of the late nineteenth century – but it removed a vital source of state weakness and/or illegitimacy: the capture of the state by a single group, dynasty, or region of the country to the exclusion of others.

State-formation in Western Europe was also a very lengthy process, dating back more than 500 years. Legitimacy of the state and the political community was gained through slow growth and struggle. France existed as a geographical expression for almost a millennium; it did not become a fully defined political community until the Revolution when all royal subjects – many of whom contested their monarch's right to rule – were re-defined as citizens, regardless of the color of their skin, their religion, or the language they spoke. The countries of eastern and central Europe and the Baltic and Balkans are of much more recent vintage. Many were created in almost a single act, in part through their own efforts and in part by the victors of World War I. They had earned, so to speak, their upgrading from nationalities to states through the efforts of nationalist elites during the latter part of the nineteenth century. The prelude to statehood lasted, in other words, for only the better part of a generation.

More important from the perspective of studies on international relations and war is that these new states had to demonstrate their state-like credentials to the satisfaction of the victorious great powers. Among those credentials, in addition to the traditional requirements of diplomatic recognition (stable population, recognized frontiers, and capacity to enter into treaty obligations), were commitments to democratic rule and observance of minority rights. The state-creation process in 1919, in other words, was partly *conditional*. Applications for membership to the League of Nations were carefully scrutinized and, in theory at least, the new states were monitored in the way they treated their citizens, their minorities in particular. But whatever the hopes of 1919, it soon became apparent that the various peace treaties and arrangements for minorities would not lead to peace. Within short order there was war or low intensity conflict between Hungary and Romania (allied with Czechoslovakia and Jugoslavia), Greece and Turkey, Poland and Lithuania, and Finland and the Baltic states versus the Soviet Republic. All of these conflicts revolved around irredentist pressures and problems of ethnic kin residing in neighboring states. The 1930s witnessed the wholesale abuse of the principle of self-determination by Nazi Germany and gross violations of minority rights in several of the new states. The idea of "natural" communities, once thought to be the answer to international strife and instability, proved to be as much a source of war as of peace. We turn next to the state-formation process since 1945 to examine the bases of state legitimacy and political community in very different environments.

4   The creation of states since 1945

State-creation in the former colonial areas, and to a different degree in some of the former Soviet republics since 1991, has taken patterns and trajectories significantly different from those of Europe since the fifteenth century.[1] In the latter, there was a lengthy historical project to give political meaning to the geographical expressions called France, Germany, Sweden, and the like. The consequence of wars, centralization, taxes, and the provision of services was to create a form of political organization called the state.

The original purposes of colonialism, in contrast, never included state-making. European overseas conquests after the fifteenth century had nothing in common with the state-consolidation projects of Louis XIV, Peter the Great, Frederick the Great, or Bismarck. Imperialism was driven by a variety of purposes: trade, slavery, exploitation of resources, "civilizing" the barbarians, religious conversion to Christianity, ending the Arab slave trade (late nineteenth century), securing strategic territories, and emulation: if the British were expanding in Africa, the Germans had to do the same in order to maintain their

---

[1]   The next chapter discusses the generic concepts of weak and strong states. They are not confined only to the areas commonly described as the "Third World." There are, of course, significant differences between the state-creation process from former Western colonies, and the emergence of the post-Soviet republics after 1989. There are also similarities. Many of the Russian colonial practices in the Caucasus, around the Crimea, and the vast stretches encompassing contemporary Central Asia (Kirgizstan, Tajikistan, Uzbekistan, Turkmenistan, Kazakstan, and Azerbaijan) during the nineteenth century resembled those of the British, French, Dutch, Belgians, and others in Africa and elsewhere. The point is that some of the former Soviet republics share in common with many post-Western colonial states the element of state weakness. (Cf. Lemaitre *et al.*, "The Crisis of Societal Security in the Former Soviet Union," in Waever *et al.* [1992: 110–30]).

status as a great power. Colonialism was as much a product of European external rivalries as of domestic imperatives. Conspicuously absent from this non-exhaustive list of the purposes of colonialism is any state-making project. Whether the colonialism of the fifteenth through eighteenth centuries, or its late nineteenth-century counterpart, the colonial leaders, encompassing the military, government officials, colonial societies, political parties, and the churches, never assumed that some day the subjugated peoples should or could create a state form of political organization. It was beyond their imagination, given their views of "native" societies, that these peoples could rule themselves – forgetting, of course, that these "natives" had ruled themselves for centuries and even millennia before the arrival of the white man.

The colonial state's main purposes had nothing to do with preparation for ultimate statehood, and everything to do with economic exploitation, building some infrastructure and communication, settling migrants, organizing plantation agriculture, introducing extraction of surplus through taxes, organizing some semblance of lower-level education and religious activity, and providing "law and order" so that these tasks could go on unhindered.

The actual patterns of exploitation, economic development, and social policy varied greatly from colony to colony. The Belgian Congo was little more than an organized system of theft based on forced labor to benefit the Belgian crown, while British rule in India directly and indirectly benefited vast numbers of Hindus, Muslims, and others. To pursue their multiple purposes the Europeans had to create *administrations*, but these were not designed to prepare the natives for the ultimate transformation of the colonies into states.

Reflecting European sovereignty practices, the colonies nevertheless had to be defined territorially. This was not the case initially, as Portuguese, Spanish, French, and British colonial domains began as little more than ill-defined and fluctuating enclaves in the vastness of Africa, North America, the Middle East, and Asia. But by the nineteenth century the enclaves had grown to vast proportions and in the scramble and competition for colonies toward the end of the nineteenth century territorial limits had to be defined, not so much to identify "our natives," but to exclude European competitors. From the beginning, then, the territorial limits of the colonies had little or nothing to do with the economic practices, identification, or the political organization of indigenous populations. As with the administrative organizations, they were transplants from European practices.

Saadia Touval (1972: 6–7) has challenged the conventional view that colonial boundaries were designed by the Europeans exclusively for European diplomatic purposes, that they were arbitrarily drawn in total disregard of local circumstances, or that they were imposed on unwilling populations. He points out that Europe's boundaries were often formed the same way. The straight lines on the map of Africa, the Middle East, and among some of the former Soviet republics were not the only frontier demarcations. There were also curves, bumps, indentations, river lines, and other trajectories that reflected complex combinations of historic, religious, ethnic, commercial, geographical, and pragmatic political concerns. There was no single pattern to the territorial definition of the myriads of colonies.

Most boundaries were artificial, however, in the sense that (1) they were mostly imposed by the colonial administrations without reference to indigenous concerns, and (2) they seldom corresponded to pre-colonial political systems. Moreover, during the era of colonial rule territorial boundaries were often changed to suit the convenience of the administrators. The considerations underlying modifications had little to do with indigenous political practices. Touval (1972: 12) provides one example, perhaps an extreme one, but nevertheless typical in organization and intent. The French created "their" Sudan – to distinguish it from Britain's Sudan – in 1890 as a distinct administrative unit. Fourteen years later western parts of the colony were detached and the original Sudan name was changed to Upper Senegal and Niger. The eastern part of this new entity was detached in 1919 and included in the new colony of Upper Volta. In 1932, Upper Volta was abolished and some of its parts were attached to the original French Sudan. Fourteen years later, these parts were transferred from French Sudan to Mauritania, and after three more years, other parts acquired in 1932 from Upper Volta were detached from French Sudan and returned to Upper Volta.

In other areas, colonies were federated, split, hived off, joined administratively, or just left alone, as was the case in most island colonial domains (cf. Young 1985: 75). In very few cases did territorial boundaries approximate communities that had any identity as such prior to colonialism (again, small islands are exceptions). In almost all cases, the relevant social and political groupings were far smaller than the territorial creations of the colonial administrations. To apply the term "ethnic" in this context is mostly meaningless. Indigenous political organizations were seldom coterminous with cultural and language groups, and political allegiances were often highly localized. Ibos may have existed as an ethnocultural category (created by ethnologists, not the Ibos themselves), but this had no practical consequences as far as politics were concerned. Warfare and predation were as common among Ibo villages as between Ibos and other groups (cf. Herbst 1989: 679).

Post-1945 states had numerous "personalities," few of which had pedigrees of more than one generation. There was the Nigerian colonial self versus the eastern Nigerian colonial self, the ancient Ethiopian historical self versus the Tigrinean historical self, or the Somali ethnocultural self versus the Oromo ethnocultural self (Neuberger 1986: 55). The Eritreans, who came together to fight a successful war of secession from Ethiopia, existed as a colony, but prior to that war never existed as a "people," either politically, culturally, or ethnically. Eritrea is composed of at least eight major language groups and even more ethnocultural groups, to say nothing of distinctions between Christians and Muslims, agriculturalists and pastoralists, and any other number of categories (Neuberger 1986: 27). Its colonial "self" never unified this diversity of peoples.

Plantation colonial economies required more labor than was often available among the local population. Colonial and Soviet administrators therefore helped create mixed communities where formerly there had been reasonably homogeneous communities. Hindus and Muslims from South Asia were transported to Guyana, Fiji, and several Caribbean islands. Chinese, Japanese, Korean, Samoan, and Okinawan laborers migrated in waves to the American imperial domain in Hawaii. Russians were transported to the Central Asian Soviet republics, and restless (anti-communist) "natives" there and in the Caucasus were liquidated, forcefully assimilated, or carried off to distant locales (cf. Lemaitre *et al.* 1992: 123). Minorities were thus often created in areas where they had not existed previously.

The main point is clear: the colonial territorial unit bore little or no relationship to any pre-colonial ethnic, religious, political, social, or religious communities or political systems.

There were, of course, exceptions. Some colonies actually approximated historical, precolonial political entities. Zimbabwe, Swaziland, Rwanda, Morocco, Egypt, Tunisia, a few of the former Soviet republics, Indochina, Burma, plus most small island colonies were simply taken over and their historic territorial limits (to the extent that they were known, which was not always the case) were accepted as the colonial boundaries. Something akin to states, defined by Harik (1990: 5) as "an established authority which enjoys jurisdiction over a core territory and people for an extended period of time," existed in most of the Arab world prior to the nineteenth century. Oman, he argues (p. 17), goes back as a separate political unit to the eighth century. The Asante in Africa, if not yet a state when colonized, constituted a national-type society on its way toward becoming a nation-state. "It possessed known boundaries, a central government with police and army, consequent law and order, an accepted national language; and beyond these it even possessed, by the 1880s, an emergent middle class capable of envisaging the role of capitalist entrepreneur" (Davidson 1992: 75). Whatever the ultimate hopes of Asante development, they quickly came to an end with colonial rule.

What of precolonial political organizations? The same generalization applies: in a majority of the colonies there was no political organization that approximated the territorial jurisdictions established in London, Paris, St. Petersburg, and elsewhere in Europe. The colonial authorities defeated, bribed, coerced, and sometimes exterminated an incredible variety of political leaderships, ranging from clan elders, tribal chiefs, hereditary kingdoms, and local sultanates to maharajas and imam-chiefs.

Colonial authorities used these local political forms and forces as the primary medium for indirect rule. They supported and worked through chiefs, caudillos, and various types of strongmen who made rules and allocated values among a variety of ethnic, clan, class, and functional or communal social units (cf. Migdal 1988: 31–9). The British in India created political, legal, and social institutions for different religious, ethnic, and caste communities when these demonstrated loyalty to colonial rule. They also recruited their armed forces from "martial races," thus separating them from the rest of society (Nafziger and Richter 1976: 93). All of this helped sustain colonial rule, but it also hindered the development of a sense of identity that corresponded with colonial territorial divisions. While in some colonies (e.g., India) a strong sense of nationalism had already developed in the early twentieth century, in many of the others colonial rule respected some degree of local autonomy and sustained traditional political structures specifically so that they would form poles of attraction and identity in competition with the early "nationalists" who were beginning to think in European terms (cf. Mazrui 1983: 42)

Much has been written on the economic and social depredations and contributions of colonialism. This complex tale does not require repetition here. For our purposes it is sufficient to re-emphasize two facts: (1) the colonial state was created for a multiplicity of purposes, none of which had anything to do with the creation of states; and (2) the territorial limits of colonies were imposed by colonial regimes, again for their own multiple purposes and convenience, and in most cases these did not correspond to historical realms or to the limits of jurisdiction and political effectiveness of local rulers. The colonies were therefore for the most part alien political *fictions*. They were ruled by administrators who had little but contempt for the "natives," but who dressed up their more exploitative activities with paternalistic rhetoric of "civilizing mission," "modernization," and "trusteeship" for the ultimate benefit of the subject populations (cf. Young 1985: 67–8).

Under the influence of the League of Nations, American prodding, World War II, and the formation of the United Nations, the idea that these colonies should eventually become self-ruling (but not necessarily independent states) began to take root. The idea of tutelage formed the basis of many post-World War II colonial regimes, although the administrators seldom acknowledged that the "natives" had yet achieved a level of civilization warranting independent political existence. As late as 1947, responding to a Colonial Office proposal to reform local political institutions in Kenya, the governor wrote: "How primitive the state of these people is, and how deplorable the spiritual, moral and social chaos in which they are adrift are things which can perhaps only be fully realized by those who are in close personal touch with the realities of the situation" (quoted in Davidson 1992: 179). Report after report to colonial offices denied that such populations were yet ready for independence. For many impatient "nationalists," independence was the only goal. The incompatible goals of the colonizers and colonized led in many cases to coercion, mass protest, armed rebellion, and "wars of national liberation," the first of which popped up in Muslim Russia when the Tsarist state collapsed in 1917. But how could these territorial units, many of which bore little or no relationship to an historic, organic, social–political identity, suddenly become states? The fact was that in granting independence to colonies, many of the resulting states had no nation; or just as bad, they had many nations (Buzan 1991: 98). Where was the emotional glue that could hold diverse populations characterized by myriads of localisms into some form of a political unit that corresponded with colonial or Soviet territorial limits? What was the social "stuff" of these fictions?

The question of nationalism

Was there an indigenous "nationalism" that drove the de-colonization process? Many have argued that even today identities seldom correspond with the legacies of the colonial state. But unless one is a captive of the great man theory of politics, it would be hard to understand the de-colonization of India, Egypt, China, Indochina, and dozens of other current countries in the absence of nationalism (Norbu 1992: 58). Clearly, de-colonization was not arranged by a few elites in the absence of popular mobilization and deep feelings of masses. The problem is with the term nationalism. It was not the same everywhere.

In many areas, the colonial societies had weathered all sorts of conquest throughout their histories. But most of these conquests either left no significant residues, or the conquerors ultimately became assimilated into the cultures of the conquered (the Mongols in China, the Moghuls in India). Many other conquerors established systems of suzerainty which required only tribute payments but not the loss of autonomy.

Western, including Russian, colonialism was fundamentally different. It imposed a system of rule, rules, and commerce that fundamentally transformed the indigenous societies. In Norbu's (1992: 106, 105) words:

> The Arabs had known the Turks since the eleventh and twelfth centuries; the Hindus, the Muslims from Iran and Afghanistan since the ninth to tenth centuries; the Han, the "barbarians" for millions [*sic*] of years. But none of these "outsiders" brought about an identity crisis to the host population to the extent the European capitalist imperialists did to the Third World. The western generalized others appeared not only more aggressive but so fundamentally different from the Asian or African social selves in terms of value-system, social organization, communication system, and above all in terms of coercive power generated by science and technology . . . [W]estern colonialism and imperialism became not economic and political questions . . . but more subtly a psychological question of survival associated with autonomous cultures.

It is not surprising that in these circumstances opposition and resistance to colonial rule should develop. Whether this constituted "nationalism" is a matter of substantial debate. Some, like Norbu, emphasize the long traditions of religion, written history, and even ethnic identity as predating colonialism. These were particularly pronounced in India, China, Southeast Asia, Muslim Russia, and the Middle East. Were such "nationalisms" evident also in Africa? Not according to Norbu. But others insist that forms of nationalism sustained empires such as those of the Tokolor, Mandika, and Fulani. "Clearly, far more African communities than commonly imagined have inherited a national tradition and a national consciousness from their pre-colonial past" (Mazrui and Tidy 1984: 84–5). Colonialism and its attending forms of direct and indirect rule, they argue, destroyed these "national" sentiments.

Whatever the case, the fact remains that there were few "nationalisms" that coincided with the territorial units called colonies. Most of these units were fictions; nationalism thus had to be created. This was no easy task, since it was never entirely clear what the post-colonial state would look like. The confusion was particularly acute in Africa, where most territorial lines coincided with no known community. Consider a statement by Attoh Ahuma, written in 1911 in a book on the Gold Coast:

> It is seriously asserted by rash and irresponsible literalists that the Gold Coast [ultimately Ghana], with its multiform composition of congeries of States or Provinces, independent of each other, divided by complex political institutions, laws and customs, and speaking a great variety of languages, could not be described as a nation in the minent [*sic*] sense of the word . . . In spite therefore of the dogmas and *ipse dixits* of those wiseacres who would fain deny to us, as a people, the inalienable heritage of nationality, we dare affirm . . . that – WE ARE A NATION! It may be a "miserable, mangled, tortured, twisted *tertium quid*," or to quote a higher authority, a Nation 'scattered and peeled . . . but still a Nation.' If we were not, *it is time to invent one* [my italics]. We have a Past – "though ungraced in story".   (quoted in Langley 1979: 162–3)

Ahuma's dilemma is clear: if there is no historical nation, then it is time to create one. But how can this be done in the context of numerous social cleavages, traditions, and languages? By the simple transformation of the colonial territory into a state by declaration, not by history.

Leader after leader in pre- and post-colonial Africa had to face the problem of how to define the nation. Early nationalist movements did not have clear territorial referents (Young 1985: 82). In Nigeria, for example, nationalist groups prior to 1934 thought in terms of regions or ethnic communities, not "Nigeria." The colonial governor himself, in the 1920s, insisted that the idea of a Nigerian nation was "inconceivable" (Nafziger and Richter, 1976: 92). Some nationalists spoke on behalf of entire regions such as West Africa. Many feared "Balkanization" of the continent – transforming colonies into states on the principle of *uti possidetis* – on grounds that the colonies as independent units would not be viable and would perpetuate the weaknesses through which the exiting colonial powers could maintain their paramountcy and privileges. Their solution was either to federate several colonies into a single entity (e.g., Nigeria) or the more ambitious project of pan-Africanism, unifying the entire continent into a single superstate that would be capable of resisting the neo-colonial hold of the metropolitan powers that was implied in the concept of Balkanization. A few, like Nyerere, saw the task of creating nation-states on the European model a hopeless one:

> it would be visionary to conceive of a nation as one people, speaking a common language, bound together by a common heritage and a shared historical experience. Africa must break loose from this alluring European model. It does not fit in with the social realities of the continent.   (Nyerere 1967, quoted in Langley 1979: 453)

Leopold Senghor took a different tack: the colony must become first an independent state, and *only subsequently* the diverse peoples and cultures must be welded into a nation. The state would be the instrument to create a sentiment that transcends local "fatherlands" (tribes and other groups). "For the proper characteristic of Man is to snatch himself from the earth, to rise above his roots and blossom in the sun, to escape . . . from his 'natural determinations'" (quoted in Langley 1979: 530).

The Senghor vision emerged as the prototype for most colonies: the state had to create nationalism as a sentiment uniting diverse peoples into the carapace of the colonial territorial unit. In some states, the project has flourished. In many others, the immediate post-colonial enthusiasm soon dissipated into the plague of African and other politics, the re-emergence of localism in its numerous varieties. Some leaders called it the curse of tribalism. But this is often an epithet masking a more fundamental sentiment that is best called nationalism. There is little validity in calling ten million Ibos a "tribe," while referring to the far less numerous Basques or Slovenes as "nations." The main point is that, to quote Joseph Mobutu, government programs had to be fashioned in order to "fight this plague which has spread to all African countries: the absence of national consciousness" (Langley

1979: 729). It is not, of course, a new plague. The consciousness of a colonially defined, territorially based community had never existed in most of the areas.

The colonial territory thus ultimately imprinted itself on most nationalist leaders; they appropriated the Western ideas of nationalism and after considerable hesitancy about its exact territorial configuration, settled for the colonial names and boundaries. An administrative fiction had to become a meaningful political community. Nationalist movements thus did not fundamentally challenge the colonial state; what was at issue was who would control it (Smith 1983: 50). Competing conceptualizations of political organization, such as regional states or pan-Arabism, were quietly dropped. The colony, which was created for a multiplicity of purposes, but not state-making, was now to become a Western-style state. For many colonies, this was not a case of a reasonably homogeneous historic, ethnic, language, and/or religious group claiming an upgrade of status from a "people" into a state, as happened in Europe in 1919. It was, rather, the literal creation of a nation out of dozens, and sometimes more, of "peoples" not unified sentimentally with anything resembling early twentieth-century European nationalism. If there was to be self-determination, the doctrine used to justify independent statehood, the "self" was the colonial administrative unit that in many cases contained many nations and peoples. In opting for the European model of the state, then, most anti-colonial leaders rejected their own histories and indigenous political forms. Liberation, according to Basil Davidson (1992: 10), "produced its own denial. Liberation led to alienation." The nationalist elites borrowed Western ideas of nationalism and the Western concept of the state, and melded the two. However, the crucial question of who, exactly, formed the new political community, the fundamental basis for the legitimacy of the state, was not often carefully defined or understood by the time of independence. It has plagued many post-1945 states since.

A taste of things to come was apparent in some national liberation movements: they were divided by regional, ideological, ethnic, or religious differences. The Muslim/Hindu split within India is well known. Less well known were separatist movements such as the União Nacional Africana de Rumbezia, which claimed that "it is necessary to form a national political organ solely for the people north of the Zambezi River . . . This region will be known as Rumbezia" (Bragança and Wallerstein 1982: 174–5). Even in tiny Portuguese Guinea, the armed national liberation movement was threatened with diversity and secession. "Experience seems to show," wrote a chronicler of the armed struggle (Chaliand 1969: 123)

> that a great deal of attention must be focused on preventing the guerrillas . . . from becoming detached from the peasantry. Is the mere fact of having started the struggle on behalf and in the name of the masses a guarantee against losing touch with them? Tribal and patriarchal structures in Africa create a tendency to accept . . . the authority of the local leader. There is thus a tremendous temptation for certain Party chiefs to display authoritarian tendencies when they have been given too much independence and not enough Party supervision. The excessive independence allowed during the first year of the struggle in Guinea had already produced a few petty tyrants by the time the Party Congress . . . was obliged to get rid of them.

In Eritrea, between 1970 and 1974 a bitter and prolonged civil war took place between two competing movements, the Eritrean Liberation Front (ELF) and the Eritrean Peoples' Liberation Front (Sherman 1980: 78–83). Similar armed conflicts broke out in Moldova, Georgia, and Tajikistan after 1991.

Many national liberation movements thus already carried within them the seeds of political fragmentation. In some cases, "nations" were quickly discovered or manufactured to justify secessionist movements that emerged shortly after independence. Not everyone accepted the idea that the colony-turned-state should automatically correspond to colonial territorial definitions, or that the act of liberation from colonial rule was the only act of self-determination. Many subnations, from Abkhazians in Georgia to Rumbezians in Mozambique, asserted themselves and, facing various forms of discrimination and predation by new central governments, proclaimed their own right of self-determination.

And so the leaders for freedom took over the colonial state; alternative forms of political organization, such as a return to traditional modes of governance, federations, or continent-wide units, lost all popularity and thus significant discussion. The colonial state, an organism that left legacies primarily of arbitrary boundaries, bureaucracy, and the military, was taken over by leaders who believed they could go on to create *real* nations and master the new state. Some succeeded. Many failed, and it is these failures that have led to wars of a third kind.

National liberation

Political legitimacy refers to the principle(s) on which the "right to rule" over an identified political community is established. In many of the post-1945 states, the principle was negative: liberation *from* colonialism. In most colonial territories, as well as in some former Soviet republics, national liberation was more a movement of colored peoples and/or different religions against Western or Soviet domination, exploitation, and racism, than a program to build something new. National liberation struggles in the post-1945 world were significantly different from their nineteenth-century European, South American, and North American counterparts. The American revolution was a war of national liberation. It was also a war to institute a new kind of political rule, namely a republican democracy. In 1919, many of the Baltic and East European countries shared that vision. They sought not just "national" independence from their respective empires, but also the chance to create parliamentary democracies based on the French, British, or American models. National liberation in the Americas and Europe was *for* something – popular sovereignty and democracy – as well as against something.

Most national liberation movements in the colonies, in contrast, emphasized the oppressions and depredations of colonialism rather than the principles on which the post-colonial state should be based. For them, liberation was frequently an end in itself, not a means toward a greater goal. If there was a broader message, it was usually socialism (or private markets in the post-Soviet republics) and instant economic transformation, not democracy or popular sovereignty. The multitudes of speeches and political mobilization efforts by liberation leaders emphasized freedom and new economic opportunities, meaning an end to foreign domination. To take just one example, a paper by Uria T. Simango of the Presidential Council of FRELIMO emphasized that "our struggle today is not primarily an ideological or class one; it is a struggle of the masses of people against foreign domination, Portuguese colonialism, for freedom and independence of these masses" (quoted in Bragança and Wallerstein 1982: 125). This statement could have been made by any of dozens of leaders of national liberation movements. In India, Tanzania, and elsewhere, more profound rhetoric emerged emphasizing the critical importance of democracy and the secular state, but such expositions were relatively uncommon compared to the emphasis on "liberation."

The leaders of the liberation movements were themselves rarely elected, and once independence was achieved they seldom subjected themselves to popular validation. Frelimo and dozens of its counterparts became the post-colonial governments, the "sole legitimate representatives" of the Mozambique and other national "selves," by virtue of waging an efficient military and political campaign on behalf of the colonial "people." As in so many historical societies, rule came to be based primarily on the legends created through war. But there were no organized methods to validate the "sole legitimate representatives." Some colonies transformed themselves into states with democratic institutions through referenda or plebiscites (Bechuanaland, Cyprus, Zambia, French Guinea, Nigeria, Ghana, Western Samoa), but most achieved the change through peaceful transfers to essentially self-proclaimed and often unrepresentative political parties or movements or through armed combat in wars of "national liberation."

International legitimation of post-colonial states[2]

Post-1945 states were not created solely by armed national liberation movements or by the co-opted indigenous elites of the colonial state. The United Nations, representing the international community and its norms, was also involved in the state-making process. It participated in three ways: (1) by defining the territorial extent and political forms of new states; (2) by establishing the philosophical and political ground rules for de-colonization; and (3) by granting membership to the organization and providing the new states with a variety of life-support assistance.

The role of the United Nations in the proposed 1947 partition of Palestine was the first major effort by the new international organization to define and help create states. It failed in this instance; even if the Palestine Liberation Organization succeeds in transforming its jurisdiction in the Jericho and Gaza areas ultimately into a state encompassing the West Bank as well, it will not have gained as much as the 1947 partition plan envisaged. On hindsight, the rejection of the United Nations plan was a major blunder by the Arabs and Palestinians.

More instructive in comparing the pre-1919 and post-1945 state-

---

[2] A more elaborate discussion of the role of the international community in creating and sustaining post-colonial states, states imbued with "negative sovereignty," is presented in Jackson (1990). Some of the points below derive from his seminal discussion of the problem.

making processes is the case of the Horn of Africa in general and Eritrea in particular (Dubois 1994). Eritrea came to the attention of the United Nations in 1949 because parts of it had been a former Italian colony and the wartime Allies, who were jointly to dispose of Axis colonial legacies, were unable to agree among themselves on its future. They therefore handed over the issue to the United Nations.

The organization set up a commission to travel to Eritrea, examine the problems, and recommend to the General Assembly how to dispose of the territory. The members of the commission could not agree among themselves. The Guatemalan and Pakistani delegates recommended full independence after a period of United Nations direct trusteeship. Burma's representative proposed an Eritrean–Ethiopian confederation, but with the right of the former to secede after a five-year period. The Norwegian delegate proposed the integration of Eritrea into the Ethiopian empire, but with the proviso that the western part of the territory be detached and, after a period of British rule, be annexed to Sudan if accepted by a plebiscite. Faced with a lack of consensus, the General Assembly decided that Eritrea should federate with the Ethiopian crown, that there should be a typical federal division of powers, and that Eritreans should write their own constitution. A United Nations commissioner helped the parties implement the resolution, including assistance in establishing a democratic form of governance in the territory. By 1952, the federation had been completed to the satisfaction of all parties – except a large number of Eritreans who were to learn quickly that Haile Selassie's interpretation of federalism was not the same as that of the United Nations General Assembly. In this manner, the United Nations, somewhat reminiscent of the Berlin Congress of 1884–5, decided the fate of a vast territory. It took a colonially defined territory with a collection of peoples of different religions, economic practices, social structures, and languages and decided to tack them on to a preexisting empire of immense comparative proportions, a state whose main groups shared nothing in common with the Eritreans, but which through this decision gained a maritime coastline. Perhaps there were no alternatives since there was no Eritrean "people" who could have formed the basis of an independent state. But the episode demonstrates the holdover of colonial assumptions and practices into the post-World War II era. The idea that a vast territory should simply become part of an empire with which it had no affinity except geographic proximity was quite in keeping with the administrative reorganizations of European and

Russian colonies in Africa, Muslim Russia, and the Middle East during the nineteenth and early twentieth centuries. The result was a thirty-year war in which the Eritreans – not without a civil war among themselves – undid the state-making effort of the United Nations by formally separating themselves from Ethiopia. The United Nations of course could not create a "nation" where none existed. It was the war itself which created an Eritrean "people."

The United Nations also assisted in the process of state-creation after 1945 by enunciating the basic terms of independence. The principle of self-determination is mentioned only twice in the Charter, and neither time does it refer specifically to the situation of colonies. In the wake of the moral and political imperatives to end colonialism, however, the *principle* in the Charter evolved into the *right* of self-determination (Hannum 1990: 33–4). This evolution culminated in the famous 1960 General Assembly Resolution, "Declaration of Independence to Colonial Countries and Peoples" (UN Document A/4684, 1960) which spelled out the meaning of self-determination: it is a right that applies only to the peoples of European overseas colonies (thus excluding Soviet colonies), as defined territorially by the colonial authorities. Colonial states, these European-defined territorial fictions, thus received international validation. The appropriation of the Western and colonially defined state was never questioned in the United Nations.

The purpose of self-determination is to bring a "speedy and unconditional" end to colonialism "in all its forms and manifestations." In this context, the "[i]nadequacy of political, economic, social or educational preparedness should never serve as a pretext for delaying independence." To make certain that the colonial territory be transformed *in toto* into statehood, the resolution further specified that "[a]ny attempt aimed at the partial or total disruption of the national [sic] unity and territorial integrity of a country is incompatible with the purposes and principles of the United Nations Charter." In other words, the "self" in self-determination referred to all the peoples within the traditional territorial boundaries of the colony. The United Nations went on record early to discourage those who might think that the "self" should be defined in terms of ethnicity, language, religion, or other attributes of groups *within* the colonies. The right of self-determination was to be exercised by the territorially defined colonial people. Nothing in the United Nations resolutions hinted at the right to secession for those who did not fit comfortably in the colonially defined state.

This interpretation of self-determination has been consistently enunciated throughout the history of the organization. Self-determination was thus to be *solely* a vehicle for de-colonization, and not an authorization for subsequent secession of diverse groups that might claim nationhood. As the late Secretary General U Thant stated, "As an international organization, the United Nations has never accepted and does not accept and I do not believe it will ever accept the principle of secession of a part of its Member States" (quoted in Buckeit 1978: 87). The organization spent over $500 million to make the point in fighting against the Katanga secession in 1960, and gave no support to secessionist movements in Tibet, Biafra, Bangladesh, and elsewhere.

De-colonization *was* the act of self-determination. There was to be no international scrutiny or questioning of the territorial or other characteristics of the post-colonial state. The United Nations, in other words, explicitly endorsed the concept of the state based on a community of citizens rather than on consanguinity or some other "natural" source.

The problem was that the United Nations failed to stipulate that freedom from colonial rule should also bring with it equal rights of citizenship for the territorial population. Membership in the organization was granted almost automatically to the newly freed colonies. All they had to do was proclaim themselves peace-loving and committed to the principles of the United Nations Charter. This they did through the simple device of a declaration, made in a formal instrument, that the new state accepted the obligations of the Charter (Kelsen 1952: 67). How the new governments ruled their peoples was of no concern to the international organization.

In 1919, the new states of Eastern Europe were subject to intense external scrutiny before they gained diplomatic recognition from the major powers and thereby subsequent membership in the League of Nations. To gain recognition, they had to have constitutions, schedules for elections, evidence of effective rule of law, and as noted, various commitments to protect the rights of minorities. In brief, they had to possess the characteristics and hallmarks of the liberal democratic state. The underlying principle for the "right to rule" in the post-1919 new states was popular sovereignty. Recognition was either denied or made conditional upon domestic improvements where the principle was denied or violated.

No such qualifications applied to the post-1945 countries. No one inquired into the domestic politics of the new states.[3] The United Nations did not carry over the regime for protection of minorities adopted in the 1920s in Europe. Some members argued specifically against such a regime on the grounds that official recognition of minority status might weaken multi-ethnic states (Ryan 1990: 157). Nor did it require any evidence of the validation and legitimation of post-colonial rule. If a state had been born through a war of national liberation, it seemingly had more legitimacy than one that came into being through a plebiscite. Armed struggle was a validation in itself. FRELIMO, for example, was recognized as the legitimate representative of the Mozambique national "self," not because it was elected, but because it had proved itself by waging a successful military campaign against Portugal. The same formula was adopted for Indonesia, Algeria, Cyprus, and all the other states that were born through armed combat. These struggles, then, were not regarded as a traditional war under Chapter VII of the United Nations' Charter. On the contrary, the "Declaration on the Strengthening of International Security" (General Assembly Resolution 2734, 1977) specifically urged member states to "increase their support and solidarity" with violent national liberation movements, which were defined by the United Nations as a legitimate means of achieving independence from colonialism.

While some jurisdictions legitimated themselves through elections or plebiscites, most did not. Having been a colony was sufficient qualification for attaining immediate membership in the United Nations. There was to be no international scrutiny of post-colonial political arrangements and practices. It was assumed that a constitution (sometimes drafted with the help of United Nations officials) and adherence to the United Nations Declaration on Human Rights (1948) were sufficient to guarantee the full rights of citizenship.

The United Nations thus validated new states without inquiring whether they met all four traditional qualifications of statehood: (1) a defined territory; (2) a permanent population; (3) an effective government; and (4) the capacity to enter into treaty relations with other

[3] Western governments' treatment of the former Soviet republics and socialist states has been substantially different, however. Since 1989, they have insisted that all post-socialist states commit themselves to market economies and democratic institutions if they wish to obtain diplomatic recognition and various forms of aid. In the case of many of the former Soviet republics, the condition has been more rhetorical than real. Despite professions of commitment to both principles, the politics of Tajikistan, Uzbekistan, Georgia, and elsewhere in the former republics have hardly become democratic (Kangas 1994; and for further discussion, Holsti 1994).

states. It is the third condition that on any objective grounds some of the new states could not meet. The most famous case was the Congo, a vast territory of Belgian plunder that had almost no university graduates, no idea of "community," no history as a distinct political entity, or any other of the many qualities that formed the foundation of statehood in Europe. Shortly after its independence, it collapsed into civil war and the secession of Katanga province. It took a major United Nations military intervention to restore some semblance of coherent statehood.

The quality of "effective government" is obviously a matter of judgment; it includes, as a minimum, the actual exercise of power and a right or title to exercise that power. Most of the new states had the latter solely by virtue of having been a colony. But many were soon to exercise power by means other than public support or constitutional law. They soon came to base rule on coercion, bribery, despotism, murder, and massive violations of civil and political rights (see chapter 6).

The United Nations has never spelled out a "rule" of government effectiveness. The subject is far too political. It granted membership to the Congo, Sudan, Nigeria, Burma, Guinea-Bissau, and many others without any scrutiny of government effectiveness. At the same time, it has denied to or withdrawn membership from certain states with very effective governments (Taiwan, Rhodesia). In practice, the recognition/granting of statehood by the UN has been based primarily on the right of colonial people to self-determination irrespective of their actual capacity and/or readiness to govern.

Finally, the United Nations, having helped to create and define the new states, provided a variety of programs to help build the economic foundations of statehood. International assistance soon came to be seen as a responsibility for the wealthy countries and an entitlement for those who should be repaid for the years of colonial economic exploitation (Jackson 1990). In addition, the great powers provided for their own strategic reasons and interests a variety of programs to strengthen the internal coherence of their allies, clients, and adversaries' enemies. Supplies of arms, economic assistance, and military training vastly strengthened their recipients and were often used by incumbent regimes to strengthen their domestic power rather than to fend off external enemies. To the extent that these supplies assisted central authorities against their ideological, ethnic, religious, or other-based domestic oppositions, they significantly aided the state-sustaining function.

The universalization of the state format

Despite the great variety of societies, cultures, languages, religions, forms of commerce and production, and indigenous political structures that existed in the precolonial and colonial eras, the process of decolonization produced a single format – the Western territorial state. The heterogeneity of political forms that had existed throughout man's organized history has now been reduced to a single form. There are today more than 185 members of the United Nations, and all of them are in theory equal as states. Political organizations that are not constructed on the principles of sovereignty and territoriality are not members of the international society and have no standing in public international law.

But official designations of sovereignty hide fundamental differences between states. The immense variations of culture, religion, commerce, and politics that has characterized the world throughout recorded history has perhaps diminished under the onslaught of global communications and their resulting transmission of ideas, tastes, fashions, and fads. It is clear, however, that the universalization of the territorial state format does not mean that all states share the same characteristics. In particular, artificial states – the creations of colonial authorities and international organizations – are in many ways fundamentally different from states that grew slowly through an organic process involving wars, administrative centralization, the provision of welfare entitlements, and the development of national identities and sentiments. The processes that took place in Europe over many centuries were bound to lead to consequences very different from processes that were imposed by colonial authorities over peoples of immense diversity and variety. Since the purpose of colonialism was *not* to create states, it is hardly surprising that the states that *did* emerge from colonialism would share few of the characteristics of their European counterparts. War in the latter half of the twentieth century has been primarily a phenomenon to (1) create states in the Western image, and (2) to try to hold them together after their creation. As we saw in chapter 2, the incidence of wars between states has declined dramatically since 1945, while the incidence of wars about and within states has increased.

The problem of war in international politics has thus been reduced primarily to the problem of state-maintenance and state failures. The history of state-creation since 1945, as varied as it has been, has nevertheless demonstrated an important point about the foundations of political orders. Successful states are based on two dimensions of legitimacy: (1) the definition of the community over which rule is to be exercised, and (2) the principle(s) upon which the "right to rule" is based. The two are inextricably connected (see next chapter). But if one dimension is missing, muddled, or maldeveloped, the state will have difficulty cohering. After the French Revolution, the principles of popular sovereignty (the "right to rule" principle) were attached to the principle of citizenship as the basis of the community around which the political order must anchor itself. Later in the nineteenth century, the doctrine of popular sovereignty became increasingly widespread throughout Europe, but the concept of the community based on citizenship increasingly gave way to the community defined in terms of "natural" attributes of groups. States created in 1919 generally adopted the latter definition of community. This led to substantial conflict and war, as the territorial limits of the state could not be made to fit perfectly within the vessel of nationality.

Since 1945, both dimensions of legitimacy have been muddled or murky. The legitimating principle of the "right to rule" was seldom more than the negative one of national liberation, combined with the legendary feats of those who led anti-colonial wars. The definition of community, once the nationalist leaders had decided to appropriate the colonial unit as the basis of the post-colonial state, necessarily had to be confused. The community of citizens was the aspiration, but the political complexities "on the ground" were such that common citizenship was not sufficient glue to hold the societies together. Despite brave efforts of those who, like Jawaharlal Nehru, sought to give meaning to the citizenship concept, to insist on the de-politicization of social, language, and religious cleavages, and to guarantee access to decisions and resources to all peoples irrespective of their attributes, many governments succumbed to the politics of segmentalism, factions, and division. The communities over which the "right to rule" is exercised became increasingly defined in terms of attributes, majorities, minorities, orthodoxies, and heretics. In some, the "right to rule" principle shifted from popular sovereignty to divinity, the old-fashioned idea that all secular rule is divinely sanctioned. This basic legitimating myth, the subject of so much war in sixteenth- and seventeenth-century Europe, is following the same path on the eve of the twenty-first century.

Colonial administrations, including Soviet authority in some of its republics, left few legacies upon which to base legitimate authority. There was a small colonial bureaucracy capable of extraction, often some clones of parliamentary institutions, and usually large and well-trained military and police establishments that could coerce. Most of these institutions drew disproportionally on one language, religion, or regional population, thus helping to undermine the concept of a community of citizens (cf. Tilly 1990: 200–1). Many other factors were involved as well. But in the absence of a clear understanding of, and commitment to, the principles upon which the "right to rule" were based, over what sort of community, many of the states born after 1945 and 1989 were weak. It is this weakness that lies at the root of wars since 1945. We turn next to examine the main differences between weak and strong states. Chapter 7 then links these characteristics to the international milieu and to the problem of war.

5   The strength of states

In the conventional international relations literature, states are primarily characterized in terms of power, that is, in their capacity to achieve and defend their purposes either through persuasion or coercion and, if necessary, to defeat their adversaries in war. Histories of international politics as well as their theoretical renderings in neo-realism thus concentrate on the activities of the "powers" which are usually defined as the great powers of a particular era. There is a strong correlation between the status of a great power and its immediately available military resources. The concept of a "power" thus traditionally has been linked closely to the phenomenon of war.

But war in the second half of the twentieth century has not been predominantly a great power activity. As the tables in chapter 2 demonstrate, most war since 1945 has occurred in the Middle East, Africa, Central America, South Asia, and Southeast Asia, and more recently in the Balkans and the Central Asian former Soviet republics. If war is the topic of contemporary analysis, then academic analysts' long love affair with the great powers will have to change. Since 1945, the great powers have primarily *responded* to the problem of war in and between weak states. They have not themselves been the sources of war, as they had been between the seventeenth century and 1945. To study war, then, the new focus will have to be on states other than the "powers." Theories of international relations will have to veer away from Rousseau's insights and recognize that anarchy within states rather than between states is the fundamental condition that explains the prevalence of war since 1945.

State strength, for our analytical purposes, is not measured in military terms. It is, rather, in the capacity of the state to command loyalty – the right to rule – to extract the resources necessary to rule and provide services, to maintain that essential element of sovereignty, a monopoly over the legitimate use of force within defined territorial limits, and to operate within the context of a consensus-based political community. It is by no means the case that all states similarly share these essential characteristics of statehood.

To this point, the concept of the state has remained undefined. Definitions abound in the literature – the concept is one of the most contested in the literatures of constitutional law, political science, and international relations – but no authoritative rendering is offered here. Our purpose is to link kinds of states to war; hence, it is important to identify those characteristics of states that give it strength or weakness. Barry Buzan helps in the task (1991: ch. 2), for his purpose was also to explore the problem of the weak state, particularly in its security concerns. Buzan suggests that the state contains three interlinked components, (1) the idea of the state; (2) the physical basis of the state; and (3) the institutional expression of the state. The idea of the state represents history, tradition, culture, nationality, and ideology. It is, in a sense, the *affective* aspect of the state, the forces, sentiments, and ideas that distinguish political communities from each other. Obviously, however, political community and territorial sovereignty are frequently not the same. The poor fit between territorial states and the distribution of political communities gives rise to social tensions and often to internal war. Where the idea of the state does not command consensus or loyalty within a population (e.g., Afghanistan, Lebanon, Canada), the political institutions and perhaps even the territorial base of the state will be weaker than in those countries (e.g., Japan, Iceland) where such a consensus exists. The physical basis of the state includes defined territory, population, resources, and wealth. All are variable, although territorial definition has become more fixed than in previous eras. The international norm today is that lineal boundaries are "sacred" and cannot be altered except with the consent of all states involved in a dispute. State institutions comprise the machinery of government and the regime, meaning laws, norms, and incumbents of official office.

All three elements of the state are interconnected and are necessary, if not always sufficient, for a state to cohere and sustain its basic functions. A state may exist as purely an idea (e.g., among Kurds and, until recently, Palestinians), but it is not an internationally recognized actor without a defined territory and government institutions capable of exercising authority over that territory. Likewise, a state may exist territorially, as did Lebanon in 1976 and Somalia in the early 1990s, but it ceases to function in the absence of institutions that command loyalty and authority. A territory without either institutions or an idea is not a state either.

Those states where all three components are well articulated, inter-connected in such a manner as to sustain and support each other, will be stronger than states with opposite characteristics.

The literature on the strength of states emphasizes instrumental capacities of statehood such as degree of institutionalization, capabilities for extraction of surplus, delivery of services, autonomy, and the like (cf. Huntington 1968; Migdal 1988). All of these are important but they do not get to the heart of the matter. It is in the realm of ideas and sentiment that the fate of states is primarily determined. A totalitarian regime, for example, may rank high on institutionalization and extractive capacity, but that does not make it a strong state. Its rule is ultimately based on fear, force, and coercion rather than on consent or voluntary compliance. It therefore suffers from a legitimacy deficit. Instrumental conceptions of state strength overlook two critical aspects of legitimacy introduced in the previous chapter: the principle(s) on which the "right to rule" is based, and the intellectual and emotional bases of political community, that is, the definition of the population over whom rule is exercised. For the sake of brevity, let us call these, respectively, *vertical* legitimacy and *horizontal* legitimacy. The first deals with authority, consent, and loyalty to the idea(s) of the state and its institutions; the second deals with the definition and political role of community.

Authority/consent

Debates on the concept of legitimacy are among the most profound and fascinating in the study of politics. The issues of the right to rule and right rule commanded the attention of Plato, Aristotle, Confucius, contract theorists, and modern liberals. This is not the place to enter into these debates, for questions of definition, types, identification, and distinction between empirical and normative notions of legitimacy could take us far afield from the problem of war. There are, however, several distinctions that need comment. First is the distinction between the popularity of a government and the legitimacy of the state. In most Western societies, the state and government are distinct in the minds of most citizens. A government may suffer from low popularity but the effort to oust it is not necessarily an attack on the state, its underlying ideas, or on state institutions. A decisive electoral defeat of an incumbent government, for example, is not usually a sign that the population seeks a fundamental change in the constitutional order. In some states, however, the state/government distinction is not so clear. When a regime bases its rule on coercion, terror, and violence and proscribes political activity by a segment of the population or denies it access to resources and decision-making, that segment may withdraw loyalty to both the regime and the state. Some rulers, in fact, may consciously strive to erase the state/regime distinction as a means of hiding personal objectives, privileges, and gains in the name of state interests (cf. Stedman 1991: 376; Buzan 1991: 89). The state becomes the virtual "possession" of the person at the helm; when he or she is gone, the state may fail as well (Ajami 1992: 27; Ayoob 1995: 86–7). In yet other cases, the government may not be particularly unpopular, but the state nevertheless loses the ability to command authority and loyalty of all its citizens. Many Québécois, for example, do not hold the incumbent Canadian federal government in particularly low esteem, but they do not accept the proposition that Quebec should continue to remain an integral part of the Canadian state. Canada thus suffers from a horizontal legitimacy deficit among a significant proportion of the francophone population; the state's "rightful title to rule" (Friedrich 1963: 234) is questioned as is the community over whom rule is to be exercised. The same condition applied in the former Czechoslovakia. The Havel government, by all measures, was reasonably popular in Slovakia, but a group of Slovak politicians decided that the artificial state called Czechoslovakia was not a rightful political vessel for two different ethnic/language communities. In brief, a minority no longer wishes to be a minority and withdraws loyalty from both the political community and the state, and develops its alternative idea of a state – in these cases based on language and culture.

Claims and titles to rightful rule have, historically, varied substantially. Weber's (1978: 216) famous ideal typology of legal-rational, traditional, and charismatic bases of authority is important but does not encompass enough variations. Nor, for that matter, do the three categories introduced in chapter 3: civic, ethnic, and religious. The following have been observed in various historical and cultural settings:

1. Force and might. An occupation regime, for example, may earn authority by virtue of a military victory and the subsequent disarming of the occupied society. There was almost no

resistance to Allied occupation regimes in Japan and Germany after World War II. The occupation regimes were considered legitimate, although they did not command loyalty as that term is usually employed in the context of a polity.

2. Religion. Priest-kings have been ubiquitous throughout history. Authority is validated by the mystic qualities of the rulers or by the claim that they are the official secular interpreters of the faith.

3. Heredity. A ruler claims authority on the basis of lineage. The claim usually dissipates as successors are unable to match the feats of the lineage's originators.

4. Leadership attributes. Rulers validate their regimes through their exploits, heroic deeds, or wisdom (Plato).

5. Ethnicity. A regime claims its right to rule on the grounds that it is a "pure" incarnation of a "people."

6. Ideological task. A group of leaders claims to have a special historical task of national/racial redemption (Hitler, Milosevic), class victory against oppressors (Lenin), or various forms of "liberation" of the oppressed, wherever they may be.

7. Consent or contract. Rule is validated through various mechanisms of consent such as periodic elections, plebiscites, popular revolutions, or elite arrangements for alternating or sharing leadership positions (pre-1975 Lebanon).

8 Task achievement. As we saw in the previous chapter, many post-colonial regimes claimed the right to rule on the basis of their leadership of liberation movements. Success in this military/political endeavor was assumed to be tantamount to public validation of rule.[1]

States and their regimes are seldom based on a single concept. Hereditary rule in eighteenth-century Europe was not based solely on lineage. The doctrine of divine right (religious validation) and various paternalistic concepts buttressed the royal mystique. Iran's current ruling clerics come close to the religious category, but they must make some gestures toward popular validation as well. Modern dynastic regimes, such as the Duvaliers of Haiti and the Kims of North Korea, find it necessary to manufacture myths of god-like accomplishments to buttress lineage claims.

---

[1] For a somewhat different categorization of principles upon which the right to rule is claimed, see Sadeniemi (1995).

These categories derive from the perspective of the rulers. Claims to authority are only that. If they are not accepted by large segments of the population, then either the claims have to be changed or the rulers have to convince the disaffected that the claims are indeed legitimate. In times of social upheavals and rapidly changing ideas, bases of legitimacy seldom last: kings become figureheads, priest-kings are deposed for failure to prevent natural calamities (performance counts!), philosopher-kings become naked emperors, and those who rule through terror and violence end up either in exile or dragged through the streets. Where, however, legitimacy claims and popular expectations overlap or coincide, the state gains substantial strength. Rule is based on consent of one form or another. "Legitimacy," according to Rodney Barker (1991: 11), "is precisely the belief in the rightfulness of a state, in its authority to issue commands, so that those commands are obeyed not simply out of fear or self-interest, but because they are believed in some sense to have moral authority."

Today most Western analysts argue that rule based on explicit consent through periodic elections is the only enduring basis of vertical legitimacy. This may turn out to be the case, but it is probably premature to claim that only democracies have strong bases of legitimacy. There are a variety of states whose regimes base their legitimacy primarily on lineage or on religious principles. In this group we would include Saudi Arabia, Oman, Iran, and Swaziland.

Community

The horizontal aspect of legitimacy refers to the nature of the community over which formal rule is exercised. What is the community? The answer is by no means obvious. In Western political thought and state-creation, communities have been defined in terms of history, religion, citizenship, or consanguinity. There are other types of communities as well, such as communities of believers and faith, communities of class, or communities of occupation and profession (the bases of many thirteenth-century free cities in northern Europe). Horizontal legitimacy refers to the attitudes and practices of individuals and groups within the state toward each other and ultimately to the state that encompasses them. If the various groups and communities within the polity accept and tolerate each other, horizontal legitimacy is high. In many countries, the question of over whom to rule is assumed or not subject to debate. If communities, in contrast, seek to exclude, marginalize, oppress, or exploit others within the same state, then there is low horizontal legitimacy, even in ostensible democracies. Northern Ireland's Protestants, for example, have formally displayed their intolerance (or fear?) through the electoral mechanism, by voting consistently for a permanent majority of Protestant candidates. The implication is that the legitimate political community does not include Catholics. Those who have the right to choose their governments also choose who is to be governed (Cooper and Berdal 1993: 119) and there is no guarantee that the *who* will turn out to be the same as the historical population of the state.

The Croatian and Bosnian Serbs' practice of "ethnic cleansing," just to mention one particularly extreme and odious form of exclusion, is a basic statement that condemns any notion of community that transcends ethnicity or religion. It says, basically, "In our political community, we can accept only those who are exactly like us. We don't want to have anything to do with anyone different. Those who are not like us should get out." The political system that institutionalizes such exclusions renders the "other" powerless in both participation and allocation of resources. Those who are excluded cannot extend loyalty either to their compatriots or to the state. Lack of horizontal legitimacy within the society may therefore lead to the erosion or withdrawal of loyalty to the state and its institutions. Those who are excluded then seek their own political arrangements. The relationship may also be reversed. Dubious vertical legitimacy may create, maintain, or exacerbate horizontal legitimacy.[2] A standard stratagem for weak regimes is to create internal scapegoats within society to deflect criticism and disloyalty against themselves. The idea is to build a stronger foundation for the "right to rule" by excluding some over whom that rule is to be exercised. The examples are many and obvious: the Jews and communists in Nazi Germany, "capitalist-roaders" in Mao's China, communists and the Baha'i community in Iran, and numerous groups in Idi Amin's Uganda. Moreover, regimes and states that are based on a fundamentally exclusionist vertical principle of legitimacy, such as religion or ethnicity, by definition divide plural communities. A religiously tolerant theocracy is an oxymoron. Those who do not follow the official faith necessarily receive differential treatment – usually of an inferior type – and thus hedge or withdraw their loyalty to the community and to the state. Governments in states based on

---

[2] I am grateful to Scott Pegg for making this point.

ethnicity find compelling reasons to define "us" and "them" as a means of sustaining their vertical legitimacy.

It is often difficult to build a community of citizens, particularly when there are deep social and/or ideological cleavages within the society. Even the French revolutionaries who (re)invented the concept of citizen soon began distinguishing between "good" and "bad" citizens, the latter to be excluded through the ultimate punishment of decapitation. Vertical legitimacy in revolutionary France was buttressed by creating an internal enemy, many of whose victims had committed no crimes other than having been born into the aristocracy. The sense of community among the revolutionaries created by an internal "threat" almost destroyed the society of citizens, but it temporarily saved the revolutionary regime.

Those who find themselves defined in special categories, usually outside the political community, have several options: (1) remove themselves from the community (exile or migration, as the Asian community fled from Uganda in the 1970s); (2) organize resistance against the majority community to defend their interests, rights, and aspirations (the Mayans in Guatemala, Tamils in Sri Lanka); (3) secede to form their own state (numerous examples, including Sudan, Eritrea, Abkhazia, Chechnya); (4) capture the state apparatus through a coup or revolution (Tutsis in Rwanda, Fiji); or (5) start a communal war (Hutus in Rwanda). We have seen these strategies used over and over again in different post-1945 states. Which strategy is chosen depends on a variety of contingent circumstances including available leadership, the size of the minority, presence of external support, neighboring sanctuaries, and the like. The point to emphasize for our purposes, however, is that any state/regime, and the community over which rule is exercised, that bases legitimacy on exclusionary categories contains an inherent weakness. "Others" will always constitute an actual or potential threat (as perceived by the rulers) to the integrity of the state and/or to the solidarity of its underlying community. By contrast, a state based on a community of citizens has an added element of strength because no categorical group can legally be excluded from economic and political power or be subject to discrimination or oppression.[3] It is not a guarantee that the community will survive,

---

[3] The generalization needs qualification. Women in many countries did not enjoy suffrage until the second half of the twentieth century. In the United States, the African-American population, though granted the vote after the Civil War, was effectively excluded from exercising the franchise in many states until the 1960s.

89

however, for even in democracies such as the United States (the Civil War), pre-1975 Lebanon, Canada (some Québécois), Finland (some inhabitants of the Aaland islands), and Belgium (Walloons) where there is no discrimination by the state against language groups or between those groups, secessionist sentiments have led to civil war in the past or threaten the integrity of the state and the solidarity of the political community today (cf. Luciani and Salamé 1990: 402).

Legitimacy is thus a variable rather than a constant. Its vertical and horizontal dimensions are critical components of a state's strength, but that strength may wax and wane.

The continuum of state strength

States may be placed on a continuum of strength. At one extreme are strong states whose main features are strong linkages between the physical, attitudinal, and institutional components, all encompassed within high degrees of vertical and horizontal legitimacy. Other characteristics within this framework are enumerated below. At the other extreme are failed states, political entities that have collapsed. There is little or no public order, leadership commands no authority or loyalty, and a variety of groups and factions are armed to resist those who might try to integrate the community or establish effective order. Communal war and local rule by warlords, gangs, and factions are the order of the day.

The two extremes outlined briefly here are ideal types. Most states most of the time fall between the poles. We have little difficulty placing Switzerland, Norway, and Tonga toward the strong end of the continuum, and Lebanon, Liberia, Afghanistan, and Somalia toward the failed state category. In the middle ranges would be countries like Malaysia and Singapore tending toward the strong, and Iraq and Algeria tending toward the weak.[4]

Over time, states move along the continuum. There is no final resting place, although it is possible that some failed states may simply

---

[4] The typology, or more accurately, a dimension of strong state to weak state, can use a different terminology. Georg Sorenson, for example, has developed a typology of states termed "pre-modern," "modern," and "post-modern." I prefer to use the concept of a continuum of state strength rather than rigid categories because Sorenson's terms imply a historical movement in only one direction – toward the modern. Sorenson is aware of this problem and allows for states to have mixed characteristics (Sorenson 1994: 26–37).

disappear by being annexed, a common practice in pre-twentieth century Europe, and most recently experienced by East Germany. Movement is not consistently in one direction, either. States strengthen and weaken depending upon numerous political, economic, social, and philosophical trends. Canada is weaker today than it was two decades ago, but in the 1960s it was stronger than in the 1860s. In some respects the United States is a weaker state today than it was during the Eisenhower years. The legitimacy of the constitutional order has not declined notably (although there is substantial cynicism toward politicians in general), but the massive ownership of firearms and the development of locales of armed power, such as private militias, place the country closer to Afghanistan than to Japan in terms of effective control over private violence. Somalia moved from a weak state in the 1970s to a failed state in the 1990s. Other states have fared better. Malaysia has moved fairly consistently from a position of weakness at its independence in 1963 to greater strength, but it is still not in the strong category. Chile has moved from a situation of chronic weakness (indicated by civil war and coups) in the early nineteenth century to a position of strength today. The list could be extended at length. There is no automatic trajectory toward strength or weakness. The relationship of state strength to war, however, is emerging: since 1945 most wars of all types have originated within and between weak states. Strong states have warred against the weak, but not against each other. The remainder of this chapter lists some of the more concrete characteristics of strong states and establishes their linkage to legitimacy and the physical, attitudinal, and institutional components of the state.

Strong states

Vertical and horizontal legitimacy are composed of sentiments or habits based on a variety of institutions, rules, norms, practices, and attitudes. In ancient civilizations (and even in some contemporary states), the mysteries of religion were used to manufacture loyalty and compliance among subjects. Resistance was sacrilege and punishable by death. In most modern states, by contrast, legitimacy is performance-based. The state has to earn and maintain its right to rule through the provision of services, including security, law and order, justice, and a varying range of welfare measures. The poorer the performance and the more biased in execution, the more likely that resistance will either bring down the regime or break up the state.

Thus, a fundamental prerequisite of vertical legitimacy – even in the contemporary older types such as heredity (e.g., Saudi Arabia) – is an implicit bargain between the state and the political community: the state has the right to extract, but it must also provide services and allow participation in decisions to allocate resources. There must be a reasonable balance between the demands of extraction, the expectations of service deliveries, and participation. When the state extracts but does not provide offsetting services or access to decisions and decision-making, it risks losing its legitimacy and may face armed rebellion. In seventeenth-century France, for example, such rebellions were as common as the changes of seasons. Their most common sources were grain shortages, economic exploitation, and excessive taxes on peasants (Braudel 1990: 387–9). When the extraction of taxes, the delivery of services, or participation consistently and severely favor some category groups at the expense of others, rebellion, war, and secession are common responses. This was the basic complaint of East Pakistanis, the southern Sudanese, Eritreans, Ibos, and Slovenians. It is important to emphasize that the implicit bargain of extraction, services, and participation is always a matter of judgment and perception subject to change. A system that is judged reasonably "fair" at time x may be judged exploitative at time y. The allegation of the favored position of some republics in the former Yugoslavia was a powerful incentive and argument for secession in Slovenia and Croatia in the circumstances of 1990–1, while it was a matter of relatively minor complaint during the 1960s. The role of leadership in fostering a sense of injustice and mobilizing people to the point of taking up arms is crucial in breaking down the implicit compact.

A second foundation of vertical and horizontal legitimacy is reasonable agreement among all sectors of the society on the fundamental rules of the political game, what Buzan (1991: 65) has called the "institutional expression of the state." These rules are usually summarized and specified in constitutions. They contain the fundamental principles of justice that underlie the state. They may include, for example, the principle of majority rule, government validation through periodic elections, guarantees of civil liberties, including rights of minorities, limits on government authority and coercion, and principles guiding the allocation of funds and services between different communities, groups, regions, or other subunits of the state and society. Such principles are usually subject to interpretation as social, economic, and political circumstances change, in which case amendments or new constitutions have to be written and enacted. Systematic violation of the principles or neglect to change them in the face of altered circumstances often leads to the erosion of legitimacy. The rapid population growth of Muslims in Lebanon led to a demand to alter the compact of 1943 by which government positions were allocated between the various religious communities. When the Lebanese Christians – by the mid-1970s, a minority – refused to alter the constitution to change the rules of the game, civil war and the ultimate collapse of the Lebanese state resulted. The "rules of the game" aspect of vertical legitimacy is captured well by Charles Anderson's (1982: 310) characterization, in which "men disagree vigorously over the policies that government should pursue or the personnel that should occupy the decision-making posts, yet . . . support common notions of the locus of decision-making authority, the technique by which decisions are to be made, and the means by which rulers are to be empowered."

Horizontal legitimacy in strong states is based on the fundamental rule that no group within the community is excluded from seeking political power and enjoying its benefits. There can be no strong sense of community within the state if one segment of its population is proscribed from participating in politics, in all its dimensions, or is systematically excluded from state allocations of funds and services. In the strong state, there is a neutral authority that guarantees and ensures the primacy of common citizenship and attending rights over privileges based on family, ethnicity, or religion (Hassner 1993: 129).

Equality of opportunity and participation is not, however, a sufficient condition for maintaining both vertical and horizontal legitimacy. Québécois in Canada and francophones in Belgium have equal political rights – and indeed some privileges not justified by numbers (e.g., number of senators or representatives on government bodies) – but that has not prevented a significant number of them from seeking "a normal state" for the francophone Canadians or Walloons. Separatist sentiments in Scotland, Wales, northern Italy, and elsewhere are similarly not based on exclusion from access to political power.

A fourth characteristic foundation of legitimacy relates to the distinction between public service and personal gain. Vertical legitimacy derives to a large extent from the popular perception of rectitude among those who rule. Populations may accept all sorts of privileges and symbolic rewards accruing to rulers, but they ordinarily will not accept the proposition that the state should be used as a vehicle or platform for excessive personal enrichment at their expense.

Next, vertical and horizontal legitimacy correlate strongly with another important aspect of the "implicit contract" between society and state, namely that the state and its institutions must provide security, law, and a reasonable amount of order. That is, the state must be internally sovereign. It has a monopoly over the legitimate use of force and effectively controls or prevents illegitimate public or private violence. Communities that are armed against each other, as in Lebanon in the 1970s, reflect the incapacity of the state to provide one of its basic services, security and public order. Through a long historical process that took place over a half-millennium or more, the populations and political subunits of European states were eventually disarmed. Hobbes's concept of a state of nature was not far off the mark as a description of sixteenth- and seventeenth-century Europe or of some societies in weak states today. Homicide rates were very high compared to today; they have declined dramatically as the state slowly gained a monopoly of arms and began to provide alternative ways of settling scores and resolving individual and group conflicts. Strong states do not contain groups or individuals that can, through armed force, resist or encroach upon state jurisdictions. Colombia fails the test because the drug cartels effectively and systematically violate state laws and have the means to resist attempts to apply the law. A "state within a state" is a fundamental contradiction of the sovereignty principle.

Strong states and the vertical and horizontal legitimacy upon which they are based are also characterized by instrumental rather than fundamental politics. Politics lose their passion and revolve around fairly technical questions of means and priorities rather than ends and grand causes (Brenner 1994: 74–5). Higher or lower taxes, priorities on research or consumption, centralizing or decentralizing government services; the extent of welfare benefits – these are the kinds of issues that define politics in the strong state.[5] In contrast, ways of life,

---

[5] The emergence of some fundamentalist religious groups and, particularly in the United States, the increasing resort to violence as a means of engaging in the abortion debate, shows that many liberal democracies still have zero-sum-type politics that go far beyond the realm of pragmatism. One can find, in fact, more pragmatic politics in some states whose other characteristics would put them toward the weaker end of the continuum.

definitions of the community, and ideological crusades are fundamental questions that are bound to lead to zero-sum situations and
thus frequently to violent conflict within the state.

Effective civilian control of the military is another basis of both
vertical and horizontal legitimacy. When the military take over the
state they necessarily exclude normal political activity; and if they
become a "state within a state" they compromise the sovereignty
principle. With their command over the instruments of violence, they
are also particularly prone to use force against segments of the
population. They become, in other words, threats to the security of
communities and other groups within the state. Even military regimes
that base their legitimacy on the argument that they are the saviours of
the constitutional order must ultimately resort to coercion and terror or
return to the barracks (see chapter 8). Only in time of war does a
military dictatorship have some reasonable prospect of generating
popular consent.

There is, finally, an international dimension to legitimacy. A state
whose frontiers are contested or which receives no international
recognition is inherently weak given the imperatives of the global
division of labor. The lack of international legitimacy may help
undermine domestic legitimacy (and vice versa), a point which was
not lost on the South African authorities during the era of apartheid
or on the leadership of Rhodesia after its unilateral declaration of
independence in 1965. Israel, Rhodesia, North Korea, South Africa,
China (until the early 1970s), and Taiwan, among others, have all
been "pariah" states at one time or another. They have suffered the
lack of diplomatic, commercial, social, cultural, and athletic ex-
changes with other states as a result. Some were formally excluded
from the United Nations and from regional organizations. The
economic and status costs of the lack of legitimacy were often very
high, in some cases helping to bring about social unrest and,
ultimately, revolution.

Strong states have a fixed and permanent international personality,
defined most basically in their territorial dimension. Most strong
states have had their territorial limits sanctified through numerous
international treaties, through customary acceptance, and through
principles of territorial integrity enshrined in international covenants
such as the Charter of the United Nations and the Charter of Paris
(1990).

This list of the foundations of vertical and horizontal legitimacy is not exhaustive; other components might be relevant as well. More-over, well-articulated and popularly supported principles of vertical and horizontal legitimacy may not be sufficient conditions for state strength, although it could be argued that they are necessary. How necessary is of course a matter of judgment. The bases of legitimacy listed here have a decidedly modern character; there is the possibility that the analysis derives too extensively from a single political tradition. Most of the criteria are found in modern democracies and the political philosophies that underlie them. It is important to acknowledge therefore that some polities are reasonably strong in the absence of many of these characteristics. In an age of successful priest-kingdoms, for example, many of the sources of legitimacy narrated here would be non-existent or irrelevant. As Woodrow Wilson (1889) noted in his analysis of the historical development of governance, primitive or ancient polities normally ruled through coercion and the threat of religious punishment; nevertheless, many sustained reasonably popular loyalty and endured for centuries. Even today, some reasonably strong polities feature charismatic or lineage-based legitimacy principles (Cuba until the late 1980s, Saudi Arabia today) that may endure for some time.

The criteria are dimensions rather than absolutes. There is no such thing as a pure strong state. A state that scores high on all dimensions remains an ideal type. There is also the problem of theory versus practice. All the guarantees of civil liberties and full political participation do not mean that the horizontal aspect of legitimacy – a true community – is sufficiently strong to preclude various forms of unofficial exclusion, discrimination, and exploita-tion. The state cannot compel individuals to love one another or attribute groups to tolerate each other, although it can do a great deal to promote tolerance and to prevent discrimination. Similarly, while there may be a significant consensus on the political "rules of the game" or the fundamental contours of economic, social, and political activity, it is rare that virtually all individuals and groups are included in the consensus. Today, there are neo-Nazi groups throughout Europe, racist groups in the United States, and Muslim groups in Egypt and Algeria that fundamentally disagree with the consensus and seek to create a new kind of state. Moreover, few states have a monopoly over the provision of justice. Random killings and high crime rates have helped turn the United States into an armed camp featuring a Hobbesian life of insecurity in ghettoes and elsewhere, and prison as a way of life for approximately one of every 250 citizens of the country. Periodic government "wars against crime" have not ameliorated the problem. Compared to most other industrial and many developing countries, American authorities do not have the means to control private and some public violence. Almost all countries have some territory in dispute with neighbors, and political corruption remains typical in many areas of the world. Tax revolts are not uncommon and many citizens withdraw their loyalty from the state by migrating abroad. They choose exit over voice. In brief, no state is strong in all dimensions. All have weaknesses. The question is the trajectory over time either toward greater strength, or toward weakness and possible collapse. For the purposes of this study on armed conflict, the critical task is to identify at what points in movements along the trajectory armed violence and war are likely to break out. The evidence in chapter 2 strongly supports the hypothesis that state weakness correlates with war.

Let us now summarize the argument. The state, following Buzan (1991: ch. 2), is founded on physical (territory, population, resources, wealth) attributes, historical memories, affections and ideologies, and institutions, broadly conceived. All are interrelated. But these "objective" bases of the state are not sufficient to explain the weakness and strength of states. The critical variable is *legitimacy*, conceived in two dimensions: the vertical which establishes the connection (the "right to rule") between society and political institutions and regimes, and horizontal, which defines the limits of and criteria for membership in the political community which is ruled. The two dimensions are interrelated in important ways, and each is linked, in turn, to Buzan's three components of the state. The relationships are identified in figure 5.1.

The sources of vertical and horizontal legitimacy, not placed in any necessary order or ranking, are listed below the vertical and horizontal legitimacy "summit." Note that some of these sources are in a particularly close relationship to one of the three state components. The numbers are listed on each corner of the triangle.

The nexus between strong states and peace will be explored in chapter 7. The next task is to examine the problem of legitimacy in weak and failing states.

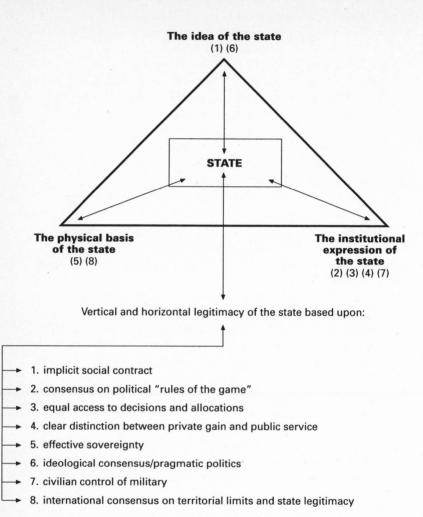

Figure 5.1

6 Perils of the weak: the state-strength dilemma

In classical and modern political thought, the state is the creation of some sort of community. In contract theories, for example, individuals band together to create a state in order to terminate life in a state of nature. In Hobbes's version, the contract is between individuals of the community and the Leviathan. In Rawls's modern version, individuals hidden behind a "veil of ignorance" congregate to create a just society and its governing apparatus.

From the perspective of this study, two interesting facts stand out in these accounts of state-creation. First, the authors do not bother to define who are members of the community. The community, as suggested in chapter 3, is assumed rather than made problematic. Second, in the act of state-creation, only members of the community are involved. Members of other communities – representatives of foreign states – have no role.

Contract metaphors for understanding the state-creation process after 1945 are inappropriate because the two assumptions, above, are incorrect. In post-1945 states, community cannot be assumed. It is the most problematic aspect of all new states, for most of them contain not a single community, but many. Nor was the act of state-creation primarily between members of a single community, or between those individuals and a Leviathan. Outside communities in the form of the metropolitan powers and the United Nations played significant and often crucial roles in laying the foundations of post-1945 states. Hobbes, Locke, and others wrote at a time when states remained relatively isolated. This condition did not prevail after World War II.

Weak states did not just happen. They emerged from colonialism, sets of practices and institutions that left important legacies for the new states.[1] We have already discussed the main legacy: the idea that the new independent states should simply transform themselves from the territorial creations called colonies into modern states. There were other legacies that must be mentioned because they are important in understanding the bases of weak and failed statehood today.

The most important legacy, after territoriality, was the nature of colonial political institutions. Colonies were not created to become participatory democracies. While the British often established quasi-parliamentary institutions and the rudiments of Western-style rule of law, ideas and practices of constitutionalism, accountability, civil liberties, and political participation were not part of the colonial political game. Fundamental decisions were made in the metropolitan capitals; resistance to them was frequently met with force (Ergas 1987: 4). Other legacies included bureaucratic structures whose personnel were trained to rule top-down rather than being responsive to local expectations and interests. They were there to control, not to respond. Colonial authorities also favored some groups at the expense of others and, as in Rwanda, sustained or even created ethnic elites to rule over supposed inferiors. Colonial authorities often created divisions of labor along ethnic lines. "In a number of instances . . . the allocation by the [colonial] state of 'differentiated rights of access' was based on a normative scale according to which some groups were seen as superior to others, and in times these normative evaluations were projected into the collective images which Africans formed of themselves" (Lemarchand 1983: 57). Ethnic politics did not begin with independence.

Finally, colonialism left organized military and police forces, instruments of coercion that were deliberately separated from the rest of society. Overall, then, colonial rule was one in which the relation between the state and society was characterized by downward links of domination but not by upward links of representation (Ottaway 1987: 172). There was nothing suggesting a social contract of any type.

[1] This is not to argue that the sole, or even most important, source of contemporary state weakness is colonialism. If our standard of measurement is the Western concept of the state, then it is unlikely that non-colonized areas would have made a successful transition from pre-modern political forms to strong states based on vertical and horizontal legitimacy. Since there were few states/empires outside of Europe that were not formally colonized (Ethiopia, Siam, China, Japan), there are insufficient test cases. Significantly, however, only Japan emerged as a reasonably strong state during the nineteenth century. Ethiopia, Siam, and China shared many of the characteristics of contemporary weak states.

The international community inserted itself in the state-making process in part to alter and reform these colonial practices and institutions. Through the metropolitan powers, the United Nations, and indigenous elites' educational experiences in London and Paris, Western political concepts and liberal constitutions were transplanted. In many instances, committees of Western diplomats and bureaucrats, and indigenous elites, wrote the constitutions of the new countries. Western academic circles, particularly in the United States, then assumed that the new, young countries would ultimately develop into carbon copies of European and North American states. Not recognizing that European and North American history differed in significant ways from the colonial experience, the American Social Science Research Council, aid agencies, governments, and innumerable international organizations and voluntary groups argued that the main item on the agenda now was "state-building" or "nation-building" that would result in modern liberal democracies. Most of the first-generation indigenous political elites – the "fathers of the country" – shared these assumptions, expectations, and aspirations.

One generation later, these expectations proved to be illusory in many countries. Some former colonies went on to thrive and even to develop political and social institutions that could be described as democratic. Despite great odds against them, some have even become strong states. But for many, the record has been one of communal wars, civil wars, rebellions, wars of secession, authoritarian and predatory rule, chronic political instability, and government change through bullets rather than ballots.

Ryszard Kapuscinski, a communist-era Polish journalist, narrated his travels through West Africa in the first years of independent rule there:

> In the course of one month [in 1963], I had driven through five countries. In four of them, there were states of emergency. In one, the president had just been overthrown; in a second, the president had saved himself only by chance; in a third, the head of government was afraid to leave his house, which was surrounded by troops. Two parliaments had been dissolved. Two governments had fallen. Scores of political activists had been arrested. Scores of people had been killed in political conflicts. Over a distance of 520 kilometers, I had been checked twenty-one times and subjected to four body searches. Everywhere there was an atmosphere of tension, everywhere the smell of gunpowder. (Kapuscinski 1990: 127)

Kapuscinski's ordeal was only too typical. Between 1958 and 1985, sixty-four "forcible changes of government" and innumerable abortive coups took place in Africa (Ergas 1987: 214–15).

If we count all the coups, attempted coups, civil wars, wars of secession, and communal wars, life in many Third World and some former Soviet republics has been dangerous. And dangerous not from external predation, as was the case in European history, but from conflicts within the state. The chief threat to many post-1945 states is not the external; it is internal. In the context of the Third World and post-socialist states, the concept of "national security" takes on an entirely different meaning (cf. Al-Mashat 1985: 74–5).

The variety of states

In the last chapter, I argued, following Buzan, that states have four components including a physical base, an idea(s), and institutions, all brought together and made meaningful in terms of sovereignty in a structure of horizontal and vertical legitimacy (cf. Zartman 1988: 6–8). A state must also have *effective* rule throughout a defined territory. If rule does not extend beyond the capital city, the state is a fiction although foreign governments may not choose to deal with it as such.

Other conceptions of the state have been seen throughout history. While all contemporary states have some things in common such as fixed territoriality, symbols, and membership in international organizations, their internal characteristics, and particularly the principles underlying vertical and horizontal legitimacy, vary greatly. We must not assume that characteristics that are different from those found typically in Western states necessarily lead to weakness. Consider some of the different types of political orders where the idea and practices of the state differ fundamentally from Western conceptions, but where the state functions reasonably well nevertheless and commands some vertical legitimacy, even if only of a passive sort.

In Africa there are some patrimonial states whose vertical legitimacy is based less on popular validation through elections or government performance than on personal loyalty. In the Middle East, there are traditional imam-chief systems that have existed for centuries and that command substantial loyalty (Oman), states created by colonialism (Syria, Iraq, Jordan), "rentier" states sustained by oil wealth (Qatar, United Arab Emirates), and virtual non-states (Libya). Except for the capital, for example, Libya is ruled primarily by local bodies, tribal sheiks, and kinship structures. To Muammar Quadaffi, the Western concept of the state is anathema; what counts is the Arab "nation." Libya is a state in the Western sense only for external purposes; otherwise, it is something entirely different (Lemarchand 1991: 147–8).

Rentier states are significantly different from their Western counterparts. A rentier state exists and commands some popular loyalty by virtue of sitting on pools of oil. In Kuwait, oil income accounts for more than 60 percent of government revenues. If one adds the income from foreign investments made from oil revenues, then 94 percent of Kuwait's government income comes from oil (Luciani 1990: 72). It allocates rich sums to a population that is mostly migrant. In the United Arab Emirates, 90 percent of the work force is foreign; in Qatar, the figure is 85 percent; in Kuwait, 79 percent (before the 1990 invasion by Iraq); in Bahrain, 59 percent; in Oman, 48 percent, and in Saudi Arabia, almost one-half the country's work force comes from abroad (Luciani and Salamé 1990: 408). Many teachers, and even a high percentage of the civil servants of rentier states, are foreigners (Sabagh 1990: 359, 386). This is a vastly different situation than that assumed in contract theories of the state. It is difficult to speak of the governance of a "community" in these states. There is little horizontal legitimacy where high proportions of the population are comprised of temporary foreign residents.

Rentier states have also been called "allocation states" (Luciani 1990) because they distribute wealth but their workers do not typically produce it. Only about 3 percent of these states' populations are actually involved in the production of oil. Most of the rest are construction workers and civil servants. Allocation is the secret of these states' success – as long as oil is in international demand. These states can literally purchase the loyalty of their mostly foreign populations by providing lavish welfare, housing, education, and employment programs. Vertical and horizontal legitimacy are not based, as in many Western countries, on patriotism, symbols, a collective history, sense of community, or even a distinct religion; they are founded primarily on the distribution of oil monies.

If there are significant differences between states in single regions such as the Middle East, there are also differences between regions. States in Central America, for example, are much older than those of Africa and law plays a different role in state–society relations. The successor states of the Soviet Union vary greatly in history, culture, longevity, and government structure. We are not looking for elements of diversity, however. The question is "what makes states weak?" What are the common properties of weak states, regardless of region, history, social makeup, and culture?

Structural characteristics of weak states[2]

Most weak states share characteristics that are structural. That is, they are not dependent upon single decisions, or even on entire programs of rulers and/or the political community. They are features and patterns created and/or sustained by larger forces, including colonial legacies and certain aspects of the world economic system.

One of the most critical characteristics is the low level or absence of vertical legitimacy. Substantial segments of their population do not accord the state or its rulers loyalty – for reasons enumerated below – and the rulers, in the name of the state, have little authority in the sense that their decisions, decrees, actions, and policies elicit habitual compliance. Yet, many of them appear strong and authoritarian. Authoritarianism is not to be confused with authority, however.

Weak states in fact display a paradox: they are at once strong in the category of despotic power, but weak in infrastructural power (Mann 1986: 109–36). Joseph Mobutu's Zaïre is a paradigmatic example. According to Thomas Callaghy (1987: 99), "[i]t is both hard and soft, authoritarian and lacking authority, extractive and strapped, coercive and loose. It is a Leviathan, but a lame one." Coercive capacity is high, as indicated by well-developed instruments of state surveillance and internal security (Dawisha 1988: 284–9), but compliance with government decrees is low. The essential props of vertical legitimacy – authority, reciprocity, trust, and accountability – are largely absent (Hydén 1992: 23). This does not mean the absence of rule; it is, rather, that rule is localized. A perennial contest exists between the "national" authorities representing the state and local power centers which command the effective loyalties of important segments of the population. In Migdal's (1988: 33) terms,

> [t]he ineffectiveness of state leaders who have faced impenetrable barriers to state predominance has stemmed from the nature of the

---

[2] The literature uses a variety of terms to denote essentially the same phenomenon of weakness. Other terms include "mashed potato state," "soft state," "gentle state," "absent state," and "imaginary state" (cf. Odhiambo 1991: 294). The preference for the term weak state arises from the recognition that weakness is a variable rather than a constant, as is implied in the terms above.

societies they have confronted – for the resistance posed by chiefs, landlords, bosses, rich peasants, clan leaders, *za'im*, *effendis*, *aghas*, *caciques*, *kulaks* . . . through their various social organizations.

These local power centers regard the state more as a threat than as a legitimate source of authority, direction, and services. In many weak states, therefore, central rule is mostly theater. "Between the ambitions of the elite and the survival stratagems of the masses, the state often appears to survive essentially as a show, a political drama with an audience more or less willing to suspend its disbelief" (O'Brien 1991: 145–6). The authorities of the state may appear to be discharging their functions, but in reality rule is local, and the gift of legitimacy – belief in the rightness to rule – is withheld or offered only conditionally and periodically by the masses. The authoritarianism of most weak states is not to be confused with the capacity to govern effectively (Ottaway 1987: 174).

A second structural characteristic is the personalization of the state – a feature common to European polities prior to the twentieth century and even beyond. In the weak state, exactly who is it that enjoys or fails to command loyalty? In Western thought – though not always in practice, as Adolf Hitler demonstrated – the state is supposed to be the vessel of authority, defined in territorial terms. Rulers come and go, but the state has a permanence not accorded to mere mortals. In many weak states, however, leaders seek to erase the distinction. They suffer from the Louis XIV (*"L'état, c'est moi"*) complex, believing that they are not mere governors but the very incarnation of the state and sometimes even of the gods. Citizens confuse the distinction between state and ruler, particularly when leaders portray themselves as saviours, emperors, "inspired ones," and "teachers" (cf. Ajami 1992: 227). If citizens have experienced only such figures, they know of no other source of authority. Many observers call these "patrimonial states," meaning that patron–client ties rather than legal–rational relationships form the basis of the polity (cf. Ergas 1987: 5). When these ties are broken, as they were in Somalia starting in 1988, the state literally collapses. The patron *is* the state. Perhaps a better way to put it is that, in patrimonial systems, the state disappears for all practical purposes, and is replaced by personality politics for which state structures are but an object of manipulation with no legitimate claims to a distinct existence or purpose (Jackson and Rosberg 1982; Marenin 1987: 66). When rulers act as if they are the state, they actually weaken it (Ottaway 1987: 173).

In the contemporary world, the state of course does not simply disappear upon the death or ousting of a supreme authority. States survive, rulers change. But some states do collapse and are sustained as legal entities primarily by international life-saving operations and by the force of the tradition of statehood as the only appropriate form of political organization. For a variety of reasons, annexation – East Germany is a rare exception – is not an option (who would want to annex Somalia or Liberia?); nor is international partition. The creation of mini-states – the Abkhazias, Chechnyas, Somali Republics, and Bougainvilles – are the only answer proposed yet, but this is not a very attractive option to the international community either (see chapter 9).

Finally, weak states lack horizontal legitimacy. There is no single community whose members, metaphorically speaking, have signed a social contract among themselves. Instead, there are numerous communities and categories that shape the nature of politics and authority structures. Most of the recent literature on "ethnic conflict" is therefore far too narrow. Ethnicity is just one of many moving lines of cleavage within post-colonial societies. Religion, class, caste, factions, language, and territorial location are just as important as ethnicity. Social cleavages, moreover, shift through time, and states deal with them in different ways. To reduce everything to ethnicity is to miss a great deal. In Islamic communities, for example, religious differences (sometimes linked to ethnicity, but not always so) are traditionally more important than ethnicity. And those differences are dealt with in many different ways. In many Arab states, for example, non-Muslim communities of monotheistic faith are tolerated and protected, while Shiite communities are frequently persecuted (cf. Corm 1988: 18–22; Rodinson 1989: 57). In India and elsewhere, religion, like nationalism, is the glue that holds many communities together but weakens the state when adherents demand exclusive access to political office and economic resources.

Societies are constituted of many different types of communities. They might include, within a single country, full nations, "peoples of the frontier" (indigenous groups), communal contenders for state power (Chinese in Malaysia, Pushtuns in Pakistan, Ibos in Nigeria), militant sects (some Shiites in Lebanon and Catholics in Northern Ireland), or ethnoclasses, such as Afro-Americans in the United States and Roma throughout Eastern Europe (Gurr 1991). For research purposes and in common parlance, such groups are commonly referred to as "minorities." But we must remember that a "minority" is

a social construction and not necessarily a self-perception. Bernard
Nietschmann (1987: 5–6) makes the point well:

> A nation people within its own territory is not an "ethnic group" or
> "minority." Sikhs may be an ethnic group in London, but not in
> Punjab (Khalistan); Samis may be a minority in Oslo or Stockholm,
> but in Samiland they are a people. A people does not automatically
> become a minority or an ethnic group because its nation is invaded.
> The French, Poles, and Dutch did not become "minorities" during the
> German invasion and occupation. States define nation peoples as
> "ethnic groups" and "minorities" as a tactic to annex their identities
> in order to incorporate their lands and resources.

It is also incorrect to assume that various nations, groups, or
categories are naturally hostile to each other. Hostility is a variable, not
a constant. It derives from a variety of sources, among which are
extended dominance of one group over another, exploitation, inequi-
table allocation or division of resources, and forced assimilation. Most
"ethnic wars" are not the result of primordial hatreds but rather of
state policies. Some states are weak precisely because they have (sometimes following colonial practice) established systems of social, economic, and political domination and injustice. Otherwise, people of
different identities can and have often coexisted peacefully for generations. Multiple loyalties and allegiances are also common in most
societies. One can be a local pastoralist, Kikuyu, Kenyan, and African
simultaneously (cf. Miles and Rochefort 1991). One cannot be,
however, a loyal citizen of Sudan if one is an African animist in a state
dominated by Muslims bent on applying the *sharia* to all non-Muslims
and expropriating the lands of African tribes.

The reality of most weak states is that they contain numerous
communities. The population of India has thirty-six major languages,
every existing religion in the world, and multitudes of ethnicities. The
Sudan which, unlike India, has not been able to create any sense of
horizontal legitimacy, contains 597 different tribes speaking 115 different languages, significant numbers of nomads who could not care
less about some fictional Sudanese "identity," and three major religious forms (Gurdon 1989: 67–71).

Horizontal legitimacy fails to develop or is destroyed when, as in
Sudan, various groups or communities clearly, systematically, and
over a period of time dominate, oppress, exploit (e.g., appropriate
resources), forcibly assimilate, or threaten the security of other groups
and communities. States of whatever format, if they lack vertical *and*

horizontal legitimacy, and if their authority structures are primarily patrimonial, will be weak. They may look like states to the outside world because they enjoy international recognition, have defined territories, flags, government offices, ambassadors, and armies. They have two of Buzan's three state components. But they lack a single "idea" of the state around which different constituent communities' affections and loyalties can converge. Inside, they are largely hollow shells in which governance is local, not national, and where communal animosities or state–group relations threaten to erupt into civil wars, communal bloodbaths, and wars of secession. The further question is: what conditions erode legitimacy and authority, or prevent them from developing? What are typical practices and institutions in patrimonial polities, where the state and personalist rule become one and the same?

Practices and policies that prevent or erode legitimacy

In the implicit contract between individuals and the state, whereby the citizen agrees to state extractions, the most fundamental service purchased, as Hobbes emphasized, is security. The Leviathan must provide law, order, and protection. In the contemporary setting of many post-1945 states, that means that the authorities must protect communities against each other, individuals from individuals, and individuals against predatory actions of authorities. If the state cannot provide security, or if the state itself becomes a major threat to the life and welfare of individuals and the well-being of communities, it can hardly exercise authority or expect loyalty in return. Populations faced with these problems cannot and do not extend the "right to rule" to such states (we will examine their options below).

Personal security is fundamental to the sustenance of any polity. In weak states it remains problematic. In jurisdictions such as Zaïre, Sudan, Mozambique, Lebanon, Afghanistan, Angola, and Chad, among others, protection remains a local matter because central institutions either do not exist or have collapsed (cf., Lemarchand 1987: 157). Even worse, in some states the authorities themselves become threats to the lives and security of citizens. Gurr (1991: 173) notes that violence is particularly likely to be used by regimes headed by minorities in highly stratified societies that have themselves gained and maintained power through violence, and that have organized secret police, revolutionary "militias," or special military contingents charged with rooting out all potential opposition. Governments can also inflame communal or group tensions and promote violence between them. In order to disrupt political opposition in 1993, for example, Joseph Mobutu deliberately set communities in Shaba (Katanga) against each other, though they had lived harmoniously for generations. The result was a half-million refugees who fled the area (Lee 1994: 38–9).

The provision of essential services beyond security varies from country to country. In industrial societies, governments that extract too much compared to the services they offer in health, education, welfare, and employment, for example, face tax revolts and burgeoning underground economies. In most post-1945 states (but not the post-Soviet republics), the idea of state responsibility to provide welfare beyond education, though prominent in the development literature, is not yet widespread. In many such societies, welfare and employment remain the responsibilities of families and local groups. We cannot therefore argue that a central government which does not deliver Western-style welfare benefits necessarily lacks legitimacy.

But the second, or economic dimension of vertical legitimacy, is important. If the state extracts to the point where livelihood is no longer possible, migration, resistance, rebellion, and secession attempts become alternatives to payment. In societies characterized by extensive poverty, virtually any government extraction imposes a severe threat. Most African states have GNPs smaller than the endowment of Harvard University (Young in 1991a: 21). Tax and price increases are a constant reality in a general environment of economic decline. It is perhaps not accidental that the erosion of state authority in Africa correlates strongly with poor economic performance.

The balance between extraction and services is not the only economic dimension of vertical legitimacy. Allocation has to reflect some standard of justice between groups and communities. In polities where scarce resources are allocated to favor some groups at the expense of others, both vertical and horizontal legitimacy decline. The breakup of Pakistan in 1970–1 was not so much a matter of ethnic intolerance or hatred – the major population groups were not intermixed or even contiguous – as of rank discrimination by Urdu-speaking elites in the capital in allocating resources and services to the Bengali population of East Pakistan (cf. Nafziger and Richter 1976; Breuilly 1982: 225).

A third source of eroding or weak legitimacy is the lack of social consensus on the political "rules of the game." Formal constitutions mean little in many post-1945 states, including some former Soviet republics. Some aspects of politics may conform to constitutional requirements, but as noted, many of these aspects are theater and hide the realities. Patrimonial systems may work quite well except that the "outs" will not consider them legitimate. The persistence of localism in politics fundamentally frustrates efforts to extend effective state jurisdiction over society. As Migdal (1988: 255) describes it:

> [S]trongmen have been wedded to state resources and personnel to maintain their local control and to gain new resources to enhance that control. Yet, their most basic purposes have been antithetical to modern norms of what a state should do. These norms have depicted the state as a mechanism to create a single jurisdiction – a rule of law in which the rules are the same from border to border; this is the desideratum of the modern state. These strongmen have worked for precisely the opposite effect. They have sought to maintain their own rules and their own criteria for who gets what within much more limited bounds; their rules have been parochial and discriminatory rather than universal.

Paradoxically, some accoutrements of democratic "rules of the game" may actually weaken the state and set the stage for secessionist and other forms of armed struggle against the polity. In multicommunity states where category distinctions are culturally, economically, and politically relevant or critical, elections and plebiscites may establish and perpetuate majority rule that permanently excludes minorities from access to power and resources (cf. Welsh 1993; Ayoob 1995: 40–1). This was the problem in the March 1962 plebiscite in Bosnia and has been a factor in the politics of Sri Lanka, Myanmar, and many other countries. It is one of the great difficulties of post-1945 states, given their usual multicommunal social makeup, that democratic rules originating in relatively homogeneous European and North American societies in the eighteenth and nineteenth century can actually amplify social tensions and, thereby, erode both horizontal and vertical legitimacy.

A fourth characteristic that prevents the development of, or erodes both vertical and horizontal legitimacy, is where one individual, family, group, or community "captures" the state and uses its authority to exclude others from participation and access to resources. In some states, elites attempt to build the political order around select groups – including families – and define it in such a way as even to deny the existence of groups that may not share their world outlook (cf. Ayoob 1995: 38). Exclusion is the daily practice of politics in countries such as Sri Lanka, Myanmar, Thailand, Turkey, Israel, Sudan, and many others. The military are no less exclusive; indeed they are the norm of Third World politics, not the exception. The average Third World state has spent more than one-half of its years of independence since 1946 in the hands of the soldiers (Tilly 1990: 213), and the soldiers who usually come to power in order to protect unity, law, and order, often end up destroying the state apparatus and its legitimacy in their search for means of staying in power (Bienen 1989: 24). Not infrequently, those means include the oppression of minorities and all actual or potential sources of opposition.

The rulers of "captured" states exclude communities and groups through a variety of policies, including *subjection* (e.g., apartheid, Ethiopian policies in Eritrea), *displacement* (Uganda's expulsion of Asians in the 1970s, Myanmar's expulsion of Indians in 1962 and Muslims in 1994), *forced assimilation* (Sudan), formal or virtual *disenfranchisement* (Sri Lanka, Croatia, Bosnia, Estonia), and *mass murder* (Uganda under Idi Amin, Equatorial Guinea under Macias Nguema) (cf. Rothchild 1986).

The lot of the excluded destroys any possibility for both horizontal and vertical legitimacy and loyalty to the state. All alternatives look better. We might add that such state practices also compromise the international legitimacy of the state. If taken to extremes, the perpetrators become pariahs and face a variety of external pressures that may culminate in global economic sanctions and ultimate armed intervention.

Politics in weak states are also characterized by passion; at issue is the idea and nature of the state itself, the nature of a political community, relations between communities, and the purposes of governance. These are the politics of "ultimate ends" (Hawthorn 1991), not the politics of tinkering with priorities. There are many leaders, movements, groups, and individual activists who reject the idea(s) and institutions of the state in which they live (this may be the case in strong states as well, although numerically such groups are relatively small). They grant no legitimacy to their rulers – they reject their claims of "right to rule" – and in the case of sectarians, they extend no legitimacy to nor hold any sense of community with fellow citizens who are not members of their group, community, or faith.

During the 1950s and 1960s, Arab nationalists spoke of the "Arab nation" and regarded the existing states, many of which were colonial fictions, as Western imports that divided and thus weakened Arab civilization. The aim of Arab nationalists, such as Muammar Quadaffi, is to eliminate existing states and to integrate their populations into a single Arab entity. Some Arab nationalists consider Western-style states as "too small clothes for the Arabs to wear." They want to add. Many secessionist groups, on the other hand, "find the same states too large or completely unsuitable" (Salamé 1990: 227; Harik 1990: 21). They want to subtract. Either way, the purposes of these integrationist and secessionist groups are fundamentally incompatible with the continued existence of states as they developed or were created originally.

Among many Muslim fundamentalists, Western-derived states are also anathema. In Islamic thought, the relevant community on which to base the state is the community of believers; territoriality is irrelevant to faith and only creates artificial divisions between believers. According to Hasan al-Banna, the spiritual father of the Muslim Brotherhood in Egypt,

> Islam does not recognize geographical frontiers and does not take into account racial differences. On the contrary, it considers all Muslims as one umma and regards all Muslim countries as one watan, regardless of distances and boundaries which separate them.
>
> (quoted in Bensaid 1987: 171)

The idea of a civil society distinct from religion and the state is also foreign to many Muslim thinkers. The purpose of the state is not, as Westerners would have it, to provide welfare or to guarantee civil liberties; it is to apply the law of God on earth (Mayall 1991: 52).

These ideas are not represented only in the essays of Muslim theologians cum politicians. They are widely held in Arab societies. In one recent survey, almost 80 percent of the respondents believed that there is a single Arab "nation" that is artificially divided and ought to be unified into a single state (Korany 1987: 54–5). The 1991 electoral victory of Muslim fundamentalists in Algeria, as well as Khomeini's revolution in Iran, demonstrate that alternatives to Western conceptions of the state command substantial following and loyalty.

These alternative conceptions of statehood are not confined to Arab or Muslim societies. In India, Hindu religious nationalists (Hindutva) seek to replace the present secular constitution with one based on the premise of a single, dominant Hindu community. In the Punjab, Sikh activists insist on creating their own religious state. During the February 1992 elections in the state, Sikh militants threatened anyone who dared to cast a ballot. Many Sikhs do not accept the legitimacy of the Indian secular state because it does not allow politicians to base their appeal on religion and excludes representatives of religious communities (Juergensmeyer 1993: 99). In Sri Lanka the extremist Sinhalese Buddhist movement (JVP) struggled to overturn the secular state – it is deemed a neo-colonial, Western import – and to replace it with a reincarnation of the ancient Buddhist kingdoms of Ceylon. Of course there would be no political role for Tamils in such a theocracy.

These kinds of challenges to Western state concepts are fundamental. The politics in which aspirations are expressed are passionate because they speak of ends, purposes, and symbols. Religious and nationalist movements of these kinds set up zero-sum situations with the spokespersons of incumbent states and with the non-believers of the community. There is scant room for compromise. To negotiate changes or to participate in elections implies legitimacy for the state, its institutional expression, and its legitimating principles, as well as accepting coexistence with other communities. Violence, in contrast, has a holy writ and a spiritual end. "By elevating a temporal struggle to the level of the cosmic, [activists] can bypass the usual moral restrictions on killing. If their struggle is part of an enormous battle of the spirit, then it is not ordinary morality but the rules of war that apply" (Juergensmeyer 1993: 167). Those who do not accept the legitimacy of the present state want to do more than just capture it. They want to use it to create a state on entirely new principles of vertical and horizontal legitimacy, usually on foundations that seek to establish an exclusive community. Such aspirations are fundamentally non-negotiable with representatives of incumbent states, meaning that violence and war are the usual means of pursuing objectives and defending the existing state (cf. Rothchild 1991: 201–3).

Another source of eroding vertical legitimacy is the prevalence of massive corruption. Some new states have been labelled "kleptocracies" (Jackson 1990), an appropriate monicker for systematic looting, predation, and confiscation by the state. State offices are not occupied in order to advance some concept of the public good, but rather to bring personal wealth, status, and acclaim to their holders, who then dispense rewards to their followers and supporters, including, first of all, family members. It is not unusual to see every family member on the official payroll – not that the incumbents are necessarily working to earn their pay. The Ceaucescu clan in Romania set a pattern that has been widely followed elsewhere, including in Iraq, Syria (where in the 1960s Salah Jalid, the real power in the country, had every person in his family over eighteen years of age on the public payroll [Ajami 1992: 53]), Haiti, and in many African countries. The distinction between public service and trust, and private gain does not exist in a kleptocracy.

The dimensions of personal enrichment and public theft in kleptocracies are truly monumental. Ergas (1987: 299, 320) estimates that the Mobutu mafia between the late 1960s and the mid-1980s smuggled out of the country between eight and nine billion dollars. The total amount of stolen money that African elites have parked in foreign banks "may conceivably be close to the total debt burden in the sub-continent," that is, about $150 billion. Ferdinand Marcos's pile of gold stashed in Swiss warehouses may have reached $12 billion, a sum double the amount held in the Bank of England at the time. The hoard was amassed through theft, bribery, kickbacks, misuse of foreign aid, and misappropriation of gold hoarded by the Japanese army during World War II. Government personnel of states that sit on great pools of resources find the temptation of skimming unearned profits and "fees" too great to resist. Most kleptocrats, however, amass their personal wealth by extracting surplus from the peasantry (Ergas 1987: 12–13). Since the perception of justice is an important prop of legitimacy, it is not hard to understand why millions of common people in new states withhold their loyalties.

Extortion becomes a way of life in kleptocracies; it is not a disease confined to the powerful. In some countries, lower-level military echelons set up rackets to dispossess citizens of their money. Political parties accept "contributions" from the non-faithful in order to sustain themselves and to gain access to a variety of gravy trains. Ryszard Kapuscinski narrates the following tale that highlights the nature of money and politics in Zaïre, a story that is common to kleptocracies.

> There were three of them. They always walked together, as three, and drove around together, as three, in a big, dusty Chevrolet. The car stopped in front of the hotel, the doors slammed, and we could hear three pairs of feet coming up the stairs. They knocked, entered our room and sat down in the armchairs. If three people go around together in Poland, you don't think anything of it. But in the Congo [Zaïre], three people can be a party.
>
> Our first conversation. They introduced themselves: "Socialists

from Kasai." Nice to meet you. After a few pleasantries one of them
came right out with it: "We need money." What for? asked my Czech
friend. "We want socialism to triumph in Kasai. And for that, we
must buy off the leaders of our province."

They were young, and you must make allowances for youth. So
[my friend] said that socialism does not triumph by means of money.
He added something about the masses . . .

The socialists sat there, downcast. For them, the masses were not so
important. Had we ever seen the millions marching here? The millions
are passive, directionless, diffuse. All the action takes place among the
leaders. Five hundred names, maximum. And it's exactly those names
that you have to buy. Once you've bought a few, you can go ahead
and set up a government, and the ones who put up the money
determine the kind of government it will be. That's how the governments of Chombego, Kalonji and Bolikango were started. There are
many possibilities, many untapped reserves. I quickly calculated that
I had 1,000 dollars left. I wondered if I could buy myself a republic.

Theft and extortion are practiced systematically by the bureaucracy
as well. Indeed, in many weak states, the bureaucracy is at best a vast
publicly funded employment scheme, and at worst a highly organized
system of graft that makes life a misery for the citizen (Corm 1988:
241). Once established, it successfully resists all efforts at reform
emanating from the society.

Colonial bureaucracies were by today's standards minuscule. After
independence, as the state claimed that it would lead the way to
"development," bureaucracies expanded rapidly and became the
personal fiefs of their leaders. In Congo (Brazzaville), for example, the
number of public employees multiplied by nine between 1960 and
1972. By 1971, salaries of the government's agricultural service ex-
ceeded the total cash income of the country's 600,000 peasants (Young
1985: 85). There are typically huge gaps between public and private
pay and incomes. In one African country in the 1960s, supervisors in
the public service were paid thirty-three times as much as daily-paid
and semi-skilled workers. This compares with a ten to one ratio in the
United States and a five to one ratio in the Soviet Union (Nafziger and
Richter 1976: 99).

In most bureaucracies, there are many more people than there are
jobs; it is simply one way the state co-opts potential followers. People
are hired without any idea of what it is that they should do (Dawisha
1988: 278). Most thus spend large portions of their time on the public
payroll actually doing private business, much of which is petty corrup-

tion. A "public service" that is deracinated from the society, predatory, inefficient, and corrupt cannot fulfill the fundamental contract of providing service for extraction. For the average citizen, the state is personified through the bureaucracy with whom he or she deals, sometimes on a daily basis. The options are either to get into the system, to resist it, or to withdraw. Otwin Marenin (1987: 67) writes:

> The modal state squats on its people like a bloated toad . . . captured by and used for private interests, unwilling and unable to serve any conception of the public good. It is linked to its social formation by exchange relations, a "what's in it for me or my group" political rationality, and cannot depend on legitimacy for compliance . . . or the willingness of powerful groups to forgo their immediate interests for long-range goals.

The state-strength dilemma

Weak states face a fundamental difficulty that is rarely resolved satisfactorily. While giving the appearance of authoritarian power, the reach of the state is seriously limited by local centers of resistance, by bureaucratic inertia and corruption, and by social fragmentation along religious, ethnic, tribal, factional, and cultural lines. The state must be strong to build more unity within the society, to help construct national identities, and to provide services which can offset high extractions. Yet, the state does not have the resources to accomplish these tasks. To obtain them it resorts to predatory and unlawful practices, which only exacerbate social tensions and erode loyalties. Vast bureaucracies are built to co-opt citizens, but extractions – usually from the peasantry or unfavored communal groups – have to increase in order to pay the civil servants. When intergroup animosities (sometimes created by ruling elites themselves) are high but the state is weak in terms of legitimacy, countries become mired in civil strife (cf. Enloe 1981: 92, 223). The state is weak not only in terms of legitimacy. It is also institutionally weak, thus precluding change and reform. The weak state, according to Marina Ottaway (1987: 173):

> has a high degree of autonomy from society, but . . . it is also very seriously weakened by its internal divisions. Decision-making is most often in the hands of a few, not of institutions. Administration is in the hands of an inefficient apparatus that the leaders do not always control . . . [I]t is a state that has autonomy (probably too much autonomy), but very little sovereignty.

116

The weak state is caught in a vicious circle. It does not have the resources to create legitimacy by providing security and other services. In its attempt to find strength, it adopts predatory and kleptocratic practices or plays upon and exacerbates social tensions between the myriads of communities that make up the society. Everything it does to become a strong state actually perpetuates its weakness. It is a system that defies even well-intentioned and honest leaders. Kapuscinski (1990: 106) noted the dilemma on the basis of his years of traveling and living in such states:

> The essence of the drama lies in the terrible *material resistance* that each [leader] encounters on taking his first, second and third steps up the summit of power. Each one wants to do something good and begins to do it and then sees, after a month, after a year, after three years, that it just isn't happening, that it is slipping away, that it is bogged down in the sand. Everything is in the way: the centuries of backwardness, the primitive economy, the illiteracy, the religious fanaticism, the tribal blindness, the chronic hunger, the colonial past with its practice of debasing and dulling the conquered, the blackmail by the imperialists, the greed of the corrupt, the unemployment, the red ink. Progress comes with great difficulty along such a road. The politician begins to push too hard. He looks for a way out through dictatorship. The dictatorship then fathers an opposition. The opposition organizes a coup. And the cycle begins anew.

We can call this situation the *state-strength dilemma*. States seek to gain the strength that would give their external sovereignty domestic content. Attempts to increase state strength generate resistance that weakens the state. In attempts to overcome resistance, governments rely on coercive measures against local power centers of various types, as well as against communal/religious/ethnic groups. "Captured" governments fare poorly in these circumstances because their claims to legitimacy become hollow. Their "right to rule" is undermined by their actions, which are frequently discriminatory, short-range, and self-serving. The exclusion of important groups by denial of access to power or to resources helps destroy horizontal legitimacy and exacerbates social tensions.

Given these resistances and problems, it is not difficult to predict that the world will continue to be populated by many weak states for years to come. The conundrums, catch-22 situations, and vicious circles of the state-strength dilemma are overwhelming. Given these conditions, what do ordinary people do in weak states? What are their options?

Individual responses to the state-strength dilemma

Four responses are common: endurance, exit, voice, and rebellion. In the first instance, individuals and groups may practice "quietism," that is, ignore the coercive and predatory practices of the state and focus life around the predominant social unit, usually the family. Quietistic acceptance has been a common response in Arab countries. Protest and opposition are limited to a few, while ordinary citizens ignore laws and regulations since government officials are notoriously unwilling or unable to ensure their application (Butterworth 1987: 110; Ajami 1992: 40). In some Arab countries, minority religious communities, such as the Shiites in Bahrain, have no possibility to participate in local politics but otherwise are not constrained in their commercial activities (Ajami 1992: 237). It is reasonably common in some weak states for the government to "buy off" potential political opposition by providing generous welfare and economic opportunities. In rentier states, oil wealth eliminates extraction through taxes: the state gives but does not take (Beblawi 1990: 89–91). The individual joins in an implicit Mephistophelian bargain: wealth and security for quiet.

Exit takes two predominant forms: migration abroad or joining the underground economy. Both are practiced on an immense scale. It is not possible to estimate what percentage of the exit-choosers migrate for economic opportunities as opposed to fear for personal and family security. Claims for refugee status number in the millions annually; a significant proportion comes from political refugees. More extensive is active participation in the black economy, a form of resistance that clearly weakens the state and amplifies its strength dilemma. Extra-legal economic activity is widespread in all types of states but reaches proportions that seriously undermine some states' capacity to provide services. In Zaïre, Ghana, Uganda, Tanzania, Guinea and several other countries during the 1980s, between one-third and two-thirds of all economic activity was estimated to be underground (Ergas 1987: 298). In contemporary Russia, racketeering and widespread corruption have become common while the quality of services in health and old age security has deteriorated seriously since the late 1980s.

A third strategy – voice – is to express resistance. In many states this is the most dangerous option. Government-sponsored death squads or special army units, as in El Salvador or Guatemala, eliminate opposition leaders and a good proportion of their sympathizers. In other

weak states, opposition commonly leads to torture, prolonged deten-
tion, and reprisals against family members.

Finally, and more commonly, resistance becomes violent. It can take
several forms, including conspiracy, attempted coups (attempts to
capture power), rebellion, intercommunal war, and the ultimate challenge to state legitimacy and the right to rule, armed secession (cf. Gurr
1991*b*; Mason 1990: 45). There are numerous explanations for armed
violence, including cost-benefit analysis, theories of justice, the "demonstration effect" of rebellions elsewhere, availability of external
support, and leadership. What crosses all secessionist and rebellion
movements, however, is the underlying idea that violence is empow-
ering (Juergensmeyer 1993: 169). As Mao Tse-tung, the leaders of the
secessionist movement in Eritrea, and analysts such as Franz Fanon
and many others have observed, violence is a major means of mobilizing those who have traditionally remained passive in confronting
predatory practices by states and/or hostile communities. Violence is
not just a means to an end of achieving power; it transforms man
(generic) from a passive object into an active subject of political
participation.

Failed states

Some states cannot resolve the state-strength dilemma. Over a period
of time, they become increasingly weaker as the sources of vertical and
horizontal legitimacy erode. Increased oppression to keep the whole
mess together only generates increased resistance. Leaders become
isolated and inhabit make-believe worlds concocted by their cronies
and dwindling sycophants. Government institutions no longer function
except perhaps in the capital city. The tasks of governance, to the
extent that they are performed at all, devolve to warlords, clan chiefs,
religious figures, and other locally based individuals or organizations
who are well armed. The state retains the fig leaf of sovereignty for
external purposes, but domestic life is organized around local politics.
The national army, the crown jewel of sovereignty, disintegrates into
local racketeering, or hires itself out to local rulers. It cannot protect the
state, for no one has the authority to command it. Blatant violations of
Lebanese sovereignty by Israeli armed forces to hunt down PLO
leaders went without any military response from the national army.
Even during the Christmas and New Year celebrations of 1968, when
Israeli units overran Beirut airport and destroyed the entire Lebanese

commercial aviation fleet, Lebanese security forces stationed at or within several hundred meters of the airport stayed in their barracks (Corm 1988: 158). The authority of a state cannot survive in such circumstances.

Lebanon collapsed from its "minority complex" (Corm 1988: 154–5) of Maronites, Druze, Shiites, Palestinians, Sunnis, Syrians and Israelis, and from the opportunities weakness provided for numerous ideological and sectarian groups. Lebanon became, in effect, an international dumping ground for revolutionaries from all over the Middle East who were no longer tolerated in their home countries (Ben-Dor 1983: 233). The Lebanese government had no way to keep them out or to control them once they were in. Lebanon became characterized by numerous "states" within the state, as well as by sustained external intervention. It no longer had the main attributes of sovereignty. We do not need to narrate the tale further except to point out that Lebanon was always somewhat of an illusion, a state created by the French in the Western mode, but which was in fact a complicated network of local rulers who held a virtual veto over every move of the central authorities. The fragile balance between local and communal groups, which expected and received "national" positions in terms of a hierarchy of entitlements and then turned these into patron–client relations, evaporated under demographic changes within the country and trends and pressures emanating from the Arab–Israeli conflict. Lebanon remained a state in the legal sense, although many foreign governments withdrew their diplomatic missions from Beirut. The country may be resurrected as a result of Arab–Israeli peace agreements and various international efforts, but in terms of the realities on the ground, Lebanon ceased to exist as a sovereign state – using the traditional criteria – for almost two decades after 1975. Most failed states do not disappear physically, but they are largely hollow shells in which the requirements of sovereignty cannot be met. Legal personality and political fact are divorced.

Somalia's collapse had a somewhat different etiology but, as in Lebanon, the state became largely an illusion. Somalia, one of Africa's few countries with purported ethnic, religious, and cultural homogeneity, collapsed amid Siad Barre's attempt to create a state on the Western model. Although Barre can take credit for instituting legal reforms for women, increasing literacy, and uplifting the status of pariah clans, his attempts to eliminate clan-based politics failed. Clan and lineage systems, not an ethnic "people," are the basis of politics in

Somalia. Barre relied increasingly on coercion and, finally, on massive violence against clans, their lands, and their animals, to fulfill his dream of creating a modern, Western-type socialist state. Persuasion, coercion, and violence failed, and ultimately Barre himself began to rely on clans and the military to sustain his rule. The civil war which began in 1988 spawned systems of local rule run by gangs of armed clan members. Somalia, even though a single nation, collapsed into anarchy (cf. Lewis 1989; Adam 1995). It remains a nation without a state despite international efforts to resuscitate it.

The roster of recent failed states includes Yugoslavia, Lebanon, Somalia, Chad, Uganda (temporarily), Liberia, Mozambique, Afghanistan, Kampuchea (restored in 1994), and, arguably, Rwanda. Candidates for future collapse include Zaïre, Algeria, Burundi, Iraq, and even Russia.[3]

Finally, some states may simply disappear – a rare occurrence in the modern states system. What will happen when oil reserves run out in the Middle East, or when fossil fuels are rendered valueless by the invention of new energy sources? Will the rulers and populations stay? Not likely. Workers, most of whom migrated to the rentier states, will either go home or locate opportunities elsewhere. Ruling elites will retire to their second, fourth, or tenth homes abroad. The "homeland" is more likely to be Switzerland, London, California, or Texas than a wasted land (cf. Luciani 1990: 83; Ajami 1992: 210). Nauru's phosphate deposits will someday have been dug up and the island's population of 7,000 souls will no longer have any land to stand on. Nauru promises to be the first state in modern times to become physically extinct. In the meanwhile, it stands as one of the post-1945 strong states; it has succeeded where many weak states have failed.

Otwin Marenin (1987: 68–9) has used the metaphor of the sinking ship to describe the situation of weak and failing states. It summarizes

---

[3] One American State Department official asserted in an interview in 1994 that "we are watching the death of a state." The "private" state in Russia is expanding rapidly. One observer estimates that 40 percent of private businesses and 60 percent of state-owned companies have been corrupted by organized crime. The Russian mafia may own one-half the country's commercial banks and up to 80 percent of the hotels, warehouses, depots, and service industries in Moscow. Corruption in the Russian armed forces is similarly widespread (Hersch 1994: 72, 66). More recently, Marshall Goldman of the Harvard Research Center on Russia, estimates that from 70 to 80 percent of all the Russian private sector, including banking, is under the control of the Mafia. Most of the profits leave the country to be invested abroad (Marti 1995: 3).

aptly the state-strength dilemma and helps explain why wars of the future will be predominantly within rather than between states:

> [A] ship which is sinking [is] kept alive and floating by the acts of some crew, passengers and passing ships . . . [other] members of the crew and passengers are busily tearing the ship apart for material for another ship. Passengers on other ships observe, shout advice, may throw life-lines or may assist some groups against others. Conflicts . . . are not only about the ship's course or the distribution of benefits and authority within an ongoing enterprise, but include most fundamentally the ship itself – whether it ought to be kept afloat and how it ought to be rebuilt or destroyed even as conflicts over allocations rage. There is, then, no state in transit but there is a transition of the state – its form, functions, and apparatus – over time.

Marenin makes it clear that some states may survive while others will founder and sink. It is not the weather on the sea – foreign predation or aggression – that is the cause of disaster, but the destructive actions of a country's rulers and population. Foreign agents, however, are more than mute onlookers. They provide advice and material aid. They are actors in the contest for the state. And that contest frequently spills over into other jurisdictions. The state-strength dilemma leads to war within states; but sometimes it results in war between states as well. And, at a minimum, weak and failing states demand some sort of international response. The killing involved in "wars of a third kind" is not a matter of indifference to the onlookers. Genocide, wars of secession, communal war, and various forms of violent rebellion begin as national events but they are soon transformed into international problems. We move next to the international sources and consequences of weak and failed states.

7 Wars of the third kind and international politics

According to popular expectations in 1989, once the decolonization process and the Cold War were over, peace should reign. The two main problems of the post-World War II era had been resolved: colonial peoples were free, and so were the subjects of communist rule. This was to be the dawn of a "new world order."

Declarations of such an order following the American-sponsored coalition victory over Iraq in 1991 were soon met with skepticism and occasionally with sarcasms such as "the new world disorder." There seemed to be a yawning gap between the hopes of the early post-Cold War era and the realities of continued carnage after 1991. The dilemmas of weak and failed states continued to spawn shocking statistics of lives lost and long lines of refugees fleeing to safe havens. Students of the Cold War, most of whom had been bedazzled by the intricacies of deterrence theory, deployment doctrines, and the introduction of new technologies capable of incinerating millions, discovered that wars of the third kind were ubiquitous in certain areas of the world and that the intellectual tools of Cold War era strategic studies were not particularly relevant to understanding them.

Decolonization and the collapse of communism solved only two problems – foreign and/or one-party rule. But gaining freedom is not the same as building viable states based on tolerant communities.

The war in ex-Yugoslavia brought to academic consciousness the factor of ethnicity in international relations. The most common understanding was that the Cold War had kept a lid on primordial ethnic hostilities, and that with its passing, old animosities were re-emerging. The problem, of course, is much more fundamental. Ethnic identities, experts agree, are malleable and variable. Hatreds did not just go underground for fifty years and suddenly re-emerge with the dissolu-

123

tion of the Yugoslav federation. Consider the number of interethnic marriages in the former Yugoslavia which, in some republics, reached almost 25 percent of the total. Politically repressed hatreds are not consistent with such figures. Ethnicity, moreover, is hardly the only problem. Societies are made up of numerous groups based on different types of affinity. Some are ethnic, some are religious, and some are little more than temporary political factions and gangs that stand to lose or gain power depending upon their relationship with central authorities. Many of these groups, in fact, coalesce to become politically significant exactly when central state authority begins to collapse. The function of social protection, no longer provided by central authority, necessarily devolves to local groups (Lemarchand 1987: 156–7) of many kinds. In some cases, as in Somalia, the groups or factions at war with each other may be little more than gangs (Hassner 1993: 128). Some may institutionalize into factions and even political parties. Others will wither away.

Ted Robert Gurr's exhaustive research project on "groups at risk" also makes the point that the "new world disorder" is not just a matter of ethnicity. While communal groups are among the most often "at risk" from central government repression, or from other communal groups, there are also religious groups, militant sects, "peoples of the frontier," and others whose primary bonds of affinity are not necessarily ethnic or language. Most of them, however, are minorities, but we must not forget that sometimes numerical minorities also repress numerical majorities (e.g., the Tutsi in Rwanda in the 1950s).

Whatever the definitions of groups at risk, the problem from the point of view of future wars of the third kind is that these groups, factions, communities, and *ethnies* are spread extensively (as of 1990) through areas populated primarily by weak states, that is, in Africa (32 percent), the Middle East (13 percent), Asia (19 percent), Latin America (12 percent), and the former Soviet Union and communist bloc countries (14 percent) (Gurr and Harff 1994).

These groups do not exist in political vacuums. Their hatreds and affinities are not primordial, but arise in certain political, social, and economic contexts. Many have coexisted for generations without major difficulties, only to find that in new political circumstances they and their interests become threatened. The threats arise from other groups and from the state, and not infrequently from both. Political aspirants using nationalist slogans and exploiting some grievances may also pursue agendas that are more personally ambitious.

"Peoples" are not always victims first, reacting only to the predation of others. A collapse of central authority may unleash all sorts of possibilities.

"Peoples," moreover, have kith and kin located nearby, which means that when fighting for their existence, resources, or access to political goods, they can turn to external locales for support and possible havens for a more accommodating political future. In fact, almost 65 percent of the groups identified in the Gurr–Harff (1994) study have kindred groups in adjacent countries.

Irredenta derives from the poor fit between state boundaries and population distributions. The doctrine of *uti possidetis*, accepted as the basis of most post-colonial frontiers, is not always regarded as the best or preferred way to delimit political territories. Africa, for example, is full of irredenta problems that have strained relations between Dahomey and Niger, Mali and Burkina Fasso, Ghana and Togo, Libya and Chad, and many others neighboring countries (Zartman 1989: 15). The possibility of subtracting from one state and adding to another (Horowitz 1991: 10) in order to meet the aspirations of various groups remains a distinct possibility throughout the Third World and in some former socialist countries. This will usually be done through armed force rather than peaceful negotiations, although the alternative of secession – the creation of new states – is even more attractive.[1]

The imperatives of state-making on the one hand, and security and cultural, political, and economic autonomy of groups on the other, are often incompatible. In European history, the long process of state consolidation took place with frequent recourse to violence and the eventual assimilation – forced or otherwise – of a variety of peoples. Mohammed Ayoob (1995), among others, is convinced that similar processes are at work among the weak states of the contemporary world. The great state-making project which is, after all, an enterprise launched and supported by European civilization, requires the "taming" of groups, sometimes entailing their forced assimilation into

---

[1] Horowitz (1991: 10–17) lists a number of reasons why irredenta is not a popular choice compared to secession. Among them is the consideration that separating from one state to join another may actually worsen the group's fortunes. From the leadership point of view, those who organize the separatist movement know that once they become part of the "home" country, their status, perquisites, and political fortunes may actually decline. It will be interesting to see whether an independent Bosnian Serb state, if it comes to pass, will ultimately seek union with Serbia; or, as among most of the separatist leaders in the Kashmir, whether it will be satisfied to become yet another independent – and weak – state.

a majority society, and also the frequent expropriation and exploitation of their historic lands. Sometimes governments promote or physically shift population groups amidst restless minorities as a means of diluting their strength. Stalin practiced this as state policy; it has occurred through less draconian means in places like India, where Nagaland became inundated with refugees from Bangladesh. For many political leaders and academic analysts, these are necessary if unsavory steps toward the creation of strong states (see chapter 9 for further discussion). For the groups involved, however, armed resistance and secession may be the only or most attractive response available (cf. Nietschmann 1987).

The enduring contest between the forces of state unification and group-sponsored fragmentation transcends both the beginning and the end of the Cold War. Whatever the new collaboration between the great powers after 1989, nothing they have done or can do puts an end to the paradoxes of state-making and community survival. Ethnic and other forms of group conflict are just a manifestation of a more fundamental process. Wars of the third kind will therefore persist for some time, characterizations of a new world order notwithstanding.

Some states, as suggested, are on the trajectory of increased strength. Others are moving toward the "failed state" end of the strength–weakness continuum. Aside from the clear failures such as Somalia and Liberia, major communal and other conflicts blight Angola, Burundi, Chad, Djibouti, Ghana, Mali, Niger, Nigeria, Sierra Leone, Sudan, and Zaïre, among others. The cycle of violence, repression, autocracy, and breakdown is already turning in many places in Africa (Lee 1994: 38) and among some former Soviet republics. Even the Russian federation may be moving into greater weakness. The state-strength dilemma there is likely to generate more wars of the Chechnya variety.

Patterns of external involvement in wars of the third kind

Numerous studies of intervention demonstrate authoritatively that domestic conflicts in weak states seldom remain isolated. Neighboring countries become involved with a regularity that borders on inevitability (Heraclides 1990: 376). The instabilities emerging from weakness tend to be exported throughout entire regions (Buzan 1991: 106, 154).

Great powers have intervened to protect client – particularly former colonial – regimes against secessionists. They have also intervened for competitive Cold War reasons and to protect access to economic resources and their nationals residing abroad. Other weak states have intervened militarily in their neighbors' affairs with even greater regularity, suggesting that weak state vulnerabilities offer all sorts of opportunities for meddling short of massive armed invasions. In Africa, for example, Nigerian troops went to Tanzania in 1964 in order to help quell a military mutiny. Guinea several times sent troops to Liberia and Sierra Leone. Libya helped Idi Amin in Uganda and organized a major armed foray into Chad. Senegalese troops have helped save the regime in Gambia, Tanzanian troops "liberated" Uganda from the depredations of Idi Amin (cf. Foltz 1991: 359), and Uganda played a major role in organizing and supplying the Rwanda Patriotic Front's invasion of its own country in 1994. Regimes facing strong domestic opposition often appeal to outsiders to provide them with military and other forms of support. The frequency of such appeals shows the extent to which alignments and external intervention are generated less by old-fashioned concerns for security of the state – as in traditional European alliances – than by concerns over internal threats. Leaders are not worried about losing their states, as realist theory suggests, but about losing their offices (cf. David 1991: 243).

Aside from the frequency of these interventions, the other interesting fact is the extent to which many are based primarily on reasons of affinity and sentiment rather than on power or more hard-headed cost-benefit analyses. Various diplomatic *démarches* and economic pressures by Muslim states and the Organization of Islamic States Conference on behalf of the Moro insurrection in the Philippines (Gopinath 1991), for example, had almost nothing to do with power politics as that term is usually used, and everything to do with religious sympathies. Heraclides' study (1990: 370–2) of seven armed secession movements makes the same point: instrumental (e.g., power, strategic) motives for intervention are less conspicuous than affective (sentiment) motives.

Whether to support incumbent governments or secessionist groups, or to try to contain the violence and massive abuses of human rights that attend wars of the third kind, intervention of one kind or another has become the norm. Sometimes it is only moral support through diplomatic statements and speeches at international organizations. It may involve humanitarian assistance. But more often, particularly among neighbors, support includes logistics, sanctuary, military training, transport, arms and supplies, advisors in the field, and cross-border raids (Gurr 1993: 4–5).

The frequency of interventions raises the question whether it is regional and systemic actions and forces that cause these wars, or whether their etiology is essentially internal. If we are looking at the origins of wars of the third kind, in other words, is it appropriate to locate the diagnosis exclusively at the level of the state and the state-making process, as suggested in the previous chapter? Or can a case be made that these wars are part of more fundamental regional and systemic processes?

Local, regional, and systemic sources of wars of the third kind: political-security approaches

The matter is complex and subject to substantial debate. As might be expected, scholars of diverse backgrounds and intellectual frameworks provide different answers to the question. Mohammed Ayoob (1991: 263) formulates the problem primarily within the weak (vulnerable is his term) state, although in his most recent book (1995) he places more emphasis on the interconnectedness of the state, regional, and systemic sources of war. Neil Macfarlane (1991: 135) finds it difficult to identify "any regional conflict that began as a result of superpower policy. The origins of conflict [in the Third World] lie predominantly in the local environment." For these analysts, as well as in the discussion above in chapters 2 and 6, the genesis of these wars is primarily domestic. I have termed the fundamental problem the state-strength dilemma: the attempt to create strong states creates the resistance that will further weaken them. For weak states, their fundamental problem is not external predation but internal challenge and possible collapse. Aside from the evidence supplied in the previous chapter, we can cite some of the regional organizations that are modeled ostensibly on traditional alliances designed to cope with groups of states' external security dilemmas. Both ASEAN and the Gulf Cooperation Council, for example, were designed primarily to contain domestic threats to their members' security (Guazzone 1988; Tow 1990: 129; Acharya 1991). Ayoob (1995: 62) summarizes it well:

> Regionalism, or, rather, subregionalism, has come full circle in the case of both ASEAN and GCC, providing evidence for the thesis that

successful regional cooperation is based primarily on the convergence of regime interests relating to internal security, especially the shared perceptions of internally generated threats to the security of states and the stability of regimes.

Further evidence of the predominantly internal generation of armed conflicts is supplied by analyzing the location and missions of military forces in many weak states. One finds that they are deployed primarily to deal with local insurrections and to protect the government of the day. External enemies and threats exist for many, but if statistics were available, it would not be surprising to find that more money is spent to protect the state/regime from its internal enemies than from its external threats. To cite just one example, the Indonesia army is concentrated on the politically crucial island of Java, especially near Jakarta, as well as in provinces experiencing rebellion. Of the army's 102 battalions, 67 are engaged in "territorial duties," meaning that they are dispersed among a large number of provincial capitals and small towns where their prime function is to ensure that political challenges to the regime do not organize and develop (Peace Research Centre 1993: 14–15). Similar inferences about the essentially domestic function of armed forces are drawn from the high proportion of expenditures on manpower and operations rather than on *matériel* (Ayoob 1991: 278). Labor-intensive organization and deployment are more typical in domestic security apparatuses than in armed forces geared to deter or defend against an external enemy.

Ayoob's most recent position underlines the importance of regional and systemic sources of wars of the third kind, but still emphasizes the domestic origins of most wars. The Third World's security problematic, he suggests (1995: 189),

> can be described as a multilayered cake in which the flavors have mingled . . . The three main layers of this cake are the domestic, regional, and global dimensions of security. Although these three dimensions . . . have influenced each other, the primary dimension – the layer that flavors the entire cake – is the domestic one. The internal vulnerabilities of Third World states are primarily responsible for the high level of conflict in many parts of the Third World.

Other analysts argue that the domestic, regional, and international sources of wars of the third kind are essentially inseparable or at least organically connected (Obasanjo 1991: xvi; Foltz 1990: 66; Buzan 1991: 157). A comprehensive analysis must therefore acknowledge the complex interweaving of domestic and external factors. How, exactly, this is to be done is not clear, however. Deep structural forces, such as the legacies of imperialism and colonialism, are obvious candidates but, to repeat, they cannot account for the vastly differing trajectories of state strength and weakness that exist today in the Third World and among the post-communist states. States that were not formally colonized, moreover, have not escaped the problem of weakness. The nineteenth-century conquests of Emperor Melenik established the Ethiopian empire independently of great-power intrusion, but his successors were unable to prevent the dissolution of the empire through bloody secession wars despite substantial support from many of the powers, and particularly from the Soviet Union.

Finally, Karen Rasler (1992) has argued that it is misleading to characterize wars of the third kind as having essentially domestic origins and then spilling over into benign regional and international systems. Using the cases of Lebanon in 1958 and 1975, she insists that external forces *create* the conditions for internal war. Both civil wars, she suggests, were inspired by regional and international politics. Her approach stresses the means by which the international system creates revolutionary situations within states as well as how the system influences war outcomes. The evidence from Lebanon is persuasive, if not totally compelling, but the study raises the question of to what extent Lebanon is typical of the general class of weak and failed states.

There is no authoritative answer to the analytical problem. I argue that the state-strength dilemma explains the downward trajectory of states toward the failed state category and that those states moving in that direction are likely to be the sites of wars of the third kind. That many of the states were born weak but were nevertheless granted recognition and aid by the international community acknowledges the role of systemic factors. Ideologies of self-determination, the concurrent de-legitimation of imperialism in the West, and the United Nations' strong support of territorial integrity are all relevant. But they are relevant primarily as factors that strengthen, or at least sustain, rather than weaken states. Nearly $100 billion of the foreign aid and military assistance the industrial countries annually transfer to the Third World and post-socialist states are typically justified on the grounds that they are essential for the "nation-building" (*sic*) or democratization tasks.

Perhaps the most telling evidence supporting the thesis that domestic dynamics are more important than regional or systemic factors is that a very high percentage of foreign interventions occur only *after* the bloodshed has begun domestically. Greek activities in Cyprus in 1974 are among the few exceptions to the generalization. While weak states offer targets of opportunity, international norms against outside intervention no doubt help reduce external involvement in those situations that have not yet broken out into armed conflict. The question is whether external involvement *created* the opportunities; only in the broadest sense, looking historically, has this been the case. Some historical-systemic conditions, as suggested in chapter 2, at least set the stage for what was to come.

Of these, the colonial legacy is the most significant. Virtually any account of a war of the third kind today begins in the nineteenth or earlier centuries. Among the legacies are the poor fit between post-colonial territorial demarcations and population distributions. Current irredenta and secessionist problems have arisen because meaningful communities were carved up between two and up to five states. Among them we would include the Somalis, Bakongo, Ewe, Zande, Fulani, Ngoni, Chwa, Lunda, Yao, and Swazis in Africa (Neuberger 1991: 104), various tribal groups in Southeast Asia and the Middle East, and, of course, the multigroup societies created by labor imports throughout the Latin, South Pacific, and Caribbean worlds. Yet, as with determinist economic theories, we have to acknowledge that there is nothing inevitable about communal conflict in these areas. Too many formerly weak states have succeeded in building societies based on citizenship rather than on ethno-religious exclusiveness or domination to accept a fatalistic or deterministic point of view about the consequences of colonialism, divided communities, or artificially created multiethnic societies. Many divided groups, moreover, have over the years developed differential interests and identities as a result of exposure to different administrations, educational systems, markets, currencies, economic policies, and political arrangements (Neuberger 1991: 105; cf. Horowitz 1991). Again, a political rather than ethnic-determinist form of analysis is more likely to be fruitful.

We can mention at least four more immediate regional and/or international factors that are often thought to generate armed conflicts in the Third World: (1) arms transfers; (2) global ethnic networks; (3) contagion; and (4) superpower competition.

Arms transfers and sales may help launch wars of the third kind. They may also prevent them. The United States by itself sells almost $30 billion annually to Third World countries, a total of $55.4 billion in the 1989–92 period when it surpassed the Soviet Union as the world's

131

largest purveyor of the instruments of war (Grimmet 1993, cited in Ayoob 1995: 101). Most of the hardware is sold to governments, however, on the theory that it will be used to enhance "national security," however that is defined. Since most great-power interventions since the 1960s have been in support of incumbent regimes rather than to help launch or sustain secessionist or resistance movements, it could be argued that these arms actually help provide a deterrent capacity. That is, they help prevent war, and they help sustain government capacity and coherence even when horizontal and vertical legitimacy are low. But the argument can be turned around just as easily. Arms transfers to despotic regimes committed to systematic repression of dissidents and resisters, as was the case in El Salvador in the early 1980s, make matters worse because they help empower those who have no local legitimacy and who often use terror and coercion to divide rather than unite societies. Official arms transfers thus have no predictable or regular consequences. They can both exacerbate tensions and inhibit violence.

In wars of the third kind, moreover, advanced weaponry obtained through official arms transfers may be less relevant than a formidable supply of small arms – the rifles, grenades, mines, Kalashnikovs, "plastic," and small rockets that are the hallmark killing devices of guerrilla bands, warlord "armies," and "militias." Currently there is an expanding demand for small arms, and the licit and illicit market for them is more extensive than ever before. Countries that used to import such weapons today produce them in large quantities. The covert trade in small arms alone is estimated to run to several billion dollars annually (Goose and Smyth 1994: 93). Most governments do not publish small arms sales figures, as they do for heavier weapons in the United Nations register, so it is impossible to know the provenance of most small arms in the arsenals of communal and other groups, and governments. Consider just one recent case, however. Most of the arms used by the Hutu and Tutsi factions in Rwanda in 1994 came from, among other sources, Uganda, France, Egypt, and South Africa. Goose and Smyth report that the Rwanda Patriotic Front and the Hutu-dominated government and its militias procured the remainder from eight other countries and from numerous private sources. It is difficult to claim, then, that any particular country "fueled" a particular war by its arms sales. Weapons are so readily available through so many channels that any group, including governments, bent on the use of force have no difficulty finding them. To say, then, that arms sales cause wars of the third kind is tantamount to saying that weapons cause them. Short of universal boycotts encompassing governments, middlemen, and gun runners, easy access to small arms facilitates violence, but it is not an immediate cause of wars of the third kind.

Global and regional dispersal of communities may also facilitate such wars. The Irish in the United States, Sikhs in Canada, Basques in Central America, and Jews around the world, to mention just a few, help create networks of connections, sources of funding, moral support, and sometimes illegitimate trade in arms and drugs. These networks reinforce and sustain communal struggles thousands of miles away (Premdas 1991: 12–13, 17). But like arms, these support networks and various non-governmental organizations do not appear to be major sources of the wars. They may help explain why wars are short or prolonged, successes or failures, but they rarely explain their etiology.

The contagion phenomenon is a more potent explanatory variable. It undoubtedly plays a role in spreading communal conflict and in providing stimulus for those who are contemplating armed resistance, revolution, or secession. Empirical studies demonstrate that contagion is a factor in domestic protest and other forms of resistance. It works similarly at the international level (cf. Vasquez 1993: 242–7). Political and military leaders learn from the experiences of others. The lessons include not just the strategy and tactics of armed operations, but also motivation. A victorious "liberation" movement in place A may have a strong impact on the motivation level of communal and factional leaders in place B. The causal link seems more clear than in the case of arms flows and global communal networks, but it remains less robust as an explanation for the sources of wars of the third kind than the state-strength dilemma. In fact, the "lesson" of most secessionist and resistance wars undertaken against the state is that they either drag on without an outcome for decades, or they are lost. For every Eritrea, there are dozens of Biafras, Khalistans, and Abkhazias.

Finally, many analysts have identified great-power competition as a primary source of wars in the Third World (though obviously not in the post-communist states). This was a standard convention in many strategic analyses of the Cold War period and helped explain, among many examples, the American support of Hissene Habre's assault on the Goukouni regime of Chad in 1980–1 (Lemarchand 1987: 161) and the breakdown of the agreements that led to the civil war in Angola between the MPLA government and Jonas Savimbi's UNITA. Aside from these and other cases, there may have been a more profound systemic situation lurking behind. The Cold War and its balance of terror provided security for the main adversaries in their homelands and backyards. Cold War competition was therefore played out in more distant venues where the risks were lower. That competition promoted and exacerbated both intra- and interstate violence in the Third World (Ayoob 1995: 273). But promotion and exacerbation are not the same as causing.

The consequences of great-power involvement in the Third World are, in fact, difficult to determine. Many observers agree that such involvement prolonged wars, raised their lethal levels and intensity, and made them more difficult to settle through negotiations (cf. Zartman 1989: 37–40; Macfarlane 1991: 135; Harbeson 1991: 139). It is also the case, however, that great-power involvement sometimes deterred incipient armed struggles and helped prevent some disputes from escalating (cf. Touval 1972: 163–4). Again, we are presented with the problem of a lack of strong correlations across a large number of cases. On a more impressionistic basis, we could test the causal assertion by looking at the war record since the end of the Cold War. Since 1989, a number of regional and intra-state conflicts have been more or less resolved (South Africa, Namibia, Nicaragua, Palestine, and Soviet intervention in Afghanistan) which suggests that great-power involvement was at least a significant factor in their genesis and solution. But on the other side of the ledger, we have seen the persistence of many lethal conflicts (Myanmar, Sri Lanka, Sudan, Afghanistan, Angola) and the outbreak of new wars of the third kind (Somalia, Rwanda, Bougainville, Bosnia, Nagorno-Karabakh, Ossetia, and the like). Long festering conflicts, like Cyprus and Kashmir, which became "frozen" (Holsti 1966) during the Cold War, remain in that state. The record seems to show that Cold War competition actually caused very few armed conflicts, but it did frequently prolong and escalate them. The origins of most wars, as Macfarlane and Ayoob suggest, were and remain essentially internal.

Systemic factors can, however, help explain the *outcomes* of many wars of the third kind. The norm of territorial sovereignty that under-lies diplomatic recognition policies, the Charter of the United Nations, and numerous regional organizations help to protect weak states in many ways. The doctrine of self-determination, as understood by most contemporary governments, has been used solely to legitimate anti-colonial struggles. The society of states and its attending organizations have never interpreted it to mean the right of peoples, whether sects, factions, *ethnies*, or communal groups, to secede from established states. It is clear from the pattern of interventions since the early 1960s that incumbent governments have attracted more support from abroad than have insurgents (Heraclides 1990: 352–3). There are significant exceptions, such as the four governments that recognized Biafra in 1967, but even where affective and emotional ties are strong, as between Muslim states and the Moro rebellion in the Philippines, or India and the Tamil minority in Sri Lanka, the intervening governments were not willing to extend much more than moral support to the insurgents. Muslim states pressed the Philippine government to negotiate with the Moros, but none acted favorably to the Moro request for diplomatic recognition of the Bangsa Moro Republic of Mindanao, Basilan, Sulu, and Palawah (Gopinath 1991: 131–3). The Indian government sought to enforce a peace agreement it signed over the heads of the Liberation Tigers of Tamil Eelam (LTTE), which in effect undercut the secession movement. The subsequent Indian peacekeeping force actually warred against the dissidents before withdrawing from a lack of success.

The risks of either stimulating an internal war or sustaining it through extensive support are too great for most countries. They have their own backyards to worry about. The Indian intervention in Sri Lanka in 1987 on behalf of the territorial integrity of the country, for example, is explained largely by the government's concern not to create a precedent in favor of secession that could be used by insurgents in the Punjab and Kashmir (Crenshaw 1993).

Sovereignty norms of the society of states thus act as a constraint on domestic wars in the sense that they implicitly and often explicitly work against the interests of rebels, insurgents, and secessionists. Groups contemplating secession or armed "redemption" of neighboring peoples (irredenta) must know that the chances of success are relatively low, given the repeated assertion of and support for the territorial sovereignty principle in previous cases. There have been, in fact, only a few successful secessionist armed struggles (Bangladesh, Eritrea, and the ex-Yugoslav states). The number of negotiated and/or peaceful secessions is significantly higher (Mayotte, Singapore, Slovakia, and most of the former republics of the Soviet Union). The international system thus operates to reduce potential armed conflicts, at least of the secessionist and irredentist variety. Weak states, many of whose European counterparts in previous centuries were annexed or partitioned by their neighbors and thus disappeared, continue to enjoy the benefits of sovereign statehood in a system that has placed this value above all others (cf. Ayoob 1995: 175). Under the ideology of "nation-building" (*sic*) and the practice of economic and military assistance, most governments most of the time do what they can to prevent or ameliorate the consequences of the state-strength dilemma in the Third World and in some of the former Soviet republics. What they do not understand is that frequently the strengthening of states and the maintenance of the autonomy and security of groups within those states are often incompatible. As we will see in the last chapter, the attempt to create strong states presents many dilemmas and, inadvertently, may help create the conditions for rebellion, armed resistance, and secession.

In the roster of sources of wars of the third kind, then, the regional and systemic explanations offered in most of the literature are not entirely convincing. While it is undoubtedly correct to argue that domestic and external influences are inextricably connected, and that Cold War competition often prolonged and made domestic wars more lethal, the etiology of these wars remains in my view essentially though not wholly domestic. The conditions of weak states, as outlined in the previous chapter, almost guarantee armed conflict, particularly among those states whose trajectory is toward failure and collapse.

Systemic sources of wars of the third kind: political-economy approaches

To this point, the analysis has employed political–military explanatory categories, assuming that the worlds of economics and politics are effectively compartmentalized. But many analysts challenge the separability of commercial and political-security realms, arguing not only that they are organically connected, but that economic forces and practices fundamentally condition the political universe. It is not so much the territorial–political aspect of colonialism that left a legacy of weak statehood, as its economic structures. For dependency theorists, for example, communal and other forms of group conflict against the state are explained by the historical class-formation process that occurred under the umbrella of imperialism. Groups and communities were set against each other for reasons of both political control and resource exploitation. The world imperialist system continues to create economic and other conditions that force communal and other groups to fight for limited resources, sometimes resulting in war between them. The weak state phenomenon is also sustained by the world economic system as a means of assuring industrial countries' access to Third World resources and making weak state governments dependent on outsiders. The weak, dependent state, according to this view, offers privileges and terms for the operation of multinational corporations that would not be available in countries with *real* governments, *real* regulations, and *real* tax systems. Neo-colonialism perpetuates state weakness, an important asset to Western capital.

But how, exactly, does the *state* remain weak in the global economic system? Here the line of reasoning relies upon a combination of personal attributes – in this case human greed – and international structures. In Johan Galtung's work (1971), for example, states in the periphery of the world (mostly former colonies) are the instruments through which surplus value, represented by profits, royalties, interest, poor terms of trade, and the like, is drained off from the Third World's hinterlands to the centers of industrial production in the North. The peripheral state is manned by the local comprador bourgeoisie, who stand to reap large personal benefits acting as the middlemen and the siphon hose through which surplus value flows from the peripheries to the centers. States in the Third World are, then, a sort of critical way station in a giant system of global wealth transfer. Their role is to make the system function smoothly; the interests of their personnel are tied directly to the interests of the center.

Because they help establish and sustain an essentially exploitative relationship between center and peripheries, the comprador bourgeoisie weaken the state by creating and amplifying class cleavages within the country. The interests of the producers of wealth and those of the middlemen are diametrically opposed. The former seek indigenous economic development where profits are reinvested and stay at home, while the comprador bourgeoisie seek to sustain the siphoning system which effectively decapitalizes the periphery and thus prevents indigenous industrial development. In such circumstances, vertical legitimacy is low and periphery–comprador bourgeoisie conflict is high. The structure of the international economic system not only created the global center–periphery structure, but helps maintain it today.

This type of explanation no doubt has some merit in explaining the origins and perhaps even the perpetuation of weak statehood – at least in some cases. However, it contains two serious flaws: (1) its one-dimensional view of human nature; and (2) its static quality. First, it

137

assumes that humans are motivated solely by greed. The comprador bourgeoisie are, to be sure, locked into a structure; but they are locked in only because they personally profit from their role as the middlemen and siphons of the international exploitative process. The analysis leaves no room for pride and nationalism. Such sentiments have, in fact, helped compel governments in countries as disparate as India, Mexico, Burma, South Korea, Peru, Argentina, Tanzania, and Brazil – to mention just a few – to adopt highly restrictive, sometimes even strongly mercantilist-exclusionist policies against the interests of the industrial countries. These have included strong controls over and even prohibitions against foreign investment, trade subsidies, currency controls, high tariffs, prohibitions against repatriation of profits, and others. Economic nationalism and Galtung's vision of an unfettered siphoning system do not fit well together.

Second, the model of exploitation is static. It does not leave room for learning or for changing power relations in commercial bargaining. The historical record does not forcefully sustain dependency theory's view of the state in developing countries as being essentially "trapped" into exploitative relationships. Granted that there are long-term global trends, such as worsening terms of trade between raw materials and industrial product producers, the state in developing countries has not remained simply a tool of capital. Particularly in dealing with foreign investment – a major dimension of exploitation – weak states go through a learning curve and are able, as they develop bureaucratic structures and industrial–technological–scientific expertise, to extract ever heavier taxes and other benefits from foreign investors (cf. Moran, 1974). The initial relationship in which international capital virtually dictates its terms for operating in a developing country ultimately changes to the point where the state begins to establish the terms under which it is willing to allow foreign capital to operate. Ultimately, the state is strengthened through its capacity to extract taxes. In some particularly weak countries the learning process may take decades. In others, as the oil-producing states demonstrated vigorously in the 1970s, the fundamental transformation of power relations may take only a few years.

Systemic-dependency explanations also fail to explain satisfactorily why some states like Malaysia, Singapore, Barbados, Indonesia, Lesotho, or South Korea are on the trajectory of increasing state strength while Somalia, Lebanon, and Liberia have collapsed. Nor do they explain why many Third World countries have had among the world's highest growth rates for more than two decades and why some of them have already surpassed income levels of many of the world's rich countries. Most small economies – not just Third World countries – find themselves constrained by international forces, yet many of them do not have weak states. The historically variegated movement of economies from subsistence to leading industrial levels is not well explained by dependency theories which predict a uniformly miserable economic level and weak statehood for the peripheries, whereas in reality there are today immense disparities of both economic development and state strength in what was once known as the Third World.

A more conventional economics approach does not rely on assumptions of particular human characteristics or on the interests of particular groups within a state. It appreciates that capitalism has not developed around the world simultaneously and that national economies march in different directions at different times. Yet, those who are late starters undoubtedly begin with serious disadvantages. The "magic of the market" for them is anything but equal. In many developing countries, producers are relatively inefficient; capital is scarce; educational, scientific, and technological levels are low; economies have not enjoyed the benefits of immense defense research, development, and spending that has helped create, sustain (and sometimes held back) progress in industrial countries; the terms of trade consistently favor producers of industrial goods; industries of developing countries that are becoming globally competitive nevertheless face all sorts of trade barriers in the industrial countries; resource-based economies face cycles of boom and bust that are unknown in most industrial countries; and debt piles up and its service charges drain national treasuries to the point where critical domestic development programs have to be jettisoned. The list of the economic disadvantages of the weak is almost endless, and it is easy to connect them with erosion of vertical and horizontal legitimacy. Because so many developing countries are so highly dependent upon international trade and financial flows – typically in the area of 35 percent of GNP (compared to less than 20 percent in most industrial countries) – the linkages between state strength and global economic conditions may be close and compelling.[2]

---

[2] Although only tangentially related to the phenomenon of wars of the third kind, there is a substantial and evolving literature that addresses issues pertinent to the state-strength dilemma. The role of capital, class, and the global economy as it relates to the

There are also specific practices that, despite the long-run intention of sustaining and strengthening states, nevertheless put immense strains on them in the short run. Financial institutions like the World Bank have been severely criticized for imposing conservative, orthodox policy prescriptions on loan recipients and applicants. In some cases, governments of weak states have few options but to accept very onerous conditions, including currency devaluations, terminating numerous subsidies that make life for the poor a little easier, and raising interest rates. The consequential hardships of these policies fall mostly upon hundreds of millions of the poor who may, in response, withdraw their support of incumbent regimes. Rebellion such as that of the Sendero Luminoso in Peru can be linked in some ways to such policies. The World Bank has also funded large infrastructure projects that require expropriation of peasant lands and force relocation of local populations. The list of depredations caused by philosophies of market magic is long. There is undoubtedly a relationship between global capitalism and state weakness, as a large literature attests, but regrettably the nexus is indeterminate. There is no simple cause–effect relationship. For every case where participation in the world economic system exacerbates social tensions and weakens the state, there is another case where significant state strengthening and growth of vertical and horizontal legitimacy result from trade, aid, and foreign investment. Thus, problems of political community definition, relations between communities, the colonial legacy, and in particular the problems of governance in weak states appear to offer more rewarding avenues of investigation.

To this point we have examined the weak state as an ideal type, in isolation. It is subject to external intervention and support in many different ways, but the perspective has been essentially from the point of view of a single state. We next have to explore regions of states, particularly those regions that are populated predominantly by one kind of state, weak or strong. This way we can infer some of the systemic and regional consequences, in terms of peace and war, of particular types of states.

articulation of social and political power in state formation, for example, is now generally constitutive of the new political economy approaches that explore the development of the Asian NICs. See, for instance, the collection of essays in Deyo (1987) and Evans (1985).

Aggregating states

Regions of the world populated by weak and failing states are zones of war. Regions populated by strong and strengthening states are zones of peace. This is the logical inference from an analysis which locates the sources of wars of the third kind primarily in the domestic structures of states. The evidence in chapter 2, as well as the extensive literature on the "democratic peace," supports the inference. Recent diplomatic agreements also support the connection. The 1990 Charter of Paris, for example, states explicitly – thus supporting Wilsonian doctrine – that if you want peace *between* states you must have democracy *within* states. This is the philosophical underpinning also of the Helsinki Final Act, numerous agreements under the auspices of the Organization for Cooperation and Security in Europe, and the belief of Western leaders in their approaches to the former socialist states, including the Russian federation (Holsti 1994). It is born out by the statistics on war. Since 1945, almost all war has taken place in the Third World and in the former Soviet republics.[3] The Irish rebellion, the 1964 and 1974 crises in Cyprus, the Soviet invasion of Hungary and Czechoslovakia in 1956 and 1968, and the Bosnian war resulted in casualty figures that otherwise would allow us to claim that no lives have been lost to war in Europe since 1945. But those wars and rebellions, it can be argued, took place in areas that are on the peripheries of Europe, where democracies were not involved. Among Western European countries, there has been no interstate war or armed intervention for more than fifty years. Ninety-nine percent of the war casualties in that period have occurred in the Third World, the Balkans, and in the former Soviet republics – all sites of weak states.

Are strong states a sufficient condition for peace? Probably not. In addition to state strength, there must be the norms, conventions, and practices associated with Bull's (1977) concept of a society of states. It is conceivable, though not likely, that a system of strong states that did not include norms such as mutual recognition of sovereignty and independence (one cannot claim to be a sovereign unless one accepts the sovereignty of others), the rules of diplomatic immunities, and the most basic norm of all that makes trade and other forms of interaction between states possible, that agreements are binding (*pacta sunt*

---

[3] This is not to imply that only states in these areas are combatants. States in the "zone of peace" have fought almost all their post-1945 wars in the Third World.

servanda), would be a system characterized by perpetual war. And was it not the case that twentieth century European history has featured two great wars between strong states? The answer is no if one accepts the definition of strong statehood outlined in chapter 5. It can be argued, for example, that both Nazi Germany and the Soviet Union had states that were captured by totalitarian parties, that the party-states systematically excluded vast classes of people from political participation and allocations, and that whatever the ostensible personal popularity of Hitler, Lenin, and Stalin, both vertical and horizontal legitimacy were relatively low. The principles underlying the "right to rule" in both countries – the *führerprinzip* and racial theories in Nazi Germany and the great revolutionary task in the Soviet Union, were inherently of short duration. The first could not outlive its mortal incarnation, the second was obviously exclusionary, and the third contained the fatal flaw of promising far more than any political system could deliver. Whether Nazi Germany and the Soviet Union were in fact strong states is questionable. I would argue, then, that any system, region, or zone populated by strong states as defined in chapter 5, will lead to predominantly peaceful relations among its components as long as the states operate within a society. Other factors may also be involved as well, which is to say that strong states may be a necessary, though not sufficient source of peace.

A zone is synonymous, in most cases, with geographical regions in which states share reasonable proximity, levels of interaction, and subjective perceptions of belonging to a space that is distinct from others. Elements of cultural similarity, such as common or related languages, religion, history, and political traditions, may buttress the contiguity and interactions. As the literature on regions suggests, there is always an element of arbitrariness in specifying such zones (cf. Kacowicz 1994: 7), but most analysts would not have difficulty agreeing on most of them. The figures in table 2.2, for example, use well-known designations such as Middle East, Africa, South America, Southeast Asia, and the like.

The problem is not entirely solved by employing geographic proximity, commerce, and cultural similarities as major criteria of zones, however. Terms like the "West" – used throughout the Cold War to include Japan, South Korea, and the antipodes – suggest that a zone may also be based on similarity of political values and practices as well as on high levels of interaction. Proximity was not part of the definition of the "West," although the concept of the "Atlantic Community" did give it a geographic core. In the contemporary world, we can argue that the OECD countries, which represent several different geographic areas, constitute a zone of non-contiguous strong states and, therefore, of peace. The term "zone," then, must be used loosely to include networks of states that may not share propinquity or a geographically compact region, but otherwise have high levels of interaction and share many or most of the attributes of strong states.

Zones of war are populated by weak and failing states. The wars typically but not exclusively begin as domestic armed conflicts but they usually bring external involvement in some form or other, and occasionally they turn into interstate or great-power proxy wars, as in Afghanistan, Angola, Ethiopia, Nicaragua, Vietnam, and elsewhere. Today, there are several regionally based zones of war. They do not constitute a single zone spanning several geographic regions, as in the case of the OECD countries, because, although their constituent units share the similar characteristic of weakness, the levels of interaction between the regions are sparse. There is little to join them, either in terms of cultural values, trade, religion, language, or political history. The non-aligned movement brought many of the states together in periodic summit meetings and caucuses in international organizations, but their mutual relations of trade and social contacts have not yet developed significantly beyond a general level of indifference. Richer densities, contacts, and mutual attention are limited primarily to specific and contiguous geographic areas, as Buzan's concept of "regional security complexes" suggests. It is for this reason, among others, that regional interstate institutions such as the Organization of African Unity and the Arab League are based primarily on geography rather than on other criteria. The Conference of Islamic States is the exception that substantiates the rule.

Zones of war have expanded as new weak states continue to be born. The addition of fourteen former Soviet republics has been accompanied in many cases by new arenas of armed conflict and weak statehood typified by poorly developed vertical and horizontal legitimacy (cf. Kangas 1994). Wars of the third kind have become a common feature of this area.

The population of strong states, however, is expanding as well. A significant number of formerly weak states are on the trajectory of gaining both vertical and horizontal legitimacy. Movement in one direction is by no means inevitable – corruption, stagnation, and turnabouts are always possible – but there are reasons for optimism when we contemplate the developing strength of states in Southeast Asia, a chronic war zone for more than thirty years after 1945, parts of Eastern and Central Europe, and, as we will see in the next chapter, in South America.

The reader familiar with the contemporary literature on international relations will object that the concept of the strong state is virtually similar with wealthy democracies.[4] Peace among strong states, they would say, is explained by their democratic and industrial characteristics rather than by their legitimacy. Why confuse the issue with yet another term? Despite some disagreements on definitions of democracy, war, time horizons, and the like, the finding that democracies do not war against each other (although they war against others just about as much as anyone else) has become one of the few solid empirical findings in the literature, as well as one of its main puzzles.

I prefer to use the strong state category because the critical criterion of state strength is the degree of vertical and horizontal legitimacy, and not particular political institutions and practices. Political units can be formed on principles other than those of classical democratic theory, and yet maintain both vertical and horizontal legitimacy. This was the idea behind the Leninist view that there would be no wars between socialist states and it is at least a dream among Muslim fundamentalists who insist that a community of believers would live in perpetual peace. In the Soviet case, practice diverged significantly from theory. Lenin's doctrine of the leading role of the Communist Party and the corollary of its infallibility prevented any possibility of developing sustainable vertical legitimacy. Mao's China enjoyed particularly high levels of popularity and legitimacy (except, of course, in areas like Tibet), but by the middle 1960s they had waned to such an extent that the Great Helmsman chose to brand a huge proportion of China's population as "class enemies" and "capitalist-roaders." It was at this time that Soviet–Chinese relations became particularly brittle and actually led to a limited border war in 1969. Neither government accepted the legitimacy claims of the other. As for Muslim states, the claim to peace within a community of believers rests on the assumption of a consensus on fundamental faith. Divisions within the faith make peaceful coexistence among states based on different versions of the truth unlikely.

---

[4] There is a strong correlation between democracies and wealthy countries (Mueller 1989; Maoz and Russett 1990).

Democracies and strong states, then, are indeed virtually overlapping categories, but to give the main hypothesis of this study a generic quality not so bound by time and location, state strength is a more encompassing term. Moreover, the concept of strength suggests a dynamic, changing variable rather than a static democracy/non-democracy dichotomy. That dichotomy is also subject to criticism on the grounds that there is no consensus on the essential components of democracy. Some emphasize regular elections, while others point to the importance of civil liberties. The election criterion overlooks the possibility that in societies deeply divided by sectarian, language, or communal lines, an election may be the means by which a majority maintains its predominance in perpetuity (see also chapter 9). Regular changes of personnel through elections, if they represent the same interests, may undermine horizontal legitimacy. In contrast, the strength concept alerts us to changing trajectories and to the possibility – denied by Francis Fukuyama and others – that even democracies may be subject to decay and loss of legitimacy. Nevertheless, at this historical juncture, the concepts of democracy and strong states are largely overlapping.

What is it about strong states, or democracies, that makes them different in their mutual relations? The literature offers a variety of speculations, including high levels of economic interdependence and institutionalization of relationships (war would not pay), societal controls over policy-makers, changes in the nature of nationalism in Western Europe, respect for international law, mutual empathy, transparency of decision-making and military capabilities, and many other candidates (cf. Doyle 1986; Russett and Starr 1989; Maoz and Abdolali 1989; Russett 1990; Nielebock 1992; Puchala 1993). Many of these explanations have been quantified, revealing both significant and relatively weak correlations. There are, however, factors that are difficult to quantify but that nevertheless must carry weight in our understanding of the genesis and sustenance of the non-war phenomenon between democracies and/or strong states.[5] Among them is the self-perception of democratic-liberal states. "[T]he enlarged scope of

---

[5] The no-war phenomenon must be distinguished from conflict in general. While there has been no war between democracies for a sustained period (researchers disagree on dates because of the lack of consensus on the candidates for war and the criteria for democracy), there have been plenty of militarized crises, that is, conflicts involving the threat of force, between democracies. What is significant is that these crises did not eventuate in armed conflict. See below for further discussion, as well as chapter 9.

obligations of liberal states toward each other," writes Christopher Brewin (1991: 202),

> is more than the sum of the plethora of post-war treaties and organizations to which they have committed themselves. Other obligations stem from their self-conceptions as liberal states. Thus, states may accept obligations on the grounds that they should not harm others by their own avoidable acts, they should do good where possible, and that they should remain faithful to their agreements and their associates, especially with kith and kin. To act otherwise, with ruthless reliance on force and fraud, would be to declare that they were not the states they conceive themselves to be.

Brewin's observation is germane to this discussion because it implicitly raises the question of legitimacy in international relations. Strong states, or democracies if you prefer, refrain from using armed force – although they may coerce through the threat of force – in their mutual relations in large part because they *share* self-conceptions. Strong states are different from other kinds of states primarily because they enjoy in common extensive degrees of vertical and horizontal legitimacy. They are, in a sense, "family," and one does not go around shooting its members. Much of international relations, despite assertions by realists, has to do with friendships and enmities based on moral judgments. It is difficult to paint as enemies those whom we know through broad experience to be essentially similar to ourselves in terms of political ideology and practice. Under certain circumstances, however, perceptions can change. The temptation to characterize those like us in evil terms can always appear. Enemies have not entirely vanished from the mutual relations of strong states today. The hostility and mistrust of the Japanese among significant sectors of the American population, quickly exploited by popular novelists for commercial gain, is a case in point.[6] We can speculate, however, that if Japan had a highly authoritarian political system based on coercion and the widespread violation of civil liberties, the perception of threat would be even higher. In general, strong/democratic states' wars against non-democratic regimes are much easier to start and sustain since non-democratic leaders and societies are much easier to demonize (Mintz and Geva 1993: 498).

[6] A major literary growth industry in the United States is dedicated to portraying the Japanese as devious, scheming, unscrupulous, and cunning in their hopes of achieving economic paramountcy in the world. A good example of a stereotype-ridden attempt to create a dangerous "other" is Tom Clancy's, *Red Storm Rising*.

Overall, however, perceptions of similar or parallel legitimacy act as constraints against the use of armed force. There have been, are, and will be future exceptions where democracies use at least subversion if not open war against their analogues abroad (American subversion of Allende's regime in Chile), but despite all the researchers' differences about empirical classifications of democracies, at least we can say that the probabilities of war among members of zones of strong states are substantially lower than those among members of zones of weak and failing states. Liberal self-perceptions and mutually accepted legitimacy are powerful constraints on the use of force (cf. Sadeniemi 1995).

To every generalization there is likely to be an important exception or an anomaly. South America is the case in this analysis. By almost any measure, the states of South America during most of the twentieth century have been neither strong nor democratic. Yet, there has been no war there since 1941, and only two wars in the entire century. On the surface, then, South America looks like a zone of peace. Yet some of the critical foundations of such a zone are missing. We will explore the anomaly in the next chapter. Here it is important, on the basis of the South American case, to offer yet another category. Zones of war are easy enough to identify by the empirical record, as I have demonstrated in chapter 2. The incidence of intra- and interstate war per state per year is high, sometimes reaching a value of more than one annually, as in South Asia and Southeast Asia since 1945. In South America, on the other hand, there has been a much lower incidence of both intra- and interstate wars, but a high incidence of militarized crises and local arms races (see next chapter for statistics). This suggests another category: *no-war zones* – areas that share many of the problems generated by weak states, including interventions, militarized crises, and all the paraphernalia of classical European international politics, including alliances and arms races, but not interstate wars.

We thus have three categories: zones of war, no-war zones, and zones of peace. Arie Kacowicz (1994) reminds us, however, that Karl Deutsch's (1954; 1957) concept of pluralistic security communities, where the incidence of militarized conflicts declines to virtually zero, is yet a higher stage in the development of peaceful relations between states. Military forces are not targeted towards fellow members of the zone, and plans for military operations against them have been either shredded or mould in unopened files. The relations between the Scandinavian states, Canada and the United States, and arguably in most of Western Europe, are of this type. The distinction between zones of peace and pluralistic security communities is not pronounced, but there are some differences of note. Let us then arbitrarily suggest that in *zones of war*, intra-state and interstate armed conflicts are intertwined and endemic, yet there may be, following Bull (1977) forces that moderate conflict, such as mutual recognition of the legitimacy of states, some fundamental rules governing their mutual relations, regularized interactions of trade and diplomacy, and some sentiments of indifference or even amity. Zones of war are not necessarily a Hobbesian world of all against all, but armed conflict recurs with sufficient frequency to cause substantial instability throughout the region, and even in the system as a whole.

In *no-war zones*, militarized conflicts are frequent; military capabilities are targeted toward specified enemies (usually neighbors); and alliances and arms races may be prominent features of the diplomatic and strategic landscape. But war does not result from these processes. An examination of South America since 1941 may help us understand why this is the case.

In *zones of peace*, militarized conflicts may break out from time to time (e.g., the Anglo-Iceland cod wars in 1972 and 1975) but capabilities are not targeted toward fellow members of the zone and operational war plans do not include "conflict hypotheses" against the same members. War has literally become "unthinkable" in mutual relations.

Pluralistic security communities are characterized in similar ways, but militarized conflicts *of any type* become "unthinkable." Following Deutsch, member states also typically share common norms, values, political institutions, and a high degree of economic and other forms of interdependence. Succinctly, a zone of peace has a foundation in the relations of states; a pluralistic security community rests on the social foundations of community between individuals and societies.

Using these categories, we would today place Africa, some of the former Soviet republics, the Middle East, Central America, South Asia, and the Balkans in the zone of war; Southeast Asia and East Asia (perhaps) in the no-war zone: the Caribbean and South Pacific in the zone of peace: and North America, the antipodes, and Western

Europe in the pluralistic security community categories.[7] But what of South America? Its war profile, particularly in terms of domestic armed conflicts, places it in the zone of war category. Yet few of its internal conflicts have become internationalized, and its record of interstate wars places it at least in the no-war category, and arguably in the zone of peace. We turn next to this important anomaly. South America not only helps us give substance to and demonstrate the changing dynamics of the war, no-war, and peace zone categories, but also sheds light on the weak state–strong state continuum and on the democracy and peace literature. Most importantly, it demonstrates that democracy is not a necessary condition for the development of no-war zones, and possibly even for zones of peace.

[7] Barry Buzan (1991: ch. 5) outlines a similar continuum of zones, but uses different nomenclature. One end of the spectrum is *chaos*, where wars recur regularly and enmity between the actors is the norm. There are no regions of this type currently in the world. Moving along the continuum, there are *regional conflict formations* (following Väyrynen, 1984), where conflict is endemic, but where amity is also possible. In *security regimes* (following Jervis 1982), states cooperate to manage their disputes, as they did in the era of the Concert of Europe. *Security communities*, following Deutsch, represent the next step. Integration – the end of international policies – forms the other end of the continuum. There are strong similarities between Buzan's categories and those outlined in this chapter. I prefer the simpler nomenclature, and the no-war zone represents an interesting category not adequately covered by Buzan's scheme.

8   Analyzing an anomaly: war, peace, and the state in South America[1]

Regions comprised primarily of weak states are zones of wars of the third kind. The etiology of these wars resides primarily within states that lack vertical and horizontal legitimacy. Many of these domestic wars cannot be contained within their frontiers, however. They become internationalized in various ways, sometimes leading to war between two or more states. Weak states are found predominantly in that vast area often inappropriately called the Third World, in the Balkans, and in some of the former Soviet republics. Does South America belong in any of these categories? Many people have so designated it. But the figures in table 2.1 show that South America has a unique profile of war. Like the other areas, it has seen a relatively high incidence of internal wars; but there have been no wars of secession. And, completely at odds with the other areas, there has been no war between South American states since 1941. South America is an intriguing anomaly. Is the war pattern of this region related to the weak state phenomenon? How can we explain the anomaly?

South America constitutes a distinct international system. It is linked

[1] In addition to the items cited in the references, some of the information and analysis is based on thirty-six interviews conducted in Rio de Janeiro, Buenos Aires, Santiago, La Paz, Lima, and Quito in May and June 1994. By role or profession, the interviews were with seventeen academic experts, eight former ministers of foreign affairs or other cabinet-level diplomats, nine military leaders with the rank of general (including two chiefs of staff of the army), one parliamentarian, and one former president. In some cases the respondent held more than one position. The interviews were conducted on the condition of anonymity; if there were serious disagreements of factual information between two or more respondents, the information was not included in the discussion that follows. I am very grateful to Paulo Wrobel, Monica Hirst, Maria Teresa Infante, Emilio Meneses, Gustavo Varas, Fernando Salazar Paredes, Eduardo Ferrero Costa, and Fernando Bustamente for their gracious assistance in organizing interviews or in other ways helping out.

to other systems, particularly to Central America and North America, but it contains its own unique properties and dynamics. G. Pope Atkins (1990: 1) defines it as an "international political subsystem." A prominent scholar of South American history (Burr 1965: 3, 28, 57) has chronicled its early years as a "continental system." Barry Buzan (1991: 207, 210) lists it among his "regional security complexes." Many other analysts concur with that categorization.

South America in the nineteenth century: a classical zone of war

In *post-hoc* explanations of the international politics of South America during the nineteenth century, many neo-realist predictions about international politics would be borne out. In less than one hundred years, there were six formally declared wars of which the devastating conflict pitting Paraguay against Argentina, Uruguay, and Brazil (1865–70), and the War of the Pacific between Chile and Bolivia and Peru (1879–84) were the most famous and have had consequences lasting into the late twentieth century. There were also five major armed invasions and interventions (cf. Goldstein 1992: ch. 17). In total, there were forty-two "militarized disputes" – defined as interactions "involving threats to use military force, displays of military force, or actual use of military force" – between 1816 and 1900 (Hensel 1994).

All the accoutrements of European diplomacy were found in nineteenth-century South America: alliances, fear of Brazilian hegemony, balances of power, and arms-racing (Meneses 1991: 346). During this era, South American governments constantly laid claims to each others' territories. In the 1830s, Chile militarily dismantled the Peru–Bolivia confederation and occupied Lima for two years. Forty years later it grabbed Antofagasta from Bolivia, and Tacna, Arica, and most of the Atacama desert – all areas containing major mineral deposits – from Peru (the War of the Pacific, 1879–84). Peru had pretensions to Guayaquil and intervened militarily in an Ecuador revolution in 1860. Bolivia also lost territory to Peru and Argentina and, after armed incidents, ceded the Acre region in the Amazon to Brazil (1903).

Brazil was the potential hegemon. It claimed territories that had been demarcated during the Spanish colonial era as belonging to Ecuador, Colombia, Peru, Bolivia, and Paraguay. Through threats, subversion, armed occupation, and the skillful diplomacy of the Baron do Rio Branco, it was able to expand its territories at the expense of its neighbors. It was also the only country in South America to proclaim itself an empire (1822–89) and was thus the object of considerable suspicion on ideological and strategic grounds. Finally, Bolivia and Peru, the down-sized losers of the War of the Pacific, had "Alsace–Lorraine complexes" that have continued to motivate their foreign policies to this day.

Looking at nineteenth-century South America, then, one sees patterns of peace and war, intervention, territorial predation, alliances, arms-racing, and power-balancing quite similar to those found in eighteenth-century Europe. This region would thus lend support to neo-realist, structural characterizations of international politics as a game of conflict, war, struggle, and survival.

There is also a correlation between the high incidence of war and intervention, and some of the typical characteristics of weak states. Nineteenth-century South America, in other words, lends support to the main thesis of this book. Brazil, for example, lacked national integration. There was little or no transportation between its major regions. As a coastal society, it looked to Europe rather than towards its own integration. Even though nominally an empire, it was in fact a loose federation of provinces, each with its own armed forces and its own political and economic agendas. Civil war flared during the 1830s and even as late as 1932 the province of São Paulo rebelled militarily against federal authorities in what was a virtual war of secession. Some of Brazil's conflicts with its southern neighbors derived more from internal considerations, needs, and threats, than from external security problems.

During the latter nineteenth century, Argentina was hardly a nation, but more a decentralized system of warlords. It was immersed in a series of civil wars until the 1860s. Chile and Ecuador (after the latter seceded from Colombia) were in a condition of chronic revolution and civil war until mid-century. Ecuador's weakness as a state prompted various claims and interventions by Peru. Bolivia in the nineteenth century was also a classic weak state. It contained geographically distinct regions, many of whose inhabitants identified with neighboring countries. Notable separatist movements developed in Tarija and Santa Cruz. The underdevelopment and weakness of the Bolivian state and its traditional dominance by Andean highlanders, contributed to decentralization and facilitated external interference from Argentina, Brazil, and Peru (Morales 1984: 175).

If states were weak, so were governments. In 168 years in Peru, there were 108 governments (Velit 1993: 214), most of which came to power through extra-legal means. Figures of similar magnitudes were found also in Ecuador, Colombia, and Venezuela.

A prime characteristic of weak states, as argued in chapter 5, is contested frontiers. A state lacks international legitimacy, and therefore security, if major portions of its territory are claimed by others. This aspect of statehood has been historically a major source of both international and domestic wars.

In nineteenth-century South America, the territorial limits of sovereignty were constantly challenged even though at the Congress of Lima in 1848 the governments agreed that the Spanish colonial boundaries as of 1810 should form the basis of future frontiers. This is the principle of *uti possidetis*, applied in a similar fashion in Africa since 1963.

The problem was that the formidable geographical barriers of the peripheral areas of South America made accurate frontier demarcations difficult. Even by 1848, almost all of the 1810 limits had been challenged or altered by armed force, and the Spanish-speaking countries, relying on the principle of the historic foundations (e.g., documents of title, treaties) of territorial extent, disagreed fundamentally with Brazil, which held that territorial limits are based on effective occupation. Until 1945 military conquest was still a valid basis for a territorial claim (Calvert 1983: 5). Calvert points out that "[i]t was therefore possible – and indeed desirable – to establish a military presence as rapidly as possible in disputed frontier regions, which could in subsequent negotiations be used as evidence of effective occupation." Vast regions of South America, in any case, had not been carefully mapped during the Spanish-Portuguese colonial periods. They included the Amazon and Orinoco river basins, Patagonia, Tierra del Fuego, and the Atacama desert – all areas of war and conflict in the nineteenth and even twentieth centuries (Burr 1965: 5). Thus, the 1848 agreement – similar to the more recent principle enshrined in the Charter of the Organization of African Unity – that the new states should define their territorial limits on the basis of colonial frontiers – never really solved the territorial identity of the new states. In the rest of the nineteenth century virtually no frontier in existence in 1848 was to remain unchallenged (Calvert 1983: 5).

Many of the contested regions were sparsely populated and difficult to control, but once they were discovered to hold resources for world trade (nitrates and guano in the Atacama desert, rubber in Acre, and oil in the Amazon basin) they became the scene of conflicts, crises, and wars.

In other respects, however, the South American countries did not have many of the features of so many post-1945 weak states. There were deep class cleavages based on color, but most South American countries did not have the multiplicity of communities found, for example, in India, Nigeria, or Sudan today. Indigenous populations had been killed off in Argentina and to a lesser extent in Brazil and Chile, or remained marginalized from the main political systems. For a variety of complex reasons and unlike their counterparts in other areas of the world in the twentieth century, the marginalized did not organize resistance around the principle of self-determination or the policy of secession. Military or civilian oligarchies ruled, but under a paternalistic framework of constitutional rules of the game. The state was not an instrument of systematic predation of one group against others (again, the indigenous populations in Argentina, Brazil, Peru and other Andean countries are significant exceptions). Political opponents for the most part were silenced through means other than widespread human rights abuses, expulsion, or genocide, and even in eras of domestic turmoil, the state was able to provide minimal services.

Twentieth-century South America: a no-war zone

The data on war incidence since 1945, introduced in chapter 2, indicate clearly that the international politics of South America have changed substantially since the late nineteenth century. Today, it stands as an anomaly among so many regions characterized by frequent wars, interventions, and collapsing states. If we exclude the Malvinas War (1982) because it was fought against an extra-regional power, there has been no interstate war in South America since 1941. This record is matched only by North America. Considering that there are four times as many independent countries in South America as in North America, on a probability basis the no-war record of the former is remarkable.

It is even more remarkable if we stretch the time horizon further back: there have been only two wars in South America since 1903. The Chaco War between Bolivia and Paraguay was a protracted, bloody conflict involving almost 100,000 casualties, while the war between Ecuador and Peru in 1941 lasted only two weeks. It is not listed in most war data sets because it had fewer than 1,000 casualties. But because Ecuador lost more than 200,000 square kilometers (about 40 percent of its territory) including access to the Amazon River (and hence to the Atlantic) as well as potential oil resources, it must be considered an important war. Further border flare-ups took place in 1981 and 1995. The first was quickly managed with a cost of less than a dozen lives. The second was substantially more serious, with about 75 casualties, but far under the 1,000 casualty threshold; its significance will be noted below.

For South America, then, the twentieth century has been an era of relative peace. If we compare it to the record of war in eighteenth- and nineteenth-century Europe, or to the twentieth-century interwar period, the contrast is even more dramatic. Except for North America, South America has been the most peaceful area in the world in the twentieth century.

Many of the other characteristics of the neo-realist version of international politics have not been duplicated in twentieth-century South American international politics. Despite substantial ideological incompatibilities between various South American regimes, the incidence of subversion, armed intervention, or other forms of interference, has been relatively low. When Brazilian exiles were trained in Chile in the 1970s for resistance/subversive activities, the Brazilian government maintained proper relations with the Allende government in Santiago, even to the point of donating limited amounts of aid to it. Despite widespread concerns throughout South America about the Allende regime, there was no joint action against it and, indeed, the military government in Argentina took a major step to arbitrate the Beagle Channel controversy with it. The military, but radical-reformist, governments of Peru during the 1970s also faced no external interference except from the United States.

The major exceptions to the general rule of non-interference or intervention include Brazilian involvement in a Bolivian coup in August 1971 and frequent Argentine interference in Bolivian politics, including assistance to the leaders of an anti-leftist government coup in July, 1980. Given the record of ideological incompatibilities, civil disturbances, and unstable regimes throughout the continent in the twentieth century, however, these few exceptions tend to prove the rule of non-intervention.

South America in the twentieth century has also seen exceptionally high rates of peaceful conflict resolution or toleration of conflicts that remain unresolved but are not likely to be settled by recourse to war (Treverton 1983). A recent study (Kacowicz 1994: 249–51) chronicles eight peaceful territorial changes (although some of them were settled only after a major, but not violent, crisis) in South America since 1900. Only two territorial conflicts were resolved by war.

Arbitral procedures for resolving conflicts have been used at extraordinarily high rates compared to other regions of the world. Since the 1820s until 1970, Argentina, Bolivia, Brazil, Colombia, Chile, Ecuador, Peru, and Venezuela used arbitration procedures 151 times (data from Puig 1985: 9ff). Since 1970, the Beagle Channel dispute was arbitrated by the Queen of England (the award was subsequently rejected by Argentina) and by the Pope. Currently, two other territorial issues are being arbitrated between Argentina and Chile.

No other region of the world has as many bilateral and multilateral documents, treaties, and charters imposing obligations for the peaceful settlement of disputes. Among the more prominent are the Treaty on the Maintenance of Peace (Lima 1865), the General Treaty of Arbitration between Argentina and Chile (Pacto do Mayo) of 1902, the Bogotá Pact of 1948, and the Charter of the Organization of American States (Puig 1983: 11–13). While few of these contain compulsory procedures, their numbers and frequent use suggest a rich regime of peaceful conflict resolution norms.

Finally, one can gain an appreciation of the war or peace proneness of a region by superimposing maps over a period of years. While there were substantial frontier changes in nineteenth-century South America (but far fewer than the European counterpart), the twentieth century includes only a few minor changes, and only the two major territorial losses to Bolivia and Ecuador as a result of the two wars of the century (cf. Goertz and Diehl 1992: 112–13). It is also significant that those same maps show the disappearance of no states and the birth of no new states as a result of armed secession. Guyana and Suriname are the only new states; both emerged from peaceful de-colonization. Again, comparisons with other regions of the world are instructive. Most states in the nineteenth and twentieth centuries were born through international and civil-secessionist violence. Since the late nineteenth century, in contrast, South America has been a no-war zone characterized by peaceful change, non-violent conflict resolution, and only infrequent interventions.

One does not find, either, the remaining mainstays of neo-realist characterizations of international politics, namely alliances and balances of power. Both were prominent practices in the nineteenth century (Burr 1965), but disappeared as major foreign policy strategies in the twentieth century despite their importance in academic geopolitical analysis that was so popular in South America until the 1990s. Brazil has more territory and greater population and economic strength than all the remaining countries of the continent combined. It has not, however, sought hegemony in the classical models of a Louis XIV, Napoleon, Kaiser Wilhelm, or Adolf Hitler. It has frequently raised suspicions among its many neighbors,[2] but the absence of any counter-Brazil coalition or neighbors' "conflict hypotheses" which include Brazil as a possible threat, indicates a significant lack of hegemonial-type behavior on the part of Brazil (cf. Selcher 1990: 85). In territorial terms, Brazil has been a "satisfied" state throughout the twentieth century.

Alliances are also absent. By far the majority of relationships within South America are bilateral. Even attempts to build tactical and *ad hoc* coalitions in times of crisis (e.g., during the Beagle Channel crisis in December 1978; see below) have generally failed.

Overall, then, the international politics of twentieth-century South America fit poorly with neo-realist characterizations and predictions. Waltz's famous recurrent outcomes of an anarchic system (war, balancing, absence of relative gains) do not apply to this area. The theory, as suggested, comes from the European and Cold War diplomatic experience; it does not fit the patterns of twentieth-century South America.

From Hobbes to Kant: South America as a zone of peace?

Is this a dramatic change from a zone of war, a "Hobbesian floor" of chronic warfare, to a "Kantian ceiling" of perpetual peace (Hoffmann 1981: 17)? Hardly. South America is not yet either a zone of peace or a pluralistic security community (Deutsch 1954; Deutsch *et al.*, 1957) as is found today in Western Europe or North America.

In the twentieth century, however, it has become at least a no-war zone ("negative peace," as termed by Arie Kacowicz, 1994) where mutually peaceful relations and non-violent modes of conflict resolution are the norm. As suggested in the previous chapter, no-war zones

---

[2] For example, in 1976, Guyana feared a Brazilian invasion in a dispute over territory.

fit somewhere between systems of chronic war, enmity, and insecurity, and zones of peace or pluralistic security communities in which the possibility of armed conflict has been reduced to almost zero.

South America in the twentieth century – or more precisely, since 1941, the date of its last war – fits into the no-war or negative peace category because since the Ecuador–Peru conflict of that year it has been the scene of forty-three militarized disputes and crises (Hensel 1994; and the 1995 Peru–Ecuador crisis) and other forms of behavior that are inconsistent with the zone of peace or pluralistic security community concepts. Indeed, the record of near wars until the 1980s would place the region only at the "introductory" levels of a no-war zone. Consider some crises and military deployments since the last war of 1941.

In 1966, the Stroessner government manufactured a contested territory crisis with Brazil (cf., Barboza 1992: ch. 5). In 1975, Peru went to the brink of war against Chile. The traditional revisionist claim by Peru for Arica (lost in the War of the Pacific) was a minor dimension of the problem. Ideological incompatibilities between two military regimes – led by General Juan Velasco Alvarado and Augusto Pinochet respectively – were significant, as were fears in Lima that Pinochet's geopolitical concepts, including the necessity for Chile to establish naval hegemony over the eastern South Pacific, would significantly increase Peru's security problems. During a period of two weeks, the Peruvian army was put on "red alert" and the air force prepared for strikes against military targets in Chile. Unlike the Argentine military regime's preparation of public opinion prior to the Malvinas campaign, the Peruvian government made no propaganda; it wanted to conduct a quick war without the complications or repercussions of public participation. The decision to launch the armed forces was rescinded only at the last moment after American sources provided Peru with satellite photographs of Chile's defenses. They were of sufficient magnitude to reduce significantly Peru's assumed military superiority in the conflict sector.

The Beagle Channel crisis of December 1978 had a similar outcome, this time resulting more from serendipity than from effective deterrence. The dispute over the islands in the Beagle Channel has a long history. The implications of the territorial distribution go far beyond the small amount of territory involved. Where exactly the border lies in the Beagle Channel determines whether, for example, Chile would be a naval power in both the Pacific and Atlantic and, with the 200-mile economic zone being formulated at the time in Geneva, whether it would also have jurisdiction over large tracts of sea containing potential resources such as krill and oil. The dispute also related to Argentine and Chilean mutually exclusive claims in Antarctica. An extension of Chilean jurisdiction into waters considered by the Argentines to be their own also seriously threatened Argentine military leaders' geopolitical dreams of hegemony over the western South Atlantic. The issues were complicated and perceived as involving national honor, prestige, national identity, and many other symbolic and commercial stakes.

Queen Elizabeth made an arbitral award in June 1977 favorable to Chile. The Argentine junta formally rejected it in January 1978. A vigorous propaganda campaign prepared the way for an Argentine show of force in the disputed area (cf. Infante 1984: 337–58). Following intense debates among the leaders of the military services in Buenos Aires (with General Videla disclaiming to South American diplomats any intention of going to war), the decision was made to resolve the issue by threatened force (for details of decision-making and military infighting, see R. Russell 1990: esp. pp. 36–59). After the necessary alerts and general mobilizations of both countries' military forces along their lengthy border, the Argentine junta sent a battle group of one aircraft carrier, two cruisers, seven destroyers, and two submarines to confront a Chilean fleet composed of three cruisers, eight frigates and destroyers, and three submarines. After four days of a face-to-face showdown in the Drake Passage (Meneses 1991: 357), a violent Atlantic storm forced the squadrons to retreat (Garrett 1985: 96–7). On December 11, Pope John Paul II sent a personal message to both presidents urging restraint and offering to arbitrate the conflict.

Not only did the events of December 1978 come very close to battle, but the crisis might well have escalated beyond the two main protagonists. Argentina, fully familiar with Peru's revisionist claims to Arica, requested a Peruvian attack in Chile's north. The request was rejected, but Peru did order a partial mobilization. Landlocked Bolivia, always looking for opportunities to redeem its losses of the War of the Pacific and gain access to the sea, also considered but decided against an attack on Chile. Chile, of course, did not sit back waiting for an Argentine–Peru–Bolivia axis to form against it. It tried to get Ecuador to stop providing oil to Peru. The Peruvians claimed that the Chilean naval attaché in Lima was involved in espionage and three Peruvian military officials were executed for providing Chile with military secrets. The classical characteristics of balance of power/threat diplomacy, espionage, and counter-balancing were all evident in December 1978.

The last major armed incident occurred between Ecuador and Peru in 1981. It was a border problem, with minimal loss of life, engineered and orchestrated by the militaries of both countries against the wishes of their civilian governments (cf. Varas 1983: 76). The 1995 flare-up, costing about seventy-five lives, indicates the extent to which crises and border incidents remain a part of the South American diplomatic and military landscapes.

Military capabilities in some regions of South America continue to be targeted toward neighbors. In addition to deployments, some South American governments continue to develop war plans, known as "conflict hypotheses," against their neighbors. Most are secret and not subject to parliamentary scrutiny or debate. Their contents are generally known, however, or can be deduced from deployments. In Chile, for example, in order of priority and probability, the four main threats – the bases of war doctrines – are (1) war against Argentina; (2) a confrontation with Peru and/or Bolivia; (3) a "maximum threat," meaning a simultaneous war against Argentina, Peru, and Bolivia; and (4) an external (great-power?) attack on Easter Island (Meneses, 1993: 398–403). Displaying the mentality of the Argentine military regime in the 1970s, as another example, there was "Plan Rosario" according to which Argentina would attack the Malvinas and then turn to settle the Beagle Channel problem by force. The sequence, according to the plan, could also be reversed.

We can cite, finally, the case of Bolivia, where the perception of threat is translated into everyday life. Until recently, Bolivia had not paved any of its roads to neighboring countries for fear that they would be used as avenues of invasion against it.

Countries in zones of peace and pluralistic security communities maintain rich and reliable communications channels between each other. It would be difficult to believe a news report that, for example, Sweden and Norway had broken diplomatic relations. In South America during the twentieth century, however, such ruptures of the most fundamental channel of communication are by no means rare. In 1953, Argentina severed diplomatic relations with Uruguay (*Keesings Contemporary Archives*, January 3–10, 1953: 12664); it broke them with Venezuela the same year because the latter refused to expel Juan Peron (*Keesings Contemporary Archives*, July 20–7, 1953: 15671). Bolivia broke diplomatic relations with Chile in 1962, and again in 1978. To 1995 they had not been restored.

The installation of military regimes throughout the Southern Cone countries and Brazil during the 1960s and 1970s tended to exacerbate preexisting regional tensions. The area was characterized by a classical arms-race mentality that included Brazil–Argentine nuclear competition, the development of indigenous arms industries, and the diversification of new armaments sources to include Soviet, French, British, German, and Canadian weapons systems (Hirst and Rico 1993: 250–3). There was also a minor arms race between Colombia and Venezuela focused on territorial disputes.

With this record of militarized crises, targeted military forces, "conflict hypotheses," diplomatic ruptures, and overall military competitiveness, South America clearly is not yet a zone of peace, much less a pluralistic security community. Nevertheless, it has been a no-war zone in which the probabilities of armed conflict are substantially lower than they were in the nineteenth century or are in many other regions of the world today. As such, it is an anomaly compared to most other regions of the world. Why did the region change from a typical Hobbesian zone of war in the nineteenth century to a predictably peaceful, if not demilitarized, no-war zone in the twentieth century?

From zone of war to no-war zone: the problem of explanation

Presently available theories of international politics do not explain the South American case. Neo-realist predictions are not borne out by the record; dependency theory would emphasize the economic roots of many of South America's conflicts, but there have also been conflicts where economic stakes were minimal; and liberal-institutionalist theories do not take us very far because until recently there have been only low levels of integration and successful multilateral institution-building in the region. Deutsch's theories of integration do not hold either because rich communications flows, democratic governments, and a common external threat have not been important features of the regional system. How do we explain the anomaly, then?

One way to proceed is to identify *types* of explanation that appear in the literature and that are offered by analysts and participants, and to

comb them for persuasive arguments. These include: (1) neo-realist/
geostrategic; (2) learning and foreign policy change; (3) domestic
politics; (4) cultural/sociological; and (5) liberal-institutional. To these
approaches I add the argument of this book: strong states are a
necessary if insufficient condition for the development of zones of
peace and pluralistic security communities.

Realist/geostrategic explanations

In their normative stance, most neo-realist and geostrategic thinkers
follow the logic of the ancient *para bellum* doctrine: if you want peace,
prepare for war. The explanation for the change from a typical war
system in the nineteenth century to a no-war or negative peace zone in
the twentieth century lies primarily in effective military dispositions
(deterrence) and an overall balance of power maintained between the
particular states and by the regional hegemon, the United States.

The absence of war between states holding incompatible claims
(Ecuador–Peru, Peru–Chile, Bolivia–Chile, Chile–Argentina, Colombia–
Venezuela, Venezuela–Guyana), according to a neo-realist analysis,
derives primarily from effective local deterrents which are promoted
and sustained by the United States. For example, Chile deploys its
highly equipped but relatively small military forces in a deterrent
posture focused on the north and south against Bolivia/Peru and
Argentina. The frontier with Peru in the north is mined. American
military aid has for the most part sought to maintain such local military
balances. When those balances tilted, as in the mid-1970s after Peru
bought large quantities of Soviet arms (as a response to American
efforts to de-stabilize the radical-reformist regime by denying it spare
parts), the United States provided Peru with satellite pictures of Chile's
defenses. This was, apparently, critical in the Peruvian decision not to
go to war in 1975. Although Argentina and Chile have often purchased
naval and other military equipment from European sources, the United
States has refused to sell certain types of potentially de-stabilizing
weapons systems. Local deterrents have for the most part been
effective in maintaining at least an "armed peace."

Brazil's generally benign or cooperative policies toward the rest of
South America can also be explained by neo-realist and geostrategic
perspectives, to which are added economic arguments. The Brazilians
are only too aware that genuinely hegemonic policies would bring
together a significant counter-coalition. More important, however, is

162

War, peace, and the state in South America

the spatial distribution of Brazil's society. It has been historically a coastal state, outward-looking to Europe and the United States. Most of its frontier regions are distant from the main urban centers, sparsely populated, and logistically difficult to supply. Like nineteenth-century America, twentieth-century Brazil has focused on internal development rather than on territorial expansion at the expense of other states. There are plenty of land and resources within the continent-sized country that it need not press further claims. From its earliest years, the great task of Brazil was to hold itself together rather than to expand outwards. Moreover, Portuguese colonial authorities specifically organized defensive buffer zones beyond major riverlines, thus creating impenetrable frontiers against incursions from Spanish colonists. Borders were fortified, and the rivers were blocked. Brazil's physical limits, in brief, were designed on defensive geostrategic principles.

Geostrategic analysis also underlines the relative weakness of South American countries' military capabilities. The low incidence of war derives perhaps less from effective deterrence than from the insurmountable problems of projecting power in peripheral regions. Child (1985: 8–9) points out that distance, mountains, rivers, and climatic extremes separate the most prominent conflict zones from the actual centers of military power, which are mostly located within or near major coastal cities. South American militaries have not solved basic logistical problems and, for a variety of historical and cultural reasons, have not developed their naval and air power in comparison to their armies' capabilities.

The no-war zone, then, might also be explained by the irrelevance of the countries toward each other (cf. Kacowicz, 1994). That is, they do not touch upon each other sufficiently to generate the bases for conflict. It is not deterrence that matters, but the lack of mutual importance.

The remarkable record of peaceful change and conflict resolution in South America during the twentieth century can also be explained by extra-regional pressures exerted on conflict parties. Sometimes it was the United States (e.g., its role as a guarantor – but also as a source of pressure – in the 1942 Rio de Janeiro Treaty which in effect sanctified Peru's 1941 conquest of Ecuadorian-claimed territory), sometimes Great Britain (in the early stages of the Beagle Channel dispute), and sometimes a variety of states exercising their influence through the Organization of American States or the United Nations. As one example, Bolivia in 1963 withdrew from the OAS (termed an "incompetent organ" by the Bolivian foreign minister), because the organiza-

163

tion had placed pressures on it rather than back up its position in a dispute with Chile (*Keesings Contemporary Archives*, 1963: 19489, 19006). According to Puig, (1983: 23), "the small and medium-sized countries of the periphery were in no position to resist the pressure exerted on them by the great powers in order that, first, they should consent to a peaceful form of solution and later, that they should accept the judge's verdict."

Such neo-realist/geostrategic explanations of peace and conflict resolution, despite some contradictions (peace through effective deterrence or peace through irrelevance or weakness?), are persuasive to a point. But in a comparative perspective they are less compelling. Logistics problems have not prevented *other* countries from warring; nor have great power pressures always constrained small and medium states from attacking each other and prosecuting wars to the point of stalemate or victory. The archives of the OAS, the United Nations, and the American State Department are littered with unheeded resolutions and diplomatic *démarches* urging conflict partners to use peaceful conflict resolution procedures or to cease fire. In the case of the Chaco War, the United States was unable to prevent, manage, or stop the fighting. Whatever the external pressures during crises and conflicts, the South American governments have displayed a unique *predisposition* to search for peaceful solutions. The number of territorial disputes and crises that have not escalated to war remains unique compared to other areas of the world.

Another weakness of neo-realist/geostrategic forms of explanation is the relative absence of conflict between South American countries despite the strong tradition of geopolitical thinking among civilian and military analysts and governments in many of them. These analytical forms were very popular after World War II. They helped form important parts of the curriculum in War Colleges, and were sustained through numerous institutes, think-tanks, and government offices. Augusto Pinochet was a student of geopolitics, wrote an influential text on the subject, and established an institute to propagate his ideas. Jack Child's admirable analysis (1985) of the substance and content of the geopolitical tradition in South America chronicles how the main advocates of geopolitics used zero-sum assumptions, held deep suspicion of neighbors' motives and intentions, and characterized their own countries as "victims."

Child and others (cf. Russell 1990: Selcher 1985) emphasize that these analytical modes had significant influence in some governments, and exacerbated long-standing territorial disputes. This was particularly the case during the 1970s when military regimes governed in the Southern Cone countries.[3]

Whatever the influence of geopolitical doctrines, they attest more to the significance of ideas in foreign policy behavior than as useful analytical tools for theoretical analysis. Geopolitical explanations of South America's no-war zone do not carry us very far. Indeed, they even contradict the realities since the expected outcomes of analysis and policy prescriptions – power projection, struggle, alliances, power balancing, and war – are the opposite of the actual record. Geopolitical ideas and analytical methods have not changed substantially, but the South American states' behavior toward each other has. Nineteenth-century South America was an area of chronic war and armed intervention; in the succeeding century it has become a no-war zone. Geography, logistics problems, and the difficulties of power projection, which have arguably changed only marginally over the past 180 years, have not been duplicated by diplomatic behavior, which has changed dramatically. Any form of geographical or power determinism in explaining the development of a no-war zone in South America does not hold up to the empirical evidence.

Learning/cognitive explanations

In anarchic systems, security dilemmas, wars, alliances, balances of power, and zero-sum situations recur. This is the "dreary" list of system outcomes noted by Waltz (1979: 66). While he acknowledges that state attributes and other unit-level properties may influence patterns of relations between individual states, the main outcomes derive from system characteristics. Yet, it is precisely these outcomes – in this case the change from a chronic war/intervention system to a no-war system between the nineteenth and twentieth centuries – that need explanation. Since the anarchic character of the system did not change,

---

[3] Many respondents, from the perspectives of the 1990s, denied that geopolitical ideas were influential as an intellectual basis for policy-making. Though various geopoliticians published profusely, today many see these efforts as relatively harmless "academic exercises." In my judgment, geopolitical ideas popular in South America during the 1970s helped create an atmosphere of mutual suspicion. The 1975 crisis between Peru and Chile was certainly exacerbated by Peruvian perceptions of Pinochet's ideas, and in the months prior to the December 1978 Argentine–Chile crisis, various influential analysts relied on geopolitical concepts to argue their case for a "final solution" to the territorial conflict (cf. Infante, 1984: 337–58).

nor was there any radical shift in the distribution of capabilities among the system members, then the change cannot be explained in system terms. We must look at the characteristics of the units that make up the system, or at the ideas of individual policy-makers.

Among the many criticisms leveled at Rousseauian/neo-realist, structural theories of international politics is the claim that if system characteristics "push" and "shove" the states to act in certain ways, then one cannot expect major changes in the character of relations between states until the system itself changes from one based on the principle of anarchy to some other principle, such as hierarchy. Systems theory, then, is basically static; it is a theory of recurrence rather than a theory of change. But there was significant change in South American international politics between the nineteenth and twentieth centuries; it took place in the absence of fundamental systemic changes, including distributions of capabilities.

One way around the shortcomings of structural theories is to assume more agency in international systems, mainly in the ability of policy-makers to *learn* and to act in new ways upon the information that has been gained through historical experiences (cf. Levy 1994). One major stimulus to learning and change is the diplomatic/military disaster, those magnificent failures of policy that lost wars, states, and empires. The Vietnam War was a great learning experience for American policy-makers, one that still has strong repercussions in America's contemporary unwillingness to use military force except under highly limited conditions. Munich was a "lesson of history" that has often been used – sometimes incorrectly – to instruct policy-makers in supposedly analogous situations. World War I was similarly a great disaster, dubbed after the fact as a "war to end all wars," because of its folly and high costs. British diplomacy in the 1930s was primarily an effort to avoid duplicating the disasters of the Great War, that is, to demonstrate that important lessons from that war had been learned (Holsti 1991: ch. 11).

In South America, the experience of war has been consistently disastrous for both military and civilian regimes that directed them. If most policy-makers have historical memories (but avoiding the question whether it is a correct memory), then the unmistakable "lesson" to be learned from South American wars is to avoid them at all costs. While in some nineteenth-century wars winners clearly emerged, they also revealed degrees of military ineptitude seldom equaled elsewhere. The military forces of Chile during the War of the Pacific were paralyzed by lack of logistics. The Chaco War turned into a carnage leading to major territorial losses by those who initiated the fighting. Ecuador lost almost one-half of its territory and access to the Amazon River after the rout of its troops by Peru in 1941. Except for the air force, Argentine military units were routed during the Malvinas War. The major winners of wars – Brazil, Chile, and Peru – made substantial gains of actual or potential resources, but in so doing earned the enmity of their neighbors for the next century.

Battlefields were not the only arenas of loss-loss situations deriving from South American wars. Unlike European wars, where populations joined together in outbursts of nationalist enthusiasm for the cause and strengthened loyalties to their governments, South American regimes that initiated wars never survived the victories, stalemates, or defeats. They were thrown out of office either during or immediately after the war. The fate of the military regime in Argentina following the Malvinas debacle was just the last in a long string of governments that paid a high price for launching the armed forces. It is perhaps because of this historical fact that many military governments in South America have "fought" to prevent wars as much as they have fought to win wars.

But there are sufficient exceptions to the generalizations to cast doubt on the learning theory as a complete explanation of the change from a war to a no-war system. Earlier, we noted two incidents in the 1970s where military regimes almost went to war but were thwarted at the last moment by serendipity or effective deterrence. It is by no means certain that knowledge of historical trends or statistical regularities pacify the bellicose when there are sufficient opportunities for major gains or when there are high states of tension during a crisis. Nor is there any substantial evidence that South American policy-makers are familiar with the history of war on the continent. Nineteenth-century experience is probably remote and only sketchily recalled, and there are too few wars in the twentieth century to constitute any repertoire of commanding "lessons." The lessons available to the Argentine generals and admirals who attacked the Malvinas, for example, were more than a century old.

Domestic politics explanations

It has become a cardinal tenet of the academic study of international politics that there is no clear line distinguishing the external from the internal. International politics is not a game with its own rules, actors, and stratagems. Ultimately, most foreign policy initiatives are taken to meet domestic requirements or needs. To understand foreign policy, then, we have to look not only at the external environment but at the domestic politics of the major actors.

With little knowledge of those politics, one might be persuaded to predict a high incidence of war in South America because the military have governed in so many countries so much of the time. By definition, the military are supposed to represent the warrior virtues, of which "national honor," victory, and loyalty are among the main ones.

It is difficult to generalize about the military in South America; their characteristics, historical origins, and sociological makeup vary significantly from country to country. Acknowledging exceptions to most generalizations, we can argue nevertheless that historically the military in South America have been institutions of politics and governance rather than armed forces trained primarily for fighting Clausewitzian-type wars against external enemies. The military have traditionally taken a paternalistic view of their relationship to society and the state. They typically see themselves as protectors of the constitution, guarantors of social order, and engines of national moral (patriotic), economic and technological development. In brief, their roles are primarily internal, not external.

Military regimes in South America have run the ideological spectrum from radical-liberal to reactionary-repressive. What unites them is their preoccupation with domestic problems. Their professionalization in the late twentieth century has strengthened their domestic roles and increased their sense of competence and incorruptibility. Compared to civilian regimes, they have often stood out as the only institution committed to the integrity of the state above private gain. During the 1970s, anti-communism gave them another plank on which to justify their predominant role in politics. José Nun (1986: 105) nicely summarizes the bases of military roles during this period:

> Professionalization of the military has . . . led to feelings of superiority, that only the military is competent, that only it has the capability to solve a wide range of social problems . . . As the military officers saw it, they had resolved "their" problem [competence] while the civil sectors and the government continued in a state of total crisis. This feeling of organizational accomplishment led to the belief . . . that the military possessed a superior capacity to confront the social problems which the civil authorities evidently could not solve.

168

Those problems included economic development and education. Under doctrines of "national security," borrowed from the United States and France, South American militaries expanded their organizational tasks to include all aspects of "development" as a means of undercutting the appeal of leftist doctrines and practices. "National security" came to mean almost any aspect of domestic political and economic life (cf. Barros and Coelho 1986: 441).

The problem was that these claims for extensive political participation (and rule in most of the Southern Cone countries during the 1970s) were not founded on a persuasive and acceptable doctrine of legitimacy. Military regimes, whatever their economic track record, came to rely extensively on human rights abuses – called "dirty wars" – to deal with dissidents and resistance. These further eroded support in the civil society. Faced with declining domestic support, they had several options: (1) pave the way for restoration of civilian rule and return to the barracks (Peru, Brazil, and Chile), (2) increase suppression of dissidence (Argentina); and/or (3) create a foreign policy crisis. Paraguay in 1966 and Argentina in 1978 and again in 1982 followed the latter path. Two – three if we include the 1995 incident – of the five major post-1945 militarized crises in South America were driven in part by the classical Machiavellian ploy of creating a foreign policy crisis in order to enhance popularity or legitimacy at home.

How do we interpret this brief analysis of domestic politics in South America? The problem is that it fails to explain the no-war zone of South America; the consequences of the institutional strength of the military are, in other words, indeterminate. All we can say is that contrary to popular assumptions, military rule does not necessarily lead to war. And civilian rule, particularly during the nineteenth century (and in 1995) did not lead to peace. There has been a South American no-war zone in the twentieth century whether civilian or military regimes governed. Domestic politics are no doubt important in explaining individual events, but variations between types of regimes do not correlate either with the overall incidence of crises and wars, or with a propensity to resolve conflicts peacefully (Treverton 1983; Morales 1984: 181).

Cultural/social explanations

More than other regions of the world, South America's diplomatic system is imbued with legal norms and a "culture" of legalism. We have already noted the profuse collection of multilateral and bilateral treaties and charters that impose obligations for the peaceful settlement of conflicts. Despite escape clauses in many of these (in cases, for example, where "vital" national interests or honor are involved), South American governments have frequently – and uniquely – chosen legal means for defusing actual or potential crises. There has also been a history of policy-makers analyzing issues from a legal rather than geostrategic perspective. Claims are based on legal interpretation instead of commercial or strategic arguments. While the latter are not ignored, concepts of justice underlie much of the discourse between governments in conflict. The Beagle Channel conflict was characterized by many in both Chile and Argentina in terms of obligations arising from nineteenth-century treaties and standard legal practices in locating sea and other territorial boundaries (cf. Infante 1984: 337–58). The Malvinas problem was similarly couched in legal discourse.

Constructing a conflict as essentially a legal dispute has its risks because arbitral procedures often result in win–lose outcomes rather than compromise. On the other hand, it also presupposes an outcome reached through argument and debate rather than through force. Once in the hands of arbitrators or mediators, there is a strong presumption against recourse to violence. There is a real cost in terms of prestige and "honor" in refusing to use peaceful conflict resolution procedures if the other party has accepted them.

But why should South America in the twentieth century be almost unique in its legalistic "diplomatic culture"? The question has not received systematic analysis, but some observers argue that in the region there is a tradition and sense of gaining honor by meeting legal obligations. The tradition is not divorced from questions of national interest. Rather, it *is* in the national interest to follow the law because it enhances reputation. Legalism is the intellectual milieu in which policy is often made. Lacking other commanding doctrines such as "manifest destiny," a civilizing mission, world revolution, or anti-communism, legalism helps establish the worth, reputation, and prestige of small countries on the margins of the central international system.

The foundations for legalism reside in the ancient Spanish and Portuguese tradition of appealing to Seville, Lisbon, or to the Pope to settle problems between the colonies, and in canon law, which is a judicial archetype. Those aspiring to be part of the South American elite have traditionally earned doctorates in civil or canon law, and until recently most foreign ministers and career diplomats held law degrees.

As with other explanations, cultural/social perspectives help us understand the unique importance of legal considerations and procedures in South American countries' policy-making and approaches to conflict. But they do not explain adequately the change between the nineteenth century, a time of chronic war and intervention, and the twentieth century, when a no-war zone developed. The plethora of bilateral and multilateral arbitration and peaceful conflict resolution treaties in the nineteenth century did not prevent numerous territorial claims, armed interventions, and wars.

Liberal-institutional explanations

At this point, liberal institutionalists would argue that the record of relative peace in South America during the twentieth century correlates significantly with the development of international institutions, democracy, and the growth of interdependence. The League of Nations was instrumental in resolving the Leticia dispute between Colombia, Peru, and Ecuador in the early 1930s. The Organization of American States and the United Nations have contemplated a number of disputes in the region since the end of World War II.

However, regional and universal international organizations have played only a peripheral role in conflict resolution in South America. Bolivia and Ecuador, the two main "revisionist" states of the continent, have appealed on numerous occasions to these bodies to help them in their claims. Results have been meager, taking the form usually of innocuous resolutions urging the parties to engage in negotiations to resolve the problem. In fact, not a single territorial/resource conflict in South America since 1945 has been resolved through the intervention of an international organization. South American governments have strongly favored *ad hoc* arbitral and mediation procedures outside of the context of international organizations. Indeed, appeals to the OAS or United Nations are made more for the purpose of embarrassing adversaries than as serious bids for resolving issues. A convincing argument that international institutions have been a primary source of peace and peaceful conflict resolution in South America does not hold up well against the evidence.

The growth of democracy fails to explain the change from a classical anarchical system of international politics to a no-war system. Most

171

governments in South America during the period up to the 1980s were not democracies. And, as we have seen, the incidence of crises and wars does not correlate with type of regime.

Economic interdependence explanations are equally unpersuasive. Trade within South America has traditionally been a minuscule proportion of the countries' total foreign trade. Communications linking national capitals are lacking or underdeveloped, with only airline routes carrying significant passenger traffic. Significant changes in trade and communications towards patterns of high density are only beginning to take place. Compared to North America or Europe, South America has remained throughout most of the twentieth century an area of low communication, social transactions, and commerce.

Strong states as an explanation

The argument of this study is that communities of strong states are sites of peace, while regions of weak states are sites of domestic and international war. In the South American case, we must keep in mind the distinction between the strength of states and the popularity of governments (see chapter 5). Domestic politics in South America are unstable, featuring a high turnover of governments and government personnel. Voters may be alienated from particular governments. However, they generally accept and defend the overall constitutional order, including its territorial dimensions and integrity.

Nineteenth-century South American states were strong at the rhetorical level of acceptance. There was both implicit and explicit acknowledgement that the new states would be the legitimate successors to the individual Spanish and Portuguese colonies. Simon Bolivar's dream of a United States of Latin America did not survive his death, and by 1846 all the former colonies (Ecuador had torn itself away from "Gran Colombia") had recognized each other's sovereignty. But states had little legitimacy in terms of mutually respecting the limits of territorial jurisdiction. Nineteenth-century South American states were inherently weak because most frontiers were not adequately defined and a number of states successfully plundered their neighbors. Governments could come and go, sometimes through elections, more often through *coups d'état*, but all faced the prospects of being downsized by a neighbor. All faced the classical security dilemma: the means to protect oneself were seen by others as a threat to their own territorial integrity. Arms-racing, regional balances of power, and war were the results.

172

Weak states also face problems of domestic vertical and horizontal legitimacy. Many South American countries in the nineteenth century lacked local acceptance, strong civil societies, and political integration. Civil wars were common and military or civilian officials ruled more through threats, coercion, and oppression than through consent. These aspects of state weakness were frequently the source of international complications and external intervention. Horizontal legitimacy was less of a problem, at least among the elites. The successors to colonial society were characterized by hierarchy and cleavages according to color. Those at the bottom, the mestizos and full-blooded Indians and blacks, were mostly excluded from politics. Their consent was neither sought nor necessary and most of them adopted passive and quietistic attitudes toward politics. They were simply not part of the political game until well into the twentieth century.

Have things changed in the twentieth century? The record of government turnovers, coups, and domestic instability would suggest not. However, on the external dimension, the territorial identity of the states has become more firmly established. Remaining territorial disputes are not likely to be resolved by armed force and most of them involve relatively small parcels of land or await only the precise demarcation of frontier lines in remote or nearly inaccessible areas. The two major exceptions are Bolivia and Ecuador, both of which hold major grievances deriving from lost wars in 1884 and 1941. Other territorial revisions of the nineteenth century have been more or less accepted by the losers.

On the domestic dimensions of state strength, vertical and horizontal legitimacy, some of the fundamental weaknesses of the nineteenth century have been ameliorated but not resolved. Recall from the figures in chapter 2 that the incidence of domestic war in South America since 1945 has not been significantly lower than the patterns found in Africa, the Middle East, South Asia, Southeast Asia, the Balkans, and among some former Soviet republics. Terrorist and guerrilla campaigns continue. Social cleavages have been expressed primarily through Marxist-inspired rebellions and armed resistance to military dictatorships and, more recently, by political action to prevent ecological depredations by national and international companies and population movements. Indigenous and other disaffected groups, however, have not sought secession as a solution to their problems. We must also acknowledge that, unlike many of the countries born after 1945, South American countries have a strong tradition of republicanism in the Kantian sense:

a polity under the rule of law, with the rules of the political game carefully defined by constitutional provisions. The habits and hopes of republicanism, despite numerous deviations in practice, remain highly embedded in citizens' political consciousness.

South American governments of whatever ideological stripe therefore legitimate themselves primarily by adopting the stance of protectors of the state and constitution. Military regimes, such as those in Brazil in the 1960s and 1970s, made themselves appear to rule constitutionally. There was an emphasis on the facades of democracy: tolerating within limits a few opposition parties, retaining a legislature, and rewriting constitutions to correct the weaknesses of the predecessors. Most military regimes also emphasized the *temporary* nature of their rule. According to Rouquié (1986: 448), "[t]hey must invoke [democratic transition] for their own legitimation and in their own policy objectives, while at the same time proposing to improve, reinforce, amend, and even protect it, but never to annihilate or destroy it as has been the case elsewhere." Thus, while publics in South America hold politicians of whatever stripe in low esteem, they are deeply committed to republican principles (cf. Fitch 1986: 32) and to the idea of constitutionalism. Military regimes have had to take these sentiments into account.

South American governments in the twentieth century, in contrast to their cousins in Central America, by and large have not used the state as an instrument of predation against subgroups of the citizenry. While treatment of indigenous populations is an important exception and leaves much to be desired even today, the brutal policies of extermination and systematic exploitation of the nineteenth century have for the most part abated. The secession phenomenon, a major indicator of state weakness in many post-1945 states, has been largely absent in twentieth-century South America. Indeed, all of South America is anomalous compared to other regions of the world because communal minority activism has taken the form of non-violent protest, and even that has declined significantly since the mid-1980s (Gurr 1991: 7–8). Respect for human rights among the indigenous has grown. There are numerous "minorities," but they are defined as citizens of the state and whatever the divergences in practice, they are slowly gaining equal rights with others (cf. Aylwin 1992). Internal wars in South America have been of the ideological rather than resistance/secessionist type.

Like Western Europe, South American states have systematically strengthened their role vis-à-vis civil society, and since the 1930s have become the "decisive motor and actor in the development process" (Nohlen and Fernandez 1990: 77). They have developed a reasonable balance between extraction and the provision of services. Many of the characteristics of weak states outlined in chapter 6 exist in South America, but at levels much lower than found elsewhere in the Third World or among some of the former Soviet republics.

Finally, levels of national identification are strengthening. Andes Indian and other indigenous peoples tend to identify with their language and cultural kin no matter where located, but politically active classes – significantly broadened since the 1930s – have pronounced sentiments of nationality. Others in South America are "cousins," but are nevertheless identified as foreigners. Unlike Western Europe, the sentiment of continental political integration is weak. Economic logic and continental identifications have not replaced the nationalist/statist logic and sentiment.

Toward a zone of peace? System transformation at the end of the millennium

In the past two decades there have been important turning points and trends in South America which suggest that the region may be moving from a no-war zone to something akin to a zone of peace.

Transformations from a no-war to a peace zone may occur suddenly after a traumatic event or learning experience, as was the case in Europe after World War II. In South America, the transformation is taking longer, but some key events and trends have propelled the process to the point where it may have become irreversible.

Brazil–Argentine relations had been for more than a century a pivot of conflict and tension on the continent. Exacerbated by geopolitical thinking in both countries, rapid Brazilian growth rates, Brazilian presence in Bolivia, Paraguay, and Uruguay, and an incipient nuclear technology race, the 1950s and 1960s were an era of substantial distrust, occasional crises, but no war.

Brazilian leadership in the late 1970s recast its relationship to Argentina primarily by "de-politicizing" it and playing down its military dimensions. President Figueiredo assumed a key role in changing the style and content of Brazil's stance toward Argentina. After forty years without a Brazil–Argentina summit meeting, he met with his Argentine counterpart five times between 1980 and 1985 (Selcher 1985). According to Selcher (1985: 31):

175

The state, war, and the state of war

> What has occurred has been termed a "conceptual leap," a new way of approaching the relationship . . . Supposition of an overarching, permanent rivalry has given way to a more reasonable, problem-solving attitude . . . With the decline of prestige considerations as motivators, the sphere of influence race in the three "buffer" states has subsided.

Issues were redefined in terms of economic progress rather than as territorial and hegemonic problems.

A second stimulus to new patterns of relationships was the Argentine defeat in the 1982 Malvinas War and the subsequent installation of the democratically elected Alfonsin government in December 1983. While South American governments (except Chile) publicly supported Argentina in its conflict with Great Britain, in private many governments were pleased with the outcome of the war. Argentina's bellicosity against Chile over the Beagle Channel problem had raised fears of escalation to include Peru and Bolivia. The Malvinas debacle spelled the end of the military regime in Argentina, a government that in addition to fighting its "dirty war" at home, also dabbled in foreign intervention (Bolivia and Nicaragua), and propounded a set of geopolitical doctrines that were seen in other countries as threatening to them. After the defeat, the geopoliticians in Buenos Aires lost influence. They were replaced by advisors with a distinct enthusiasm for economic cooperation and integration.

These trends and events multiplied into a blizzard of Brazil–Argentine agreements, the foremost of which was the 1979 Itaipú treaty to regulate exploitation of the Parana River's hydroelectric potential. Subsequently Argentina signed the Treaty of Tlatelolco and for lack of funds, an external enemy, and American pressures, abandoned its Condor II IRBM missile program (Hirst and Rico 1993, 253–4). Brazil and Argentina then agreed to forgo the development of nuclear weapons. They are now constructing a major highway linking São Paulo to Buenos Aires; trade between the two countries has increased from $2 billion in 1990 to $6 billion in 1993 (*New York Times*, April 8, 1994).

A second major turning point was the 1984 settlement of the Beagle Channel dispute between Argentina and Chile. This agreement was followed up by economic cooperation and other agreements that include oil and gas pipelines between the two countries – formerly an Argentine strategic taboo (Hirst and Rico 1993: 256 fn. 3) – a railroad tunnel, and the settlement of numerous frontier location problems in the Andes (*New York Times*, April 8, 1994; Selcher 1990: 88).

176

Table 8.1 *Changing roles and tasks of the military in South America* (from Varas 1987)

Dimensions	Conceptions of security	
	Traditional	Modern
Internal	Military repression	Political action
Interstatal	Equipment and men	Mutual confidence-building measures
Regional	Military equilibrium	Military cooperation
Global	Defense of the West	Social interests

South American military institutions are undergoing important doctrinal and capability changes. Augusto Varas (1987: 7) has urged reform of military tasks along the lines of table 8.1.

Though Varas may not have made his analysis in the expectation that South American military establishments would actually follow academic advice, some have recast their tasks in similar terms. In Brazil, the tasks have been defined increasingly in terms of dealing with subversion (a holdover from the 1960s and 1970s) and socio-political threats, as well as controlling narco-traffic and illegal migration from neighboring countries. Another relatively new task is to promote scientific–technological progress throughout the country. More traditional tasks seek to unify the country through developing transportation systems and inculcating national values through education. Conceptions of helping to "defend the West" against communism or promoting naval power projection into the vastness of the South Atlantic have been discarded (cf. Bustamente 1993: 129–53).

Elsewhere in South America military institutions are trying to define new concepts of security, roles, and tasks (for detailed discussion, see Hirst and Rico 1993: 257–68). The concept of providing services is slowly lowering the classical priority of protecting territory. Even retired generals are writing significant and sophisticated proposals for altering traditional concepts and organizations for security (cf. Jarrin 1989, esp. p. 64 and chs. 7, 9. and 11). In Ecuador, environmental protection, education of marginal populations, preventing "spillover" of guerrilla activities from neighboring countries (Colombia), and controlling narco-trafficking are current priorities. It is particularly significant that environmental protection has become one of several "permanent national objectives" that must be achieved by the Ecuadorian military (Chamorro 1994).

What is significant about these new tasks, services, and roles is that most can be fulfilled only through cooperation with the military authorities of neighboring states. While remaining a largely autonomous and non-transparent[4] institution within society, the notion of social service, albeit in a paternalistic mode, is developing rapidly.

There is also increasing transparency in capabilities and deployments. In August 1988, Chile and Argentina held joint naval exercises in the Beagle Channel (*Keesings Contempory Archives*, December 1988, 36346). Following practices developed in the Organization on Security and Cooperation in Europe, there are now numerous South American bilateral arrangements for observing maneuvers, exchanging military information, and exchanging officers in the various countries' military academies. Commanders-in-chief of the armies, navies and air forces hold annual conferences in different capitals.

Finally, economic stringencies have compelled the military establishments to scale down arms acquisitions. Military spending declined steeply for all South American countries in the 1980s, as much a function of recession and severe debt and budget deficit problems as a recasting of military tasks. South American countries are, in effect, disarming due to financial constraints. Peru's capabilities, for example, are only 30 percent effective at the time of writing.

The signs of expanding commercial and political networks are evident everywhere in South America. Complementing the more than quarter-century-old Andean Pact (Grupo Andino), the Mercosur free trade area has dramatically helped increase commerce among the Southern Cone countries; in 1994 Colombia, Venezuela, and Mexico drafted their version of NAFTA; the resurrected 1978 Amazon Treaty fosters military cooperation among eight signatories, primarily in civic roles; and the annual Ibero-American summits bring together the heads of state of the entire region, along with those of Central America, Spain, and Portugal.

The democratization of the continent has underlain all this growing network of activity, economic liberalization, and re-definition of

[4] In many countries of South America, there is no parliamentary control of military budgets. Funding remains secret. In many other ways, the military are kept separate from the rest of society.

military tasks.[5] Democratic institutions are fragile in some countries, but there are few available options. Most of the military regimes of the 1970s and 1980s were thoroughly discredited. On the other side, many guerrilla groups look increasingly like bandit organizations rather than ideologically inspired political formations. A small armed group in Ecuador threw in the towel in June 1994, and the fortunes of the Sendero Luminoso have withered though not disappeared since the capture of its leadership.

There is growing mutual support for civilian political authority. In meetings in Macchu Pichu and the Galapagos in 1989, South American governments agreed not to recognize governments that came to power through means other than elections. There have even been preliminary discussions to create a multilateral force to sustain or restore democratic regimes under assault. The idea has not been approved by several governments and remains primarily a matter of academic discussion rather than military planning, but similar ideas have appeared in discussions of a South American "peace force," perhaps as the next logical step for Mercosur.

Finally, some governments are approaching traditional tension areas with bold new proposals that alter win/lose situations into possibilities for mutual gains through cooperation. In the first-ever visit by a Peruvian president to neighboring Ecuador in 1992, Alberto Fujimori proposed a variety of areas where the two countries could cooperate for mutual advantage. While not conceding Peru's claim that the territory it gained in 1941 is an integral part of the country, the proposals seek to promote joint Peru–Ecuador exploitation of resources, development of agriculture, transport and communications, energy, tourism, and fishing, and to undertake educational and health programs among the vast territory's sparse population. These ambitious programs would be overseen by a bi-national executive committee (Ecuador 1992). However, the fragile and tenuous nature of such initiatives is indicated by yet another armed incident between Peru and Ecuador in January 1995. If there is significant movement toward a zone of peace, particularly in the southern cone, it is not yet achieved in some areas. Bolivia and Ecuador remain territorially dissatisfied states.

The overall trends of the last two decades of the millennium – with

---

[5] For a theoretical discussion and case studies linking democratization to integration and other foreign policy problems, see Nohlen and Fernandez (1991).

Colombia as a probable exception – is in the direction of stronger states, increasing vertical and horizontal legitimacy for governments, broadening civil societies, economic liberalization, dramatic increases in personal contacts between the countries' political and military leaders, and a slow but evident re-definition of military tasks from protection of territory and national honor to providing social services. As these developments continue, the prospects for armed crises recede. South America appears to be moving from a no-war zone toward a zone of peace.

The theoretical significance of the South American states system

The recent flurry of studies of the theory of the "democratic peace" follows upon Kant's argument that a necessary condition for peace between states is constitutional republics. Recent research (cf. Doyle 1986) has established what Jack Levy (1989: 270) calls one of the few empirically established generalizations in the study of international relations: democracies do not make war against each other.

There are some empirical problems with the generalization. They arise primarily from the Clausewitzian definition of war that is used in the analysis. The "democratic peace" is identified by the lack of armed combat between the organized military forces of two or more states. This type of analysis overlooks the use of coercive techniques short of formal war. Democracies have with some regularity subverted popularly elected regimes through clandestine actions, subversion, and economic coercion. The joint American–British destabilization of the Mossadeq regime in Iran in 1951; American subversion of a freely elected government in Guatemala in 1954; French armed intervention to sustain beleaguered military regimes in Africa *against* popular movements; and the American destabilization of the elected Allende government in Chile during 1972–3 are just some of the documented cases. Western democracies may not war against each other, but Western democracies also seem to hold a veto over the politics and policies of democracies elsewhere.

But the peace-through-democracy theory has gone beyond celebrating an empirically valid generalization in a field of study. Theorists and researchers have taken the next normative step, following Kant's argument: democracy is a *necessary* condition for peace. This proposition is implicit in the work of Deutsch where, almost by definition, expanding communication flows, development of mutual empathies and responsiveness, and growth of common values cannot develop between closed societies.

The analysis in this chapter raises the question whether in fact democracy is a necessary condition for peace. In South America since 1941 there has been a no-war zone despite the fact that in that period many governments were not democratic in the original sense of the word (e.g., periodic elections; civil liberties; free press; legal opposition). Empirical research (Treverton 1983) in the South American case shows that in fact the nature of a regime tends to be irrelevant to the incidence of crises, wars, and successful conflict resolution (cf. Morales 1984: 181). The 1981 and 1995 border incidents between Peru and Ecuador occurred when elected governments were in office. The 1981 story reveals more about the autonomy of the military (which launched the incident) in the countries than it does about relations between democracies (Varas 1983: 77), while the 1995 episode shows that even constitutional and elected leaders may use a crisis for enhancing their personal popularity during an electoral campaign. Both suggest that democracy may not be the key explanation for absence of armed combat; it is, rather, the strong state in combination with several other forms of explanation reviewed above.

The strong state explanation of the no-war zone is not in itself sufficient, however. But it is necessary. There is a significant correlation between growing state strength in South America between the nineteenth and twentieth centuries, and decline in the incidence of internal wars, armed crises, interstate wars, and interventions. Other explanations for the South American anomaly are nevertheless necessary as well. Local deterrents have worked; revisionist powers, in particular, might have been tempted to right historical wrongs (in their view) in the absence of countervailing military power. The South American system cannot be understood adequately, either, without recognition of the strong legal tradition that has underlain regional diplomacy. The pattern of conflict resolution in the twentieth century is unique when compared to other regions of the world. That uniqueness can best be understood as deriving from historical traditions, culture, and the importance small states place on laws and norms as protective devices. This chapter has sought to provide further evidence for the strong state–peace connection. But it acknowledges that other forms of explanation, including elements of neo-realism, also increase our understanding of this theoretically important anomaly in the history of international politics.

The transformation of international politics in South America, as well as in Europe, during the late twentieth century suggests that Rousseauian, neo-realist characteristics of international relations can change and even become obsolete. States can overcome the security dilemma and learn to live in reasonable harmony with each other. But there is scant evidence that the trajectories of these two continents are being emulated elsewhere. Weak states persist and some will collapse bringing in the wake of their downfall millions of civilian casualties, more millions of refugees, and unpredictable international responses. A sense of optimism deriving from an examination of the South American move from a classical zone of war and all its accoutrements toward a zone of peace must be tempered by the critical difficulties weak states continue to pose. The final question is: what can the international community do about the state-strength dilemma and its legacies of death and despair?

9 International responses to the weak state: managing and resolving wars of the third kind

What to do? If the diagnosis of future wars of the third kind is essentially correct, then the solution to the problem lies predominantly within states themselves. Weak states must become stronger, and those on the trajectory of failure must turn themselves around. The only other possibility is to develop an alternative to the state, or at least to the state as it has been so far conceived and institutionalized in practice. This would mean, in effect, to reverse the long historical process of political homogenization. But this is a hypothetical subject that needs separate treatment. The more immediate solution is to strengthen existing states.

This is eminently simple in theory and extremely difficult in practice because of the state-strength dilemma. Students of international relations are not, in any case, particularly well equipped to provide advice. Development analysts with vision and sensitivity, as well as comparative politics analysts have no doubt more to offer. Most important is the knowledge gained by those who have succeeded in transforming colonial entities into states on the trajectory of strength.

The fundamental problem is the state-strength dilemma: many of the steps governments take to strengthen the state and to enhance vertical and horizontal legitimacy bring about unintended consequences that actually undermine the coherence of the state. The dilemmas are numerous; some examples are worth underlining.

A standard post-1989 policy solution has been "democratization." Through the mechanism of regular elections and the institutionalization of political parties, many have argued, both the horizontal and vertical dimensions of legitimacy will be strengthened. Despots, militaries, and regimes based on the oppression of out-groups by in-groups will give way to regular turnover of officeholders. It is not clear, however, exactly how formal voting mechanisms will help deal with central-centrifugal conflicts, corruption, patrimonial ties, bureaucratic perquisites, and many of the other problems that afflict weak states, but at least they might help establish new modes of political competition in which individuals and communal groups attain prospects for gaining access to decision-making and to the distribution of government services. The implicit state-extraction-for-state-services contract might shift, in other words, toward the service side for most segments of the population.

But democratic institutions in certain social environments have their own risks. In a society characterized by strong group cleavages, elections might become little more than a census (see below in connection with Bosnia) through which majorities and minorities become permanent. Equal opportunity for access to decisions and government allocations then becomes difficult and, as has often been shown in practice (e.g., Sudan, Sri Lanka, Myanmar), even impossible. Democratic institutions such as elections and parties may not solve the state-strength dilemma in milieux where political programs and identities revolve primarily around social cleavages.

Another solution, taken in conjunction with democratization, is to devolve political power along territorial lines. This is the federalist principle, for which there are numerous arguments and diverse arrangements. This is not the place to explore all the ramifications of this alternative, one that has many advantages, including flexibility. But how it works in socially fragmented societies may differ from how it works in predominantly single-culture societies. A flexible and substantially decentralized federal system, as in Canada, has not prevented the Parti Québécois and its adherents from wanting "un pays comme les autres" – an independent state. Nor did the complicated arrangements in Yugoslavia prevent several bloody wars. In situations where the state is already weak – as is not the case in Canada and was not in ex-Yugoslavia – a loose federal system may actually strengthen the separatist forces by guaranteeing them central government revenues, local police forces, and other assets they can convert to the secessionist cause. In the Gorbachev era, the re-negotiation of the Soviet federal system led not to a re-defined horizontal legitimacy principle, but to the collapse of the federation. In Zaïre, Chad, and Sudan splintering administrative boundaries – a form of devolution – acted as a stimulus for the rise of factions. Though intended to accommodate ethnic pressures, devolution and administrative map re-drawing resulted in a proliferation of local disputes, often focused on competition over new sources of patronage created by the multiplication of administrative units (Lemarchand 1987: 157).

Federalism is also no guarantee for the security and well-being of small populations such as "people of the frontier," indigenous tribes, and religious sects. In their case, it is not so much their perpetual marginalization in *any* constitutional arrangement, but the depredations that "economic development" may make upon their territories and cultures. No federal system prevents this. Central and regional governments claim, of course, that economic development is a major ingredient of the state-strengthening process. The state cannot deliver the services necessary for enhancing vertical legitimacy without exploiting forests, lands, and seas. But the policies that governments pursue to augment their economic and bureaucratic capabilities may actually undermine or erode their authority and legitimacy among those who are the victims of development. This is the heart of the state-strength dilemma. There are, in other words, no simple solutions, but many contradictions and quandaries.

To address such dilemmas in a manner that is not self-defeating requires knowledge of relatively successful states. This does not mean the United States, Germany, Canada, or Switzerland, but India, Malaysia, Mauritius, Lesotho, Tunisia, and many others. None is yet a strong state, but all have moved in the direction of strength despite enormous odds. India, in particular, has defied with some success all the fissiparous tendencies that would have been natural to a geographical expression made up of every major religion in the world, numerous ethnic groups, dozens of major languages, and a formal caste system. Yet, by insisting upon a secular state based on citizenship, combined with elaborate programs to instill a sense of Indian nationhood, the creation of many states based primarily on language (rather than the historical state frontiers), and rigorous efforts to separate state institutions from religious cleavages, India has more or less worked. Jawaharlal Nehru's philosophy of "unity through diversity" was translated into political institutions that carefully balanced localisms and the need for strong central government. Above all, he sought to prevent religious and language differences and affinities from becoming issues of political significance. He emphasized instead issues of development, equality, education, employment, and foreign policy independence. "A nation's foremost duty is to strengthen and preserve its freedom," he suggested.

> If we give importance to other things, like our religion, our [regional]
> state, our language or our caste, and forget our country, we shall be
> destroyed. All these have their proper place, but if we place [them]
> above the country, the nation will be destroyed.
>
> (quoted in Chand 1989: 101)

Nehru's philosophy did not rely solely on constant efforts at persuasion. The 1947 constitution and subsequent amendments – the sixteenth (1963) in particular – attempted to proscribe separatist political
activities. Advocacy by word or deed of anything against the sovereignty or territorial integrity of India is a penal offence not protected
by the fundamental rights provisions of the constitution. All officials,
including state and federal legislators, are required to take an oath to
uphold the sovereignty and integrity of the country (Kodikara 1991:
108).[1]

Constitutional provisions cannot prevent political fragmentation.
Indeed, they may raise other problems. One risk of such provisions is
that those who are committed to separatism are forced into extra-legal
channels. They have no opportunity to make their case through legal
means. However, constitutional provisions may have a certain deterrent effect on secessionists by (1) putting the onus of change on them,
and (2) by guaranteeing access to decisions and allocations to all
segments of the population.

India has continuing problems in Punjab, Kashmir, and elsewhere.
Religion has become a major political issue, as Nehru's secular philosophy has been breached by adherents of Hindu and other fundamentalisms. One political party, the BJP, is a thinly disguised Hindu
revivalist organization which has found nevertheless that holding
power under a secular constitution and promoting Hindu supremacy
are incompatible. Given the choice, maintaining political power has
been more important.

India is no perfect model of a strengthening state, but if one wants to
learn some of the techniques of state-creation and survival under
extremely difficult circumstances, then it is worth serious examination
both for the dos and don'ts.

There are too many states, however, which are not successfully
solving the state-strength dilemma. As a result, there will be many
wars of the third kind, or as Leslie Gelb has termed them (1994: 6),

[1] Such constitutional provisions are not rare. A French law of 1936 similarly makes the
advocacy or planning of any action inconsistent with France's unity an indictable
offense.

"wars of national debilitation." They will have consequences for the international system as a whole, thus rendering the idea of a universal no-war zone or zone of peace highly problematic (cf. Buzan 1991: 157). Some states will also collapse, and since annexation and territorial expansion are unavailable as means of solving the problem, the international community in general, and the United Nations in particular, will have to do something about them. Standard policies of state strengthening, such as foreign aid and arms sales, will no doubt continue but, as indicated in chapter 7, their consequences are problematic; in some instances they work to exacerbate the state-strength dilemma, not solve it. The international norm of the maintenance and sustenance of states' territorial integrity may also help, but in recent years this norm has come under question because of ambiguous positions taken by the United Nations and various of its members. Whatever the case, there will continue to be international involvement in the affairs of weak and collapsing states. Concern for massive human rights abuses and for streams of refugees guarantees it.

Is the United Nations philosophically and politically equipped to take on state-sustenance and state-resuscitation projects? How can an organization designed to regulate and manage relations *between* states deal effectively with the problem of war *within* states? This is an issue of the fundamental purposes and nature of the organization. In its constitutional dimension, the problem is that by using effective action to prevent, contain, or end wars of the third kind, the United Nations must necessarily violate the fundamental Westphalian norm of non-interference in the internal affairs of states. But the constitutional problem is ultimately less significant than the philosophical problem of what *kind* of state the United Nations will sustain or restore. In some cases, it is also a problem of what kind of state the UN will help to create.

This second problem of the United Nations' role in state-making and perpetuation is seen most notably in the organization's efforts at conflict resolution and peacemaking. To date, the long-range results of United Nations actions in these domains have been generally ignored; the emphasis has been, perhaps understandably, just to stop the killing. But containing a conflict is not the same as making a settlement or peace. And if the peace is to command domestic and international support, it must be founded on certain principles, particularly those that enhance vertical and horizontal legitimacy. If the principles are wrong, then the peace may become just a prelude to revisionism and future war. To appreciate more adequately the difficulties in the constitutional and state-sustaining problems, it is necessary to review briefly how United Nations tasks have changed during the past decades.

The founding fathers' image of the United Nations

Go back to San Francisco in April 1945 when the delegates of fifty-two countries met to negotiate the final text of the United Nations' Charter. This was a time of great hope – Nazi Germany was on the verge of surrender – but also of sorrow. The human and material costs of World War II were historically unprecedented – even before the first atomic bombs were dropped on Hiroshima and Nagasaki. The record of serial military aggressions of the 1930s was also unprecedented in the history of the European states system: Germany had militarily conquered seven countries in addition to a large portion of the Soviet Union. Prior to the Nazi invasion of Russia, Stalin had annexed the three Baltic states, and large parts of Poland, Bessarabia, and Finland. Italy had conquered Ethiopia and Albania. Japan set up a satellite state in Manchuria, launched a war against China, and invaded European colonies in Indochina, Malaya, Burma, Hong Kong, Singapore, and Indonesia, and the American colony in the Philippines. Not since the Thirty Years War of the seventeenth century had there been such an orgy of military aggressions.

Given this record and the immense human misery it caused, it is not surprising that the delegates at San Francisco sought to create a particular kind of international organization. Looking backward rather than to the future, they defined its main tasks in light of the events of the previous decade. The United Nations was to provide general international security and to protect the smaller states of the system. In the Charter's original format negotiated by Roosevelt, Stalin, and Churchill during the war, the great powers would take on special responsibilities for maintaining international peace and security. This predominant position of the great powers was diluted through the negotiations in San Francisco, but the tasks of the organization were not altered fundamentally. The United Nations was designed to prevent, and should that fail, to help resolve armed conflicts *between states*. Threats to security, as Rousseau maintained, were external to the state. What went on within states was of no immediate concern to the organization; indeed, the Charter (Art. 2, par. 7) specifically prohibits

United Nations actions that touch upon matters "essentially within the domestic jurisdiction" of states.

The United Nations' Charter is a Westphalian document *par excellence*. Only states can become members of the organization. Membership requirements are only two: a commitment to the principles of the Charter, which sustain the territorial sovereignty principle, and a declaration of being "peace-loving." There are no entrance requirements that refer to the internal arrangements of states. The Charter prohibits actions dealing with members' domestic politics. The major purpose of the organization is thus to protect the territorial integrity, sovereignty, and independence of its members. Concerns with the conditions of populations within states are secondary, perhaps only negligible. The only constraint on sovereignty is the prohibition against the threat or use of force except for self-defense or when ordered by the Security Council.

Shortly after the creation of the organization in San Francisco, wars of the third kind, called "wars of national liberation," became increasingly frequent. They had not been anticipated by the drafters of the Charter, and they presented some new intellectual challenges. If there were no declarations of war, classical-type campaigns, and organized armies, was there in fact a war? Who were the victims? Where was the "threat to peace, breach of peace, or act of aggression" that must occur before the Security Council can take action?

Because new Third World countries constituted a majority within the General Assembly, these wars were characterized as legitimate armed struggles to give effect to the principle of self-determination of colonial peoples. Wars of national liberation, their defenders argued, were not wars between states; their antecedents were not the aggressions of the 1930s, but the American, Greek, and other wars of independence. They were wars of a different kind, a kind of "just war" not covered in the Charter. Numerous resolutions, and even Article 7 of the Definition of Aggression (General Assembly Resolution 3314 [XXIX], 1974), recognizes the legitimacy of the struggle of peoples under colonial or alien domination. This implies the right of peoples to struggle by every means available to them, including by the use of force (cf. Espiell 1980: 14–20). Wars between states are outlawed in the Charter; anti-colonial wars are actively promoted in post-1945 resolutions, pronouncements, and practice.

Expanding tasks and changing norms since 1989

But if secession, resistance, and liberation wars remain a frequent occurrence resulting from weak and failed states, how can the United Nations constitutionally deal with them? It has resorted to the device of labeling virtually any situation under Chapter VII as a "threat to the peace." This need not entail a state threatening another state, as the founders of the United Nations envisaged. It is enough that domestic populations are either at risk or actually suffering. Peace, in other words, has been redefined as a condition *within* states rather than one between them. Thus, Security Council Resolution 794 of December 3, 1992 stated that the condition of starvation in Somalia was a "threat to the peace" justifying the use of "all necessary means" including a massive United Nations-sponsored military intervention, to provide security for the delivery of humanitarian assistance (Thakur 1994: 395). Similarly, it was not necessary for the Cedras regime in Haiti to threaten a neighbor; it was enough for it to murder several hundred opponents and to cause a refugee outflow headed for the United States to warrant international sanctions and eventually armed intervention. In such instances, the United Nations has taken on the tasks of state sustenance, resuscitation, and restoration without great concern for legal niceties.

In dealing with internal wars and failed states, the Security Council has recently passed a number of other resolutions that undermine or alter the norms of sovereignty and non-interference. These resolutions and the follow-up actions provide evidence of a fundamental change in the purposes of the United Nations. They are evidence of the adaptability of the organization to deal with problems of weak and failed states unforeseen in 1945. They include:

1. organizing a massive military intervention to provide security for the delivery of food and medicine to war and starvation victims in Somalia, without a request from or the consent of the government of the country;
2. establishing non-combat corridors to provide relief to civilians (Bosnia);
3. establishing safe havens for civilians (six towns in Bosnia) which precludes any form of military attack by the belligerents in those areas;

4. creating no-fly zones *within* sovereign states, without the consent of the government (Iraq and Bosnia);

5. creating a protected area for the Iraqi Kurdish population under threat of massacre by Iraqi troops;

6. dispatching a force to Macedonia to deter (symbolically) a Serbian military attack against Albanians in Kosovo and Macedonia;

7. authorizing members to use military force to oust the military regime and to restore a popularly elected government in Haiti.[2] This resolution is all the more significant since many United Nations members are themselves ruled by military regimes that have ousted popularly-elected presidents.

There are other resolutions as well, but this list makes the point that United Nations actions toward internal wars have fundamentally stretched – or in some cases violated – the Westphalian norms incorporated into the Charter in 1945. Like many domestic constitutions, the principles of the founders are altered and sometimes jettisoned in new circumstances. It is hard to imagine that the delegates to San Francisco in 1945 would have approved any of these resolutions. Only a very broad interpretation of the United Nations' Charter could justify them. But most significantly, the purpose of the United Nations in the case of restoring states has not been just to re-establish public authority and some semblance of coherent governance. It has also been to create a particular *kind* of government, namely a democracy, no matter how unlikely this could be in places like Somalia (cf. Thakur 1994: 404). There was an implicit acknowledgement, in other words, that other types of political systems will not resolve the state-strength dilemma. Kampuchea is one apparent success. Bosnia may be a failure.

United Nations' actions in Kampuchea illustrate how the organization has vastly expanded its responsibilities to accord with the new purpose of state restoration. In addition to the usual peacekeeping (monitoring) functions, the United Nations took on a vast programme of state reconstitution that included police activities, engineering (road

---

[2] The relevant parts of this significant resolution read: "Determining that the situation in Haiti . . . continues to constitute a threat to peace and security in the region, [and] . . . acting under Chapter VII of the Charter of the United Nations, [the Security Council] authorizes Member States to form a multinational force under unified command and control and, in this framework, to use all necessary means to facilitate the departure from Haiti of the military leadership [and] the prompt return of the legitimately elected President (see *New York Times*, August 1, 1994).

and bridge-building), health and sanitation, organizing and monitoring elections, and the actual administration of Kampuchean government programs and agencies. The United Nations was the *de facto* government of a sovereign state for a limited period in the early 1990s. It maintained some semblance of authority until the warring factions negotiated an arrangement that approximated Western concepts of popular government. Most significantly, the new government had to base its legitimacy on popular sanction. There was never any thought that a reconstituted state should be created paternalistically by the United Nations, with itself naming governors and assigning them their tasks. Kampuchea may not retain its outward semblance of a democracy, but if it returns to prewar patterns of clientelism and virtual rule by divine right, the blame will not go to the United Nations but to the Kampucheans themselves.

To date, this operation seems to have been a success although it has received little publicity and even fewer accolades. It stands in stark contrast to the apparent failure of the state-resuscitation project in Somalia and to the failure to prevent the massacres of Rwanda and Liberia. What is particularly notable about the Kampuchean operation is the innovative activities that the United Nations' organized and administered. They went far beyond normal peacekeeping tasks to include state re-building and governance. Most of this was accomplished with the consent of most of the Kampuchean factions. While the United Nations operation was basically a resuscitation of a failed state under previous foreign occupation, there was never any question about the legitimacy of the overall purpose: it was to create a viable, sovereign, and democratic Kampuchea.

The creation of states and conflict resolution: the Bosnia prototype

The operations in Bosnia are more problematic. United Nations resolutions and actions raise numerous legal and political problems, not the least of which is the moral foundations of a political community. At issue in Bosnia, which is prototypical of wars of the third kind and the state-strength dilemma, are three fundamental problems: (1) what does "conflict resolution" mean in a civil war involving not just political factions but entire communities?; (2) what does peace mean, or what is a settlement?; and (3) if the ex-Yugoslavia is to be reconstituted into several independent states, what should be the philosophical and moral bases of those states? On what principles should the international community seek to establish viable states with reasonable vertical and horizontal legitimacy?

Conflict resolution in Bosnia: the dilemmas of United Nations intervention in wars of the third kind

The founders of the United Nations provided mechanisms for preventing war. Chapter VII of the Charter enables the Security Council to apply economic and military sanctions in the event that it has determined a member's actions to be a threat to or breach of the peace, or an act of aggression. To provide the means of deterrence, the United Nations was to design a multinational armed force made up of contingents – primarily from the great powers – of member states. The Military Staff Committee (MSC) was charged with the task of organizing this armed force and, presumably, of directing its operations in the field. The paralysis of the United Nations caused by the Cold War extended to the MSC. It continued to meet regularly during the 1940s, but the various plans for organizing a United Nations deterrent and coercive force were never reconciled and the MSC lapsed into sterile debate and, ultimately, virtual non-existence. The end of the Cold War has not resulted in a new project designed to create a deterrent/ coercive force. Secretary General Butros Butros-Ghali's proposal for creating a permanent United Nations military capability has received scant support. The United States has made it clear that it will not supply contingents to any force under United Nations command. Other members have not been willing to champion Butros-Ghali's initiative either.

What would be the role of such a military force? In 1945, it was primarily to deter armed aggression by smaller states. But can "wars of the third kind" be deterred by *any* military force? Uprisings of resistance, secessionist wars, and communal strife are not likely to be deterred by the armed forces of an international organization even if such forces are deployed prior to the outbreak of armed violence – a rare event. The United Nations has seldom taken preventive measures. In most cases, it does not intervene until the killing has started; and as Somalia and Rwanda illustrate, the intervention is not effected until late in the game. The United Nations and its regional counterparts remain primarily *reactive* organizations. For a variety of reasons, the organization has little early-warning capacity, and even when its members can begin to see the writing on the wall, they do little until the major powers decide to lead in organizing some form of action.

In the failing Yugoslavia, the action of the great powers was mostly unhelpful. In the case of Bosnia, it was destructive. Breaking ranks with its fellow members of the European Union, Germany granted recognition to Bosnia without any conditions. The war in Bosnia had started after a plebiscite transformed the Serbians from a major "nation" within Yugoslavia into a minority in Muslim-dominated Bosnia. German diplomatic recognition without conditions added a patina of international legitimacy to the plebiscite and to its predictable outcome. Bosnia thus became an independent state without providing any guarantees to protect the rights of minorities, without establishing democratic credentials, and without committing itself to the norms and principles of the Charter of Paris, which emphasize democracy, human rights, private markets, and respect for minorities. The United Nations became engaged in Bosnia only after it was too late. Perhaps the collapse of Yugoslavia was inevitable, but armed conflict was certainly made more probable by the lack of any collective effort, whether NATO, OSCE, or United Nations, to manage or influence the process. Typically, the United Nations became involved only after the war in Bosnia had already begun.

What of conflict resolution? This is the domain in which both the League of Nations and the United Nations accomplished the most in terms of assisting the conflict parties to negotiate cease-fires. But limiting the killing is just one step. There is an immense difference between a cease-fire negotiated by two governments involved in an interstate war, and a settlement enshrined in documents of legal, political, and psychological validity and legitimacy between warring communities, warlords, and other parties operating in the chaos surrounding collapsing states. It is this settlement stage of conflict resolution that is so difficult to achieve in wars of the third kind.

Historically, almost all state-creation wars ended with the victory of armed forces and not by diplomatic negotiations. Similarly, wars of secession, as in Biafra, Eritrea, and Bangladesh, were concluded by military victories. Some wars were mercifully brief (Bangladesh); most, however, continued for decades (Eritrea, Palestine) and many continue unresolved to this date (Myanmar, Sri Lanka, Sudan, the Punjab, Kashmir, and the like). Finally, some have resulted in "frozen" stalemates where numerous and extended efforts to create a final settlement have yielded no results. The Cypriot communal war began in 1964; it remains unresolved today. So do the wars in Myanmar, Sri Lanka, Kashmir, Sudan, Punjab, and elsewhere.

This pattern of either settlement by armed victory or of non-settlement raises troubling questions for the theory and practice of conflict resolution. For example, can anyone "settle" communal conflicts? Is there a hypothetical point of compromise between those intent on maintaining the territorial integrity of the state and those bent on secession? What is there to negotiate when political purposes are so fundamentally incompatible? Can communities within states dedicated to the exclusion or marginalization of "minorities" (and sometimes of majorities) be persuaded suddenly to stop fearing those who have excluded or murdered them? Do the Christian and animist southern Sudanese really have any realistic alternatives except to rebel against a fundamentalist Muslim regime expropriating their lands, excluding them from any form of national political participation, and attempting to convert them forcibly to Islam?

The urge to have a state, to create a state, and to belong to a state is one of the most fundamental political–psychological values of an era obsessed with questions of community and identity.[3] It is also sometimes a *requirement* for group survival. The original function of the state was to provide security of both life and group values such as religion. That has not changed. Some groups are truly at risk; they are convinced that sovereign statehood is the only solution to their security problem. Where "minorities" are excluded from political life, where communities find no security from their tormentors, and where the divides of language, religion, and ethnicity are profound, then the concept of "conflict resolution" may appear naive because it implicitly suggests that the solution can be found in the context of the maintenance or restoration of a preexisting state that in its essence was weak, ineffective, predatory, and/or patently unjust.

But the opposite strategy – the strategy of support for secession or partition – raises its own dilemmas. Can the international community, through the United Nations or regional organizations, support the

---

[3] The critical value of statehood is indicated by a Palestinian Arab leader who claimed "[a] flag, a sense of nationality, a passport are essential. In the modern world, State membership is a fundamental part of identity . . . With a passport we would not be pariahs. We could be the beneficiaries of reciprocity . . . We would have a place to go back to if in plight" (quoted in Branthwaite 1993: 51).

dismantling of a member state when a major purpose of the organization is to protect the sovereignty and territorial integrity of its
members? This is the quandary presented by conflicts such as Cyprus.
On the face of it, the Cyprus problem has been "solved," and as in so
many instances in the nineteenth and twentieth centuries, solved by
armed force. But the United Nations cannot bring itself to accept this as
a "settlement" because in so doing it would violate its own norms of
maintaining territorial integrity and denying the legitimacy of gains
made through armed aggression, in this case the Turkish invasion of
1974. For more than thirty years, the United Nations and its peacekeeping units have patrolled a *de facto* Cyprus partition and sponsored
negotiations that have more the appearance of charade and theater
than of conflict resolution. Formal partition is the most obvious
solution to the problem, but no one can accept it because it would set a
dangerous precedent for any number of weak states facing the threat
of secession. This is a philosophical quandary that seems to have no
solution: you cannot force communities to live together – particularly
communities that believe their physical survival is at stake (Horowitz
1985: 175–81) – but you cannot separate them either. The conflict
becomes frozen rather than settled. This is not conflict resolution; it is
conflict perpetuation.

The Bosnian war, like its counterparts in Rwanda, Sri Lanka, Liberia,
and elsewhere, raises other problems that appear to defy solution.
Here, the members of the warring communities have good reason to
fear for their lives. Given mass murders, widespread rape, sniping at
civilians, and "ethnic cleansing" over a period of more than three
years, how can the United Nations help resolve the mess? This conflict
shows nicely, if unfortunately, that in wars of the third kind, you are
likely to get a permanent cease-fire – just a first step towards a distant
settlement – only when one or more of three conditions develops: (1)
one party is on the verge of certain military defeat; (2) both parties
conclude, without negotiations, that there is no possibility or prospect
of further gains by military means or by mobilizing external support;
and (3) both parties become militarily, economically, and morally
exhausted. Zartman (1989: 267–9) calls these conditions "plateaus" and
"precipices." None of these conditions came to pass in the first four
years of war in Bosnia and the many years of war in other locales.
Until the autumn of 1995, cease-fires in Bosnia were tactical ploys to
gain time or diplomatic support; they seldom lasted for more than
several days. Diplomatic negotiations sponsored by the United

Nations and the European Union were theater, not serious bargaining. Referenda were used to buoy intransigence rather than to resolve anything.

In these circumstances, the United Nations was stuck between several incompatible activities. It saved countless civilian lives (humanitarian assistance), but in the process of delivering aid and establishing safe havens it was humiliated by local warlords and "national" armies whose consent for passage – often withheld – is necessary. United Nations troops were virtual hostages of one of the warring factions. They could not employ coercion for fear of becoming targets of military action that would threaten their humanitarian assistance tasks. Or, if they used coercion against one of the factions, they compromised their status as neutral peacekeepers – as if there were a peace to keep in Bosnia. And if they became engaged even in limited military operations, how could they meet the requirements of non-partisanship in sponsoring negotiations between the factions? The demands of non-partisanship, effective humanitarian relief, and coercive peacemaking are incompatible. The United Nations teetered between these roles, sometimes successfully, but more often in a manner to undermine its credibility and public support. A succession of commanding officers expressed their frustrations with these seemingly incompatible tasks by resigning in despair.

These dilemmas cannot be resolved and so, in effect, the United Nations cannot become an agent of conflict resolution as that term is usually employed. It can provide humanitarian assistance, an achievement of substantial magnitude given that the Bosnian war, like almost all wars of the third kind, was long, nasty, and brutish, but can it help achieve a legally, politically, and psychologically legitimate peace?

It is unlikely to do so until one or more of the three conditions listed above develops on the battlefield. In the meantime, the United Nations must ponder what sort of peace can eventually be put together. The problem of the long-term consequences of putting an end to the killing have not been thought through, either in the United Nations or anywhere else. But what happens in Bosnia is likely to have significant implications for the futures of weak and failing states.

Bosnia at peace: a settlement or a prelude to more war?

In the modern world there are various principles underlying vertical and horizontal legitimacy, but three are most prominent: the civic, the ethnic/communal, and the religious. Civic states are based on the concept of citizenship. This concept extends rights, responsibilities, and services (including protection and security) equally to all members of the community. The community is defined through history or through government policies which hold all citizens to be legally equal. Ethnicity, religion, language, and other attributes play no role in defining citizenship. There are no permanent majorities or minorities in a civic state. There are only the shifting political majorities determined by periodic elections.

A state based on a manufactured and variable "natural" community has very different characteristics. A state which is defined in terms of these attributes necessarily distinguishes "us" from "them." Citizenship is automatically extended at birth to any one of "us," but is *granted*, if at all, to a "minority." One of the first acts of the new Croatian government in May 1990 (even before it became independent!) was to amend its constitution to declare that only Croatians are citizens. All others – in particular, the large Serbian population – became "others" through the status of "official national minority" whose rights and access to services henceforth were to be granted only on certain conditions, namely that the Serbs behave as good Croatians. While frequently a state based on a "natural" community officially extends full civil and political rights to minorities, various policies of exclusion/marginalization are the norm. The fear of or actual practice of exclusion, discrimination, and injustice then drive separatist/secession movements. This is not a problem confined to the former Yugoslavia. Gurr and Scarrit's empirically based work indicates that currently minorities are "at risk" in ninety-nine countries (Gurr and Scarrit 1989: 381).

A state based on ethnicity, language, and/or religion tends toward differential treatment of "others." Lord Acton (1907: 192–3) summarized the problem almost one century ago:

> The greatest adversary of the rights of nationality is the modern theory of nationality. By making the State and the nation commensurate with each other in theory, it reduces practically to a subject condition other nationalities that may be within the boundary. It cannot admit them to an equality with the ruling nation which constitutes the State, because the State would then cease to be national, which would be a contradiction of the principle of its existence. According, therefore, to the degree of humanity and civilization in that dominant body which claims the rights of the

community, the inferior races are exterminated, or reduced to servi-
tude, or outlawed, or put in a condition of dependence.

This is exactly the situation in Bosnia. The plebiscite of the spring of
1992 organized by the Muslim government was less a referendum than
a census. Naturally, all the Muslims voted for an independent state; in
doing so, however, they automatically altered the status of the Serbs
from a major community in Yugoslavia to a minority in Bosnia. War
was the result. An instrument of democracy – a plebiscite – became a
source of war. It created permanent majorities and minorities. It cannot
therefore be a means of resolving conflicts where definitions of
community are concerned.

The third basis of community – religion – was of fundamental
importance and a major source of war in Europe until the Peace of
Westphalia resolved the issue. Since then, religion has been undermined as a basis of state legitimacy by the doctrine of popular
sovereignty and more recently by the idea of the "natural" community. Nevertheless, it has re-emerged as an issue in recent years,
primarily in the form of Muslim fundamentalism. The state, in this
view, should coincide with the "community of believers." This community is torn apart by Western territorial definitions of the state; a
main task of the devout is therefore to destroy those states and to
reunite the entire community of believers into a single realm under
religious governance. In such an order, of course, infidels and non-
believers become "minorities" subject to various forms of oppression.
To the extent that the non-devout represent a significant proportion of
the population, the state will necessarily be weak. The religious
versus civic concepts of statehood are locked in combat in the Middle
East today and constitute a major source of violence and war. It is not
the major problem in Bosnia, Serbian propaganda notwithstanding.
The Bosnian Muslims are identified in the media not so much as a
religious community as some sort of "people" who are entitled to a
state. There is scant evidence, in any event, that the current Bosnian
authorities see themselves as the center of a Muslim revivalist movement throughout the region, a kind of Iran-in-the-Balkans. Since the
Serbs and Croats have defined themselves as a people, the Muslims
must do the same *despite* their religion. In holding the plebiscite, it
was clear that the Muslims saw themselves as a distinct community,
albeit with rather fuzzy bases for the claim. But within the remnant of
Bosnia, hundreds of thousands of Serbs remain in reasonable security.

199

The Bosnian constitution establishes a political system based on the concept of citizenship. Many Bosnian Serbs would like to restore, for all, the pre-war political system including its borders. The United Nations and NATO members, in contrast, have supported the opposite principle, the idea of ethnically based states carved out of the original Bosnia.

The largely theatrical negotiations hosted by David Owen and Thorvald Stoltenberg on behalf of the United Nations and the European Union during the early 1990s produced a peace plan that would have divided Bosnia into a hotchpotch of separate, communally based "states" held together only by some loose association. Aside from the impossibility of policing such a peace, given the territorial configuration of Bosnia (mountains, valleys), this was surely a recipe for further war, not for peace. Populations down to the smallest villages would have to be transferred, but virtually no state could have been made "communally pure" as desired by the Serbs, Croats, and Muslims. It is also questionable whether these communal bantustans could have survived economically. The delimitation of frontiers for these enclaves would have taken decades, and those years would have been marked by raiding, pillaging, and constant squabbles about exact locations of boundaries. It is hard to imagine a more uncertain basis for peace.

The Contact Group's (Russia, France, Great Britain, Germany, and the United States) peace proposal, rejected by the Serbs in 1994 because it would require them to abandon some of their military gains, avoided some of the more blatant faults of the Owen–Stoltenberg plan. But it enshrined as the basis of state legitimacy the principle of a "natural" community. Contrary to customary liberal thought that argues warring communities should ultimately be integrated, this proposal sanctified the principle of community separation. It in effect partitioned Bosnia, although it retained a single, loosely federated state with its traditional international frontiers. This could indeed be the only workable principle for Bosnia in the short run. But if the Bosnian Serbs ultimately succeed in creating their own *de facto* state by force of arms, and that state is endorsed by NATO and the United Nations, then an important precedent will have been set. Until recently, governments have on the whole resisted granting recognition to secessionist movements prior to victory (the French and Tanzanian recognitions of Biafra were exceptions to the rule). A communally partitioned Bosnia, blessed and even promoted by the international community, creates a precedent that is bound to amplify the hopes of those with similar aspirations. We can expect the Turkish community in Cyprus to be among the first to cite the Bosnian example as justifying the formal partition of the Mediterranean island. Many others will follow.

The problem, of course, is that there are very few places in the world where populations are homogeneous in terms of ethnicity, language, culture, religion, and other communal characteristics. While it has become possible to produce a homogeneous Serbian–Bosnian state through "ethnic cleansing" and mass murder, the same cannot be said for the dozens of other countries experiencing secessionist rebellions and wars of "national" liberation. We then face the well-known phenomenon of the infinite regress of claims to self-determination. Minorities now become majorities with their own minorities. The demand for statehood escalates, while the prospects of creating viable political and economic entities declines. The United Nations thus may become a creator of more weak states, some or many of which will fail and will have to be bailed out yet again.

Perhaps this characterization of the Bosnian dilemma is too pessimistic. Perhaps the *only* basis for a strong state is a community based on consanguinity/religion/language rather than civic rights. It is one of the great paradoxes of our era that as the workings of economics and communications become increasingly globalized, political sentiments and psychology become increasingly tribalized (Barber 1992). The two processes may even be related: cultural homogenization caused by international communication may spawn movements to assert autonomy, cultural identity, and distinctness. Globalism helps create the demand for statehood based on "natural" communities and on religious orthodoxy (Holsti 1980).

There is no certain answer to the dilemmas posed by Bosnia and its many parallels in the contemporary world. One can sympathize with the efforts made by the United Nations and NATO to put an end to a disgusting war. Ending the killing and raping might be the highest priority. But two troubling questions remain: (1) is the "peace plan" currently in play really a basis for a settlement, or will it be the father of more war and turmoil?; and (2) what sort of precedent will it set? We cannot guess the future, but the ultimate settlement of the Bosnian catastrophe may turn out to be about as successful as the Treaty of Versailles.

The ultimate question

⌈To repeat: the Charter of the United Nations is a Westphalian document. It enshrines the principles of sovereignty and territorial integrity.
To provide humanitarian assistance, to prevent massacres of civilians,
and to put an end to killing requires the United Nations to violate the
sovereignty principle.⌉ The July 1994 Security Council resolution on
Haiti is just the most dramatic step in a long list of recent innovative
actions that, while morally and politically defensible, nevertheless
deviate substantially from the basic norms of the organization. This
may be a good thing but it is not without pitfalls. In the last half-dozen
years, the United Nations has moved beyond peacekeeping – a helpful
step in classical wars between states – to the much more problematic
tasks of peacemaking, peace enforcement, and governance within
states. What have not been accomplished yet, however, are formal
settlements, the creation of governance arrangements that are politically acceptable and that enhance rather than undermine or erode
vertical and horizontal legitimacy. To be enduring, some choice will
have to be made between the civic and ethnic/communal or religious
concepts of statehood. The first type may be impossible to create, given
communal hatreds, warfare, and atrocities in so many weak and failed
states. But the second type creates another set of problems, not the
least of which may be the filip it gives to the disintegration of many
existing weak states.

The international community is receiving mixed signals on the
question of statehood. On the one hand, Security Council resolutions
have refused to partition sovereign states. This is the situation in
Cyprus, and it was substantiated by the refusal of either the United
Nations or the United States to carve out a separate state for the
beleaguered Kurds immediately after the Gulf War in 1991. On the
other hand, the Owen–Stoltenberg formula and its less explicit reincarnation in the Contact Group's proposals for Bosnia in 1994–5 may lead
ultimately to two or three new states based on the principle of
ethnicity/communalism. It may in effect validate the results of a
Serbian war of secession, with negotiations focusing not on the general
principle but on the exact territorial limits of the new states. Secessionist movements from Bougainville, through Chechnya, to the Sudan
no doubt watched the process with considerable interest. While the
ethnic/communal formula may ultimately work for Bosnia, the
problem of weak and failed states will remain with us. The condition

of states in Africa, in particular, raises questions about their long-run viability as states *per se*, never mind just democratic states.

The most fundamental question, therefore, is whether the Western concept of the state is an appropriate construct for societies that have had fundamentally different types of political systems throughout their history. The United Nations is an organization of states. But some states do not thrive in their Western incarnation. Siad Barre's attempt to create a Western-type state in a society that had fundamentally different forms of governance based on clans is a glaring example of the problem (cf. I. M. Lewis 1988; Samatar and Laitin 1987). This is not a justification for a new era of United Nations-sponsored paternalism, but a question that must be answered before solutions to the Bosnias and Somalias of the world can be fashioned. Is it realistic to think solely in terms of Western state concepts? Are there no other alternatives – choices that would involve less warfare and killing?[4] In particular, the Western concept of the "nation-state" may not be a feasible template for many other societies, including those of the Balkans and former Soviet republics. The attempt to create states based on variable and often manufactured "national identities" has led to weak states, intolerance, suppression of "others" that do not fit the template, and resulting bloodshed. It may be worth repeating Julius Nyerere's warning in 1967:

> None of the nation states of Africa are "natural" units . . . [Boundaries] are senseless . . . [It] would be visionary to conceive of an [African] nation as one people, speaking a common language, bound together by a common heritage and a shared historical experience. Africa must break loose from this alluring European model. It does not fit in with the social realities of the continent.

Nyerere might have gone further to query whether even the Western concept of the state makes sense in every social–political milieu. The United Nations, academics, nationalist leaders, and millions of others have simply assumed that there is no alternative political format to the centralized, territorially-defined, hierarchical state. The state has not been problematized, but given the weakness and failures of so many states, it would seem prudent to begin a discussion of this fascinating and complex subject.

[4] The problem is beginning to stimulate some serious thought. See, for example, Gottlieb, (1993). The subject is vast and vastly interesting, but beyond the scope of this book. A reasoned argument against the idea that there are alternatives to the Westphalian state is in Ayoob (1995: 27–8).

To date, the literature, whether of the "nation-building" or "state-building" genre, often assumes that the historical processes that have unfolded in Europe since the fifteenth century must extend to the other areas of the world. Thus, all the wars and suffering they have caused are simply a part of an inevitable historical evolution that was once European but now has necessarily become universal (cf. Cohen, Brown and Organski 1981; Herbst 1990; Ayoob 1995). In Europe, as we have seen, war and state-making were intimately connected. So they will also be in other areas of the world, the literature suggests. The implication is that not only must we accept "wars of national debilitation," but in some senses even applaud them because ultimately out of the carnage strong states will emerge. One alternative, of course, is to re-think the concept of the state.

One problem with the view that warfare is a necessary step toward strong statehood – the Europe-as-source-of-a-universal-trajectory thesis – is that the contexts differ fundamentally. In European history there was no international community to feel the consequences of the rivalry between the forces of centralization and continued fragmentation. The Fronde in France in the mid-seventeenth century had little impact on Sweden, Russia, or even on England. That is not the situation today. There are more than 49 million domestic and international refugees camped out in various way-stations. They are the result of wars of the third kind, or to put it into the state-making-through-war school, the inevitable consequences of the "political conflicts for control over the power resources of [developing states]" (Cohen, Brown and Organski 1981: 902). Refugees are not today a matter of moral or financial indifference. They create immediate ecological problems, a crush of people seeking entry into the industrial states, international health problems and, not infrequently, they help prolong and even escalate civil wars (Lee 1994). The world's media also make it certain that international indifference cannot be sustained.

Moreover, many states in the Third World have resolved the state-strength dilemma without war and carnage. Singapore, Fiji, the Caribbean countries, Mauritius, Ivory Coast, and Lesotho, just to name a few, are prominent examples. Today there are numerous ways to strengthen the state without recourse to violence and predation. But for the failures, the international community has little choice but to address the problems in one way or another. And when it does, it should have in mind the long-run consequences, as well as the philosophical bases, of its actions.

The problem of weak states and the long, nasty, and brutish wars they spawn will be with us for some time. The United Nations was not created to deal with these kinds of problems. It is now facing them with pronounced adaptability and innovation but, as shown in Bosnia, it is also dealing with them clumsily and sometimes with unintended and unfavorable consequences. The questions that have to be asked get to the heart of concepts such as the state, sovereignty, conflict resolution, and peace. In typical bureaucratic fashion, the United Nations is muddling through from case to case without much concern for ultimate directions. But partial settlements, peace plans, and other life-saving devices also may have long-run consequences. It is best to know exactly where one is going and what the long-run implications of tactical decisions are. So far, those implications have not been thought through.

War, the state, and the study of international politics

There are implications of weak states not only for those who must deal with the moral, political, and military problems they create, but also for academic analysts of international politics. For more than 200 years they have employed a number of analytical and theoretical tools to examine the sources of war and the conditions of peace and stability. These have included game theory, deterrence theory, analogies such as Rousseau's "stag hunt," balance of power theory, and the sources and nature of alliances – in brief, those approaches generally placed under the rubrics of realism and neo-realism.

The world from which these theoretical devices and approaches have derived is the European experience of war since 1648 and the Cold War. They have also drawn heavily upon the experiences of the great powers, thus relegating lesser states to the objects of great-power rivalry and cooperation rather than as self-directed actors with their own interests and unique roles in international politics.

The problems of war and the great powers have not disappeared with the end of the Soviet–American rivalry. The mountain of literature that examines the future security "architecture" of Europe attests to the vibrancy of traditional security concerns. Ideas of some sort of a twenty-first-century Concert of Powers abound, while balance of power thinking continues to inform the debate about whether or not to expand NATO to include former Warsaw Pact members from Central Europe and how to deal with a rapidly growing China (cf. Huntington 1994). The wars of ex-Yugoslavia have undermined the euphoria of 1989 which found expression in proclamations of a new, more benign world order, in scenarios of peaceful transitions from socialism to free market democracy (Fukuyama 1989) and in predictions of the obsolescence of major power wars (Mueller 1989). Both in some of the former Soviet republics and in many areas of the Third World, security dilemmas, the possibility of interstate wars, and local arms-racing remain with us. So do interstate wars originating over water disputes and other resource shortages. There is also, finally, the risk that internal wars will escalate through foreign interventions into interstate wars. Security studies as a field concerned with the relations between states will not disappear.

[Nevertheless, the major sources of war in the future will derive less from the character of relations between states than what goes on within states. The historical, political, and psychological processes that drive communities to demand their own state have not been altered or terminated by the end of the Cold War. On the contrary, as almost every observer of Central Europe and the Balkans has noted, war and chauvinist nationalism have been the consequences of the collapse of the socialist states (cf. Snyder 1993: 81). The domestic politics of some Third World countries may have taken a turn toward democratization in the short run – particularly in South America – but elsewhere politics have mostly remained as usual which means that the forces of secession will remain vibrant, some states will fail, and governments will search, usually unsuccessfully, for more enduring bases of legitimacy.]

Realist and neo-realist approaches to the study of war offer little in the way of understanding these dynamics and how they affect weak states. In the absence of actual or potential hegemons in many areas of the Third World, there are few alliances and even fewer balances of power (Holsti 1992: 42–6). Nuclear deterrence is irrelevant in all areas of the Third World, among the former Soviet republics, and in the Balkans; it remains a possibility only between India and Pakistan and possibly later among Iran's neighbors. Many of the other accoutrements of traditional European-style power politics are notable either for their absence or for their scarcity. In brief, there is little remaining in the traditional literatures of security studies specifically and international politics more generally that has analytical value for understanding or explaining the persistence of war in weak and failed states. The comparative study of states – how they are formed, how they develop legitimacy and strength, and how they persist or fail – seem better avenues for future research on the problem of war. But since local and domestic wars also have external sources, as noted in chapter 6, then the linkages between systemic characteristics and domestic politics need to be developed into prominent analytical foci in future studies (cf. Buzan 1991: ch. 4).

Another significant change in the study of international politics is the shift from exclusive focus on the activities of the great powers to a concern with what have traditionally been considered peripheral actors. The theoretical paraphernalia of realist and neo-realist studies, in which virtually everything is explained by great-power behavior or systemic characteristics such as global balances of power, is much less relevant in the marshes of national debilitation wars. Despite the floundering of NATO in the Bosnian war, most of the great powers in future are going to be concerned primarily with economic issues, that is, with the domain called today international political economy. The *problematique* of war now moves to their peripheries. It is in the context of United Nations efforts to sustain and resuscitate weak and failed states that the military capabilities of the great powers will be most relevant, that is, in the great variety of peacekeeping activities that are the legacies of wars of the third kind.

For analysts of the United Nations, the fiftieth anniversary of the organization brought forth a wave of proposals for Charter amendment. But attention has focused primarily on the problem of representation on the Security Council. The more fundamental problem is whether and how an organization designed for one set of tasks should and can take on new tasks without violating its basic rules. Recent innovations demonstrate the capacity of the organization to improvise and to stretch the meaning and intent of the Charter to cover a variety of new and novel challenges arising from weak and failed states. It might make United Nations actions in these areas less subject to controversy if Charter revision were to specify more clearly, for example, that collective humanitarian intervention can be undertaken in the absence of a member state's consent, or that the Security Council can take action to save lives even where there is no obvious threat to international peace and security. The question of using coercive means to create a cease-fire or more permanent arrangements also needs serious inquiry and debate.

There are enough constitutional and political reforms required for the United Nations to deal more effectively with wars of the third kind to keep academics and diplomats engaged in inquiry and debate for a long time. To make this debate more profound, however, it is also necessary to examine the assumptions of statehood surrounding United Nations practices and to raise ultimate questions about the future of those polities that have failed or are not likely to succeed in making the transition from artificial colonial creations to full-fledged states. Clearly, the hopes of the 1960s were in many cases too great; "liberation" from colonialism was to be the beginning of a new era not just of freedom but of fraternity and economic well-being. For many, it has been a dramatic failure on all three counts.

This suggests that the study of the successes is also important. How have the Malaysias, Singapores, Mauritiuses, Jordans, Ivory Coasts, for example, made a reasonably successful transition from colonialism to stronger statehood? What has distinguished their policies from those of Liberia, Somalia, Lebanon, or Myanmar? This is a slightly different question from the debates current among comparativists regarding the reasons for the successes and failures of democracy. But it is a supremely important issue if we wish to see the growth and development of no-war zones, zones of peace, and pluralistic security communities in the world.

Immanuel Kant's pacific federation (foedus pacificum) was to be an expanding union of republican states (Kant [1795] 1963), where members would be encouraged to collaborate as a consequence of both the growth of commercial exchange and "nature's plan," the learning that results from increasingly ruinous wars. Today, Kant's argument has found favor among a number of theorists who have discovered empirically that democracies do not war against each other. Leaving aside the fact that Kant's idea of a republic of citizens is not exactly the same as most modern definitions of democracy (Kant emphasized law and constitutional rule, not elections), the idea of a pacific union of democracies underlies many contemporary diplomatic testaments. The Charter of Paris (1990), for example, is a thoroughly Kantian and Wilsonian document that emphasizes the formula: if you want peace between states, you must have democracies within states. The whole Western approach to the former socialist states has been founded on similar ideas. The great project of building a "commonwealth of democracies" stretching from Vancouver to Vladivostok, to use James Baker's concept, is basically a compact among states sharing similar characteristics of democracy and private markets (Holsti 1994). It would be a great zone of peace and ultimately, in Deutsch's (1954) terms, a pluralistic security community. The expansion of the European Union is rooted in similar expectations.

Chapter 8 demonstrated that it is not necessary to have democracies to have no-war zones, and perhaps even zones of peace. The lack of war in South America since 1941 – an achievement perhaps more significant than the record of Western Europe since 1945 – cannot be explained by the presence of democratic governance on the continent. It is better explained by the growing strength of South American states since the turn of the century. While the peace-through-democracy hypothesis warrants further study, it should not deflect interest from the scrutiny of strong statehood: how it develops, when it emerges, and how it is sustained. Vertical and horizontal legitimacy are the key preconditions. The correlation between democracy and strong states is significant, but popular sovereignty, historically, is not the only basis for state legitimacy. It is at least conceivable that regions made up of Singapores or Taiwans – limited democracies but republics in Kant's sense – could coexist peacefully. The South American anomaly thus alerts us to the possibility that no-war zones or pluralistic security communities can develop in the absence of Western-style democracies. This study thus ends with the theoretical proposition that in the years to come it is not so much the state of the international system that matters – as traditional approaches to international politics and war would have it – but rather the state of the state.

Appendix
Major armed conflicts by region and type, 1945–1995

Included in the following tables are the major instances of armed conflict that have occurred in the international system since 1945 up to, and including, 1995. The list is comprehensive and includes conflicts that would not necessarily be defined as war in the Eurocentric conception (i.e. a contest fought between two distinct national armies who engage each other with the objective of inflicting enough casualties/destruction to compel one party to surrender, with a minimum of 1,000 battle-related deaths). As such, it utilizes the rationale employed by the author in Holsti (1991), pp. 272–3.

A Western Europe

Conflict	Conflict type
Greece (1945–9)	Internal factional/ideological. Communist opposition vs. forces loyal to constitutional monarchy of King Paul (UK, Yugoslavia, Bulgaria and Albania intervention)
Spain (1968–93)	Irredenta/secession/resistance. Spanish government vs. Basque opposition (predominantly ETA)[a]
UK (Northern Ireland) (1969–95)	Irredenta/secession/resistance. Protestant paramilitary (predominantly UVF, UFF, UDA),[b] UK government vs. Catholic opposition (predominantly PIRA, INLA)[c]

[a] ETA   *Euskadi ta Askatasuna*
[b] UVF   Ulster Volunteer Force
     UFF   Ulster Freedom Fighters
     UDA   Ulster Defence Association
[c] PIRA   Provisional Irish Republican Army
     INLA   Irish National Liberation Army

B Former USSR

Conflict	Conflict type
Azerbaijan (1989–95)	Irredenta/secession/resistance. Azerbaijan government vs. rebel forces in Nagorno-Karabakh (Armenian intervention)
Moldova (1992)	Irredenta/secession/resistance. Moldovan government vs. Slav rebels in Transdnestr region
Georgia (1992–4)	Irredenta/secession/resistance. Georgian government vs. rebels in South Ossetia
Georgia (1992–4)	Irredenta/secession/resistance. Georgian government vs. rebels in Abkhazia
Georgia (1992–4)	Internal factional/ideological. Georgian government vs. rebel forces loyal to Zviad Gamsakurdia
Tajikistan (1992)	Internal factional/ideological. Tajik government vs. PDA[a] rebels (Uzbek and Russian intervention)
Russia (1995)	Irredenta/secession/resistance. Russian government vs. rebel Chechen separatists

[a] PDA   People's Democratic Army

C Balkans/Eastern Europe

Hungary (1956)	Interstate/lethal intervention. USSR intervention to preserve alliance (WPO)[a] unity
Czechoslovakia (1968)	Interstate/lethal intervention. USSR intervention to preserve alliance (WPO)[a] unity
Croatia–Serbia (1991)	Interstate/lethal intervention
Croatia (1990–5)	Irredenta/secession/resistance. Croatian government vs. Serbian rebels in Krajina (UN intervention)
Bosnia–Herzegovina (1992–5)	Irredenta/secession/resistance. Bosnian (Muslim) government vs. Serb irregulars vs. Croat irregulars (UN intervention)

[a] WPO   Warsaw Pact Organization

D Africa

Conflict	Conflict type
Madagascar (1947–8)	Conflict of anti-colonial liberation. French colonial administration vs nationalist opposition
Tunisia (1952–6)	Conflict of anti-colonial liberation. French colonial administration vs. nationalist opposition (Neo-Destour Party)
Kenya (1952–63)	Conflict of anti-colonial liberation. UK colonial administration vs. nationalist opposition (KAU/ Mau Mau)[a]
Cameroon (1955–60)	Conflict of anti-colonial liberation. UK and French colonial administrations vs. nationalist opposition
Rwanda (1956–65)	Irredenta/secession/resistance. Hutu government vs. Tutsi rebels
Zaire (1960–5)	Irredenta/secession/resistance. Zairean government vs. FNLC[b] rebels in Shaba (Belgian and UN intervention)
South Africa (1960–94)	Internal factional/ideological. South African government vs. ANC/MK, PAC, AZAPO and APLA[c] rebels
Angola (1961–74)	Conflict of anti-colonial liberation. Portuguese colonial administration vs. nationalist opposition (FNLA)[d] (USSR and South African intervention)
Guinea–Bissau (1962–74)	Conflict of anti-colonial liberation. Portuguese colonial administration vs. nationalist opposition (PAIGC)[e]
Somalia–Ethiopia (1963–4)	Interstate/lethal intervention
Somalia–Kenya (1963–7)	Interstate/lethal intervention
Mozambique (1965–75)	Conflict of anti-colonial liberation. Portuguese colonial administration vs. nationalist opposition (FRELIMO)[f]
Chad (1966–78)	Internal factional/ideological. Chadian government vs. FROLINAT[g] (Libyan intervention)
Uganda (1966)	Irredenta/secession/resistance. Ugandan government vs. Bugandan rebels
Namibia (1966–89)	Conflict of anti-colonial liberation. South African government vs. nationalist opposition (SWAPO)[h]
Nigeria (1967–70)	Irredenta/secession/resistance. Nigerian government vs. Ibo rebels in Biafra
Rhodesia (1967–80)	Conflict of anti-colonial liberation. Rhodesian government vs. nationalist opposition (ZANU/ ZANLA, ZAPU/ZIPRA)[i]

Conflict	Conflict type
Ethiopia (1971–92)	Irredenta/secession/resistance. Ethiopian government vs. EPLF[j] rebels
Burundi (1972)	Irredenta/secession/resistance. Tutsi-led government vs. Hutu rebels
Angola (1974–94)	Internal factional/ideological. Angolan government vs. UNITA[k] rebels (South African, Cuban intervention)
Ethiopia (1975–92)	Irredenta/secession/resistance. Ethiopian government vs. ALF[l] rebels
Ethiopia (1975–92)	Irredenta/secession/resistance. Ethiopian government vs. EPRP[m] rebels
Mozambique (1975–94)	Internal factional/ideological. Mozambique government vs. RENAMO[n] rebels
Ethiopia (1976–92)	Irredenta/secession/resistance. Ethiopian government vs. TPLF[o] rebels
Ethiopia (1977–92)	Irredenta/secession/resistance. Ethiopian government vs. OLF[p] rebels
Zaire (1977–8)	Irredenta/secession/resistance. Zairean government vs. FNLC[b] rebels (French and Belgian intervention)
Somalia–Ethiopia (1977–80)	Interstate/lethal intervention
Uganda–Tanzania (1978–9)	Interstate/lethal intervention
Chad (1979–82)	Internal factional/ideological. Chadian government vs. Habre (FAN)[q] rebels
Nigeria (1980–4)	Internal factional/ideological. Nigerian government vs. rebel Islamic forces
Ghana (1981)	Irredenta/secession/resistance. Tribal fighting (Nanumbas vs. Konkombas)
Uganda (1981–5)	Internal factional/ideological. Ugandan (Obote) government vs. UFM and UNRF[r] rebels
Somalia (1981–91)	Irredenta/secession/resistance. Somali government vs. SNM[s] rebels
Chad (1982–7)	Internal factional/ideological. Chadian (Habre) government vs. Oueddai rebel forces (Libyan, French and OAU[t] intervention)
Mali–Burkina Faso (1985)	Interstate/lethal intervention)
Uganda (1985–6)	Internal factional/ideological. Ugandan (Okello) government vs. NRM and NRA[u] rebels
Uganda (1986–93)	Internal factional/ideological. Ugandan (Musveni) government vs. UPA/DA, HSM and UDCM[v] rebels
Chad (1987)	Interstate/lethal intervention

Conflict	Conflict type
Burundi (1988–92)	Irredenta/secession/resistance. Tutsi government massacre of Hutu civilians
Mauritania–Senegal (1989–91)	Interstate/lethal intervention
Somalia (1989–91)	Irredenta/secession/resistance. Somali government vs. SPM[w] rebels
Somalia (1990–4)	Irredenta/secession/resistance. Somali government vs. USC (Ayeed faction) and SNA[x] rebels (US and UN intervention)
Chad (1990–1)	Internal factional/ideological. Chadian (Habre) government vs. MPS and IL[y] rebels
Mali (1990–4)	Irredenta/secession/resistance. Mali government vs. Tuareg rebels (primarily MPA and FIAA)[z]
Niger (1990–4)	Irredenta/secession/resistance. Niger government vs. Tuareg rebels (primarily FLAA)[aa]
Djibouti (1991–4)	Internal factional/ideological. Djibouti government vs. FRUD[bb] rebels (French intervention)
Liberia (1991–4)	Internal factional/ideological. Liberian government vs. NPLF and INPLF[cc] rebels (ECOMOG[dd] and Burkina Faso intervention)
Sierra Leone (1991–4)	Internal factional/ideological. Sierra Leone government vs. NPLF[cc] and RUF[ee] rebels
Rwanda (1991–3)	Irredenta/secession/resistance. Rwandan (Hutu led) government vs. Tutsi-dominated RPF[ff] rebels (UN intervention)
Chad (1991–3)	Internal factional/ideological. Chadian government vs. CSNPD and MDD[gg] rebels
Zaire (1993)	Internal factional/ideological. Mobutu backed Zairean (Birindwa) government vs. pro-democracy opposition forces (primarily HCR[hh] supporters)
Zaire (1993–4)	Irredenta/secession/resistance. Government sanctioned ethnic "cleansing" in Shaba
Rwanda (1994)	Irredenta/secession/resistance. RPF[ff] government vs. Hutu rebels

[a]	KAU	Kenya Africa Union
[b]	FNLC	*Front national pour la liberation Congolaise*
[c]	ANC/MK	African National Congress/*Umkhonto we Sizwe*
	PAC	Pan Africanist Congress
	AZAPO	Azanian African People's Organization
	APLA	Azanian People's Liberation Army
[d]	FNLA	*Frente de Liberatacão de Mocambique*
[e]	PAIGC	*Partido Africano da Independencia da Guine e Cabo Verde*

f	FRELIMO	*Frente de Liberatacão de Mocambique*
g	FROLINAT	*Front de liberation nationale du Tchad*
h	SWAPO	South West African People's Organization
i	ZANU/ZANLA	Zimbabwe African National Union/Zimbabwe African National Liberation Army
	ZAPU/ZIPRA	Zimbabwe African People's Union/Zimbabwe People's Revolutionary Army
j	EPLF	Eritrean People's Liberation Front
k	UNITA	*União Nacional para a Independencia Total de Angola*
l	ALF	Afar Liberation Front
m	EPRP	Ethiopian People's Revolutionary Party
n	RENAMO	*Resistencia Nacional Mocambicana*
o	TPLF	Tigray People's Liberation Front
p	OLF	Oromo Liberation Front
q	FAN	*Forces armées du nord*
r	UFM	Ugandan Freedom Movement
	UNRF	Ugandan National Rescue Front
s	SNM	Somali National Movement
t	OAU	Organization of African Unity
u	NRM/NRA	National Resistance Movement/National Resistance Army
v	UPA/DA	Uganda People's Army/Democratic Army
	HSM	Holy Spirit Movement
	UDCM	United Democratic Christian Movement
w	SPM	Somali Patriotic Movement
x	SNA	Somali National Alliance
y	MPS	*Mouvement patriotique du salut*
	IL	Islamic Legion
z	MPA	*Mouvement patriotique de l'Azaouad.*
	FIAA	*Front islamique arabe de l'Azaouad*
aa	FLAA	Liberation Front of Air and Azawad
bb	FRUD	Front for the Restoration of Unity and Democracy
cc	NPLF	National Patriotic Front for the Liberation of Liberia
	INPLF	Independent NPLF
dd	ECOMOG	Economic Community of West African States Monitoring Group
ee	RUF	Revolutionary United Front
ff	RPF	Rwandan Patriotic Front
gg	CSNPD	Committee of National Revival for Peace and Democracy
	MDD	Movement for Democracy and Development
hh	HCR	High Council of the Republic

E Central America and the Caribbean

Conflict	Conflict type
Costa Rica (1948)	Internal factional/ideological. Costa Rican government vs. anti-government rebels
Guatemala (1954)	Internal factional/ideological. Guatemalan government vs. conservatives/right wing rebels (Honduran and Nicaraguan intervention)
Cuba (1956–9)	Internal factional/ideological. Cuban (Batista) government vs. left-wing (Castro) rebels
Nicaragua–Honduras (1957)	Interstate/lethal intervention
Nicaragua (1960–79)	Internal factional/ideological. Nicaraguan (Samoza) government vs. Sandinista rebels
Cuba–United States (1961)	Interstate/lethal intervention
Dominican Republic (1965)	Internal factional/ideological. Dominican Republic (Bosch) government vs. rebel military units headed by General Wessin y Wessin (US intervention)
Guatemala (1966–94)	Internal factional/ideological. Guatemalan government vs. URNG[a] rebels
El Salvador–Honduras (1969)	Interstate/lethal intervention
El Salvador (1979–91)	Internal factional/ideological. El Salvadoran government vs. FMLN[b] rebels (US intervention)
Nicaragua (1981–90)	Internal factional/ideological. Nicaraguan (Sandinista) government vs. CONTRA[c] rebels (US intervention)
Grenada (1983)	Internal factional/ideological. Grenada (Bishop) government vs. rebel army forces loyal to Bernard Coard and General Austin (US, Jamaica, Barbados and OECS[d] intervention)
Panama (1989–90)	Interstate/lethal intervention. US invasion to arrest Panamanian leader Manuel Noriega for drug conspiracy
Haiti (1991–4)	Internal factional/ideological. Haiti (Aristide) government vs. rebel army forces loyal to General Cedras (US and UN intervention)

[a] URNG   Guatemalan National Revolutionary Unity
[b] FMLN   Farabundo Marti Front for National Liberation
[c] CONTRA Counter-Revolutionaries (the Democratic Forces of Nicaragua [FDN] was the largest CONTRA group)
[d] OECS   Organization of East Caribbean States

F South America

Conflict	Conflict type
Colombia (1948–58)	Internal factional/ideological. Colombian government vs. rebel right-wing military
Bolivia (1952)	Internal factional/ideological. Bolivian government vs. rebel left wing opposition forces (primarily supported by MNR[a])
Colombia (1965–94)	Internal factional/ideological. Colombian government vs. FARC, ELN, EPL[b] rebels
Chile (1973)	Internal factional/ideological. Chilean (Allende) government vs. rebel army forces led by General Augusto Pinochet (US intervention)
Argentina (1976–83)	Internal factional/ideological. Argentinian government vs. rebel left-wing guerrilla/opposition forces
Peru (1981–94)	Internal factional/ideological. Peruvian government vs. SL[c] rebels
Argentina–UK (Falklands) (1982)	Interstate/lethal intervention
Peru (1984–94)	Internal factional/ideological. Peruvian government vs. MRTA[d] rebels
Suriname (1986)	Internal factional/ideological. Surinamese government vs. pro-democracy rebels led by Ronnie Brunswijk (primarily Jungle Commando/SLA[e])

[a]	MNR	*Movimiento Nacionalista Revolucionario*
[b]	FARC	*Fuerzas Armados Revolucionarias Colombianas*
	ELN	*Ejercito de Liberacion Nacional*
	EPL	*Ejercito Popular de Liberacion*
[c]	SL	*Sendero Luminoso*
[d]	MRTA	*Movimento Revolucionario Tupac Amaru*
[e]	SLA	Surinamese Liberation Army

Appendix

G Middle East

Conflict	Conflict type
Syria (1945–6)	Conflict of anti-colonial liberation. French colonial administration vs. nationalist opposition (SNB)[a]
Israel (1946–8)	Conflict of anti-colonial liberation. UK colonial administration vs. nationalist Jewish opposition (Irgun, Stern Gang)
Israel–Arab League[b] (1948–9)	Interstate/lethal intervention
Morocco (1953–6)	Conflict of anti-colonial liberation. French colonial administration vs. nationalist opposition (*Istiqlal* Grouping) (Spanish intervention)
Algeria (1954–62)	Conflict of anti-colonial liberation. French colonial liberation vs. nationalist (FLN)[c] opposition
Sudan (1955–94)	Irredenta/secession/resistance. Sudanese government vs. insurgent southern provinces
Cyprus (1955–60)	Conflict of anti-colonial liberation. UK colonial administration vs. nationalist opposition (EOKA)[d]
Israel, UK, France–Egypt (1956)	Interstate/lethal intervention
Oman (1957)	Internal factional/ideological. Omani government vs. rebels led by Ghalib and Talib (UK intervention)
Lebanon (1958)	Internal factional/ideological. Lebanese government vs. left-wing Moslems and nationalists (US and Syrian intervention)
Iraq (1959)	Irredenta/secession/resistance. Iraqi government vs. Shammar rebels
Iraq (1961–94)	Irredenta/secession/resistance. Iraqi government vs. Kurdish rebels (primarily DPK and PUK)[e] (Iranian intervention)
Yemen (1962–7)	Internal factional/ideological. Republican government forces vs. royalist rebels (Egyptian and Saudi Arabian intervention)
Algeria–Morocco (1962)	Interstate/lethal intervention
Cyprus (1963–4)	Irredenta/secession/resistance. Cypriot government vs. rebel Turks (UN and UK intervention)
South Yemen (1963–7)	Conflict of anti-colonial liberation. UK colonial administration vs. nationalist opposition (NLF and FLOSY)[f]
Israel (1964–94)	Irredenta/secession/resistance. Israeli government vs. PLO[g] and non-PLO[h] rebels

Conflict	Conflict type
Israel–Egypt, Syria, Jordan (1967)	Interstate/lethal intervention
Oman (1968–76)	Irredenta/secession/resistance. Omani government vs. Dhofari rebels (primarily DLF and PFLOG)[i] (UK, Iranian and South Yemeni intervention)
Jordan (1970)	Irredenta/secession/resistance. Jordanian army vs. PLO[g] rebels.
Yemen–South Yemen (1971–90)	Interstate/lethal intervention (Saudi Arabian intervention)
Israel–Egypt, Syria, Jordan (1973)	Interstate/lethal intervention
Cyprus (1974)	Irredenta/secession/resistance. Cypriot government vs. rebel Turks (Turkish intervention)
Morocco, Mauritania/ Western Sahara (1975–93)	Irredenta/secession/resistance. Morocco, Mauritania (to 1979) governments vs. POLISARIO[j] rebels
Lebanon (1975–91)	Internal factional/ideological. Civil war among Christian (primarily Phalangist militia), Palestinian (primarily PLO)[g], Muslim (primarily pro-Syrian *Amal* and pro-Iranian *Hizbollah*) and Druze (primarily PSP)[k] groups. Syrian (1976), Israeli (1978, 1982), UN (1978) intervention
Syria (1976–87)	Internal factional/ideological. Syrian government vs. Sunni Muslim Brotherhood rebels
Libya–Egypt (1977)	Interstate/lethal intervention
Iran (1978–9)	Internal factional/ideological. Iranian (Shah) government vs. fundamental Islamic (Khomeini) rebels
Iran–Iraq (1979–89)	Interstate/lethal intervention
Iran (1979–94)	Irredenta/secession/resistance. Iranian government vs. Kurdish rebels (primarily KDPI)[l] (Iraqi intervention)
Iraq (1980–95)	Internal factional/ideological. Iraqi government vs SAIRI[m] rebels (Iranian intervention)
Turkey (1984–95)	Irredenta/secession/resistance. Turkish government vs. *Pesh Merga* rebels
South Yemen (1986–7)	Internal factional/ideological. Forces loyal to President Muhammad vs. forces loyal to Prime Minister Abu Bakr al-Attas
Kuwait (1990)	Interstate/lethal intervention. Iraqi invasion of Kuwait in pursuit of "Greater Iraq" territorial designs

Conflict	Conflict type
Iraq–Gulf Allies (1991)	Interstate/lethal intervention (UN intervention)
Egypt (1992–5)	Internal faction/ideological. Egyptian government vs. fundamental Islamic rebels (primarily *Gama'a el-Islamiya*, and *al-Jihad*)
Algeria (1992–5)	Internal factional/ideological. Algerian government vs. fundamental Islamic rebels (primarily FIS/AIS and GIA)[n]
Lebanon (1992–5)	Interstate/lethal intervention. Israeli intervention in southern Lebanon/self-declared security zone against Lebanese-based *Amal*, *Hizbollah*, and *Hamas* guerrillas
Yemen (1994)	Irredenta/secession/resistance. Northern forces loyal to President Saleh vs. southern forces loyal to vice-president al-Baid

[a]	SNB	Syrian National Bloc
[b]	Arab League	Transjordan, Syria, Egypt, Iraq, Lebanon
[c]	FLN	*Front de Liberation Nationale*
[d]	EOKA	*Ethniki Organosis Kipriakou Agono*
[e]	DPK	Democratic Party of Kurdistan
	PUK	Patriotic Union of Kurdistan
[f]	NLF	National Liberation Front
	FLOSY	Front for the Liberation of Occupied South Yemen
[g]	PLO	Palestine Liberation Organization (main groups include *al-Fatah*, PFLP/Popular Front for the Liberation of Palestine, DFLP/Democratic Front for the Liberation of Palestine, ALF/Arab Liberation Front, PSF/Popular Struggle Front, *al-Sa'iqa*, PLF/Palestinian Liberation Front and PPP/Palestinian People's Party
[h]	Non-PLO	Main groups include ANO/Abu Nidal Organization, *Hizbollah*, PIJ/Palestinian Islamic *Jihad*, *Amal*, PFLP-GC/Popular Front for the Liberation of Palestine-General Command, *Hamas*, *al-Fatah* – Revolutionary Council, *al-Fatah* – The Uprising and the PLF *Tal'at Ya'qub* Faction
[i]	DLF	Dhofari Liberation Front
	PFLOG	Popular Front for the Liberation of Oman
[j]	POLISARIO	Popular Front for the Liberation of Saguia el Hamra and Rio de Oro
[k]	PSP	Progressive Socialist Party
[l]	KDPI	Kurdish Democratic Party of Iran
[m]	SAIRI	Supreme Assembly for the Islamic Revolution in Iraq
[n]	FIS/AIS	Islamic Salvation Front/Islamic Salvation Army
	GIA	Armed Islamic Group

H East Asia

Conflict	Conflict type
China (1946–58)	Internal factional/ideological. Chinese nationalists vs. Chinese communists (US intervention)
North Korea–South Korea (1950–53)	Interstate/lethal intervention (Chinese, US, and UN intervention)
Tibet (1950–1)	Interstate/lethal intervention. Chinese annexation of Tibet/Xizang province
China (1958–95)	Irredenta/secession/resistance. Chinese government vs. Tibetan rebels in Xizang province (primarily supporters of Dalai Lama)
China (1966–83)	Internal factional/ideological. Chinese government vs. "bourgeois reactionary" rebels during the Cultural and Spiritual Revolutions
China–USSR (1969)	Interstate/lethal intervention

I South Asia

Conflict	Conflict type
India (1946–7)	Internal factional/ideological. Hindus vs. Muslims in British colonial India
India–Pakistan (1947–9)	Interstate/lethal intervention
Hyderabad (1948)	Interstate/lethal intervention. Indian annexation of Hyderabad
India (1955–69)	Irredenta/secession/resistance. Indian government vs. Naga rebels
India (1961)	Conflict of anti-colonial liberation. Indian government vs. Portuguese colonial administrations in Goa, Daman, and Diu
India–China (1962)	Interstate/lethal intervention
India–Pakistan (1965)	Interstate/lethal intervention
India (1966–8)	Irredenta/secession/resistance. Indian government vs. Mizo rebels
Sri Lanka (1971)	Internal factional/ideological. Sri Lankan government vs. Maoist PLF[a] rebels
Pakistan (1971)	Irredenta/secession/resistance. Pakistani government vs. Bangladeshi rebels in East Pakistan (Indian intervention)

Conflict	Conflict type
Pakistan (1973–7)	Irredenta/secession/resistance. Pakistani government vs. Baluchi rebels (Afghan intervention)
Afghanistan (1975–91)	Internal factional/ideological. Afghan government vs. *Mujahideen* rebels (USSR intervention)
India (1977–94)	Irredenta/secession/resistance. Indian government vs. Naga NSCN[b] rebels
India (1981–95)	Irredenta/secession/resistance. Indian government vs. Sikh rebels (primarily KLF and KCF)[c]
India (1982–95)	Irredenta/secession/resistance. Indian government vs. Kashmiri rebels (primarily JKLF[d] and *Hizbul Mujahideen*)
Sri Lanka (1984–95)	Irredenta/secession/resistance. Sri Lankan government vs. LTTE[e] rebels (Indian intervention)
India (1988–95)	Irredenta/secession/resistance. Indian government vs. Bodo rebels in Assam (primarily BVF, BPAC, BSF and ULFA)[f]
India (1992–5)	Irredenta/secession/resistance. Indian government vs. Tripura Tribal rebels (primarily ATTF)[g]
Afghanistan (1992–5)	Internal factional/ideological. Afghan troops loyal to President Burnhanuddin Rabbani vs. forces loyal to Prime Minister Guluddin Hekmatyar and his ally General Abdul Rashid (from Uzbek militia)

[a]	PLF	People's Liberation Front
[b]	NSCN	National Socialist Council for Nagaland
[c]	KLF	Khalistan Liberation Force
	KCF	Khalistan Commando Force
[d]	JKLF	Jammu and Kashmir Liberation Front
[e]	LTTE	Liberation Tigers of Tamil Eelam
[f]	BVF	Bodo Volunteer's Force
	BPAC	Bodo People's Action Committee
	BSF	Bodo Security Force
	ULFA	United Liberation Force of Assam
[g]	ATTF	All-Tripura Tribal Force

J Southeast Asia

Conflict	Conflict type
Indonesia (1945–9)	Conflict of anti-colonial liberation. Dutch colonial administration vs. nationalist opposition
North Vietnam (1946–54)	Conflict of anti-colonial liberation. French colonial administration vs. nationalist opposition (*Vietnam Doc Lap Dong Minh/Viet Minh*)
Malaysia (1948–60)	Internal factional/ideological. Malay colonial nationalists vs. CPM[a] rebels (UK intervention)
Myanmar (1948–94)	Irredenta/secession/resistance. Myanmar government vs. Karen rebels (primarily KNU and KNLA)[b] (Chinese intervention)
Myanmar (1949–94)	Irredenta/secession/resistance. Myanmar government vs. Shan rebels (primarily *Mong Tai* [Shan State] Army/Shan United Army)
Indonesia (1950)	Irredenta/secession/resistance. Indonesian government vs. South Moluccan rebels
Philippines (1950–5)	Internal factional/ideological. Philippine government vs. communist Huk rebels
South Vietnam–North Vietnam (1958–75)	Interstate/lethal intervention (US intervention)
Indonesia (1958–9)	Irredenta/secession/resistance. Indonesian government vs. West Sumatran rebels
Laos (1960–74)	Internal factional/ideological. Laotian government vs. Path Lao rebels (US and North Vietnamese intervention)
Myanmar (1961–95)	Irredenta/secession/resistance. Myanmar government vs. Kachin rebels (primarily KIO/A)[c]
Indonesia (1962–3)	Conflict of anti-colonial liberation. Dutch colonial administration in West Irian vs. Indonesia
Brunei (1962)	Irredenta/secession/resistance. Brunei government vs. rebels in Sarawak and North Borneo opposed to entry of Brunei into Malaysian Federation (UK intervention)
Indonesia–Malaysia (1963–6)	Interstate/lethal intervention (UK, Australian, and New Zealand intervention)
Indonesia (1965–6)	Internal factional/ideological. Indonesian government vs. communist rebels in Western Java (UK intervention)
Indonesia (1965–94)	Irredenta/secession/resistance. Indonesian government vs. OPM[d] rebels in Irian Jaya
Philippines (1968–94)	Internal factional/ideological. Philippine government vs. NPA[e] rebels

Appendix

Conflict	Conflict type
Cambodia/Kampuchea (1970–5)	Internal factional/ideological. Cambodian/ Kampuchean government vs. DK[f]/*Khmer Rouge* rebels (US and North Vietnamese intervention)
Philippines (1972–95)	Irredenta/secession/resistance. Philippine government vs. MNLF and MILF[g] rebels (US intervention)
East Timor (1975)	Interstate/lethal intervention. Indonesian annexation of East Timor
Indonesia (1975–95)	Irredenta/secession/resistance. Indonesian government vs. FRETILIN[h] rebels
Cambodia/Kampuchea (1977–9)	Internal factional/ideological. Cambodian/ Kampuchean government(DK[f]/*Khmer Rouge*) vs. KNUFNS[i] rebels (Vietnamese intervention)
Cambodia/Kampuchea–Vietnam (1978–79)	Interstate/lethal intervention
China–Vietnam (1979)	Interstate/lethal intervention
Cambodia/Kampuchea (1980–95)	Internal factional/ideological. Cambodian/ Kampuchean government vs. PDK/*Khmer Rouge*, KPNLF and ANS[j] rebels (Vietnamese and Thai intervention)
Papua New Guinea (1988–94)	Irredenta/secession/resistance. Papua New Guinea government vs. BRA[k] rebels
Indonesia (1989–94)	Irredenta/secession/resistance. Indonesian government vs. Aceh rebels (primarily NLFA[l] and *Acheh Merdeka*)
Laos (1992)	Internal factional/ideological. Laotian government vs. LNSF[m] rebels

[a] CPM   Communist Party of Malaysia
[b] KNU   Karen National Union
    KNLA   Karen National Liberation Army
[c] KIO/A   Kachin Independence Organization/Army
[d] OPM   *Organisasi Papua Merdeka*
[e] NPA   New People's Army
[f] DK   Democratic Kampuchea
[g] MNLF   Mindanao/Moro National Liberation Front
    MILF   Moro Islamic Liberation Front
[h] FRETILIN   *Frente Revolucionara Timorense de Libertacão e Independencia*
[i] KNUFNS   Kampuchea National United Front for National Salvation
[j] PDK   Party of Democratic Kampuchea
    KPNLF   Khmer People's National Liberation Front
    ANS   *Armée Nationale Sihanoukiste*
[k] BRA   Bougainville Revolutionary Army
[l] NLFA   National Liberation Front of Acheh
[m] LNSF   Lao National Salvation Front

References

Acharya, Amitav, 1991, "The Association of Southeast Asian Nations: Security Community or Defence Community?" *Pacific Affairs*, 64 Summer, pp. 160–77.
1992, *Third World Conflicts and International Order*. Singapore: Department of Political Science, National University of Singapore.
Acton, John Emerich Edward Dalberg, Lord, 1907, "Nationality," in J. N. Figgis, ed., *The History of Freedom and Other Essays*. London: Macmillan.
Adam, Hussein, M., 1995, "Somalia," in William Zartman, ed., *Collapsed States: The Disintegration and Restoration of Legitimate Authority*. Boulder, CO: Westview Press, pp. 69–90.
Ahuma, S. R. B. Attoh, 1979, "Extracts from 'The Negro Race Not Under a Curse'" in J. Ayo Langley, ed., *Ideologies of Liberation in Black Africa 1856–1970*. London: Rex Collings, pp. 161–72.
Ajami, Fouad, 1992, *The Arab Predicament: Arab Political Thought and Practice Since 1967*. Cambridge: Cambridge University Press.
Al-Mashat, Abdul-Monem, 1985, *National Security in the Third World*. Boulder, CO: Westview Press.
Anderson, Benedict, 1983a, *Imagined Communities: Reflections on the Origins and Spread of Nationalism*. London: Verso.
Anderson, Benedict, 1983b, "Old State, New Society: Indonesia's New Order in Comparative Historical Perspective," *Journal of Asian Studies* 43, May, pp. 477–96.
Anderson, Charles. W., 1982, "Toward a Theory of Latin American Politics," in Howard J. Wiarda, ed., *Politics and Social Change in Latin America*. Amherst: University of Massachusetts Press, pp. 239–54.
Aron, Raymond, 1954, *The Century of Total War*. New York: Doubleday.
Ashley, Richard K., 1988, "Untying the Sovereign State: A Double Reading of the Anarchy Problematique." *Millennium* 17, 2, pp. 227–62.
Atkins, G. Pope, 1990, "South America in the International Political System," in G. Pope Atkins, ed., *South America into the 1990s*. Boulder, CO: Westview Press, pp. 1–26.

References

Awolowo, Obafemi, 1979, "Extracts from The People's Republic," in J. Ayo Langley, ed., *Ideologies of Liberation in Black Africa 1856–1970*. London: Rex Collings, pp. 487–505.

Aylwin, José, 1992, "Les droits des peuples indigènes au Chili pendant la transition chilienne des droits de l'homme," in Jacques Zylberberg and François Demers, eds., *L'Amérique et les Amériques*. Sainte-Foy, Quebec: Les Presses de l'Université Laval, pp. 644–57.

Ayoob, Mohammed, 1991, "The Security Problematic of the Third World," *World Politics* 43, January, pp. 257–83.

  1995, *The Third World Security Predicament: State Making, Regional Conflict, and the International System*. Boulder, CO: Lynne Rienner.

Ayubi, Nazih, 1990, "Arab Bureaucracies: Expanding Size, Changing Roles," in Giacomo Luciani, ed., *The Arab State*. London: Routledge, pp. 129–49.

Azikiwe, Nnamdi, 1979, "The Future of Pan-Africanism," in J. Ayo Langley, ed., *Ideologies of Liberation in Black Africa 1856–1970*. London: Rex Collings, pp. 307–27.

Baker, John and Martin Kolinsky, 1991, "The State and Integration," in Cornelia Navari, ed., *The Condition of States. A Study in International Political Theory*. Milton Keynes: Open University Press, pp. 102–24.

Ball, Nicole, 1991, "The Effect of Conflict on the Economies of Third World Countries," in Francis M. Deng and I. William Zartman, eds., *Conflict Resolution in Africa*. Washington, DC: The Brookings Institution, pp. 272–91.

Barber, Benjamin, 1992, "Jihad vs. McWorld," *The Atlantic* 269, 3, March, pp. 53–65.

Barboza, Mario Gibson, 1992, *Na Diplomacia, o Traço todo da Vida*. Rio de Janeiro: Editora Record.

Barker, Rodney, 1991, *Political Legitimacy and the State*. Oxford: Oxford University Press.

Barkin, Samuel and Bruce Cronin, 1994, "The State and the Nation: Changing Norms and the Rules of Sovereignty in International Relations." *International Organization* 48, 1, pp. 107–30.

Barros, Alexandre and Edmundo Coelho, 1986, "Military Intervention and Withdrawal in South America," in Abraham F. Lowenthal and J. Samuel Fitch, eds., *The Military and Politics in Latin America*. New York: Holmes and Meier, pp. 437–43.

Bayart, Jean-François, 1991, "Finishing with the Idea of the Third World: The Concept of the Political Trajectory," in James Manor, ed., *Rethinking Third World Politics*. New York: Longman, pp. 51–72.

Beblawi, Hazem, 1990, "The Rentier State in the Arab World," in Giacomo Luciani, ed., *The Arab State*. London: Routledge, pp. 85–98.

Ben-Dor, Gabriel, 1983, *State and Conflict in the Middle East: Emergence of the Post-Colonial State*. New York: Praeger.

Ben-Israel, Hedva, 1991, "Irredentism: Nationalism Reexamined," in Naomi Chazan, ed., *Irredentism and International Politics*. Boulder, CO: Lynne Rienner, pp. 23–36.

Bensaid, Said, 1987, "Al-Watan and Al-Umma in Contemporary Arab Use," in Ghassan Salamé, ed., *The Foundations of the Arab State*. London: Croom Helm, pp. 149–76.

Bienen, Henry, 1983, "The State and Ethnicity: Integrative Formulas in Africa," in Donald Rothchild and Victor A. Olorunsola, eds., *State Versus Ethnic Claims: African Policy Dilemmas*. Boulder, CO: Westview Press, pp. 100–26.

1989, *Armed Forces, Conflict and Change in Africa*. Boulder, CO: Westview Press.

Birch, Anthony, 1978, "Minority Nationalist Movements and Theories of Political Integration." *World Politics* 30, pp. 325–44.

Bloomfield, Lincoln, 1989, "Coping with Conflict in the Late Twentieth Century." *International Journal* 44, 4, pp. 772–802.

Bragança, Aquino de and Immanuel Wallerstein, 1982, *African Liberation Reader*, vol. II: *Wars of National Liberation*. London: Zed Press.

Branthwaite, Alan, 1993, "The Psychological Basis of Independent Statehood," in Robert H. Jackson and Alan James, eds., *States in a Changing World: A Contemporary Analysis*. London: Clarendon Press, pp. 46–66.

Brass, Paul, 1985, ed., *Ethnic Groups and the State*. London: Croom Helm.

Braudel, Fernand, 1988, *The Identity of France*, vol. I: *History and Environment*, trans. Sian Reynolds. London: Collins.

1990, *The Identity of France*, vol. II: *People and Production*, trans. Sian Reynolds. New York: Harper Collins.

Brenner, Michael, 1994, "Discord and Collaboration: Europe's Security Future," in Douglas T. Stuart and Stephen F. Szabo, eds., *Discord and Collaboration in a New Europe: Essays in Honor of Arnold Wolfers*. Washington, DC: The Foreign Policy Institute, Paul H. Nitze School of Advanced International Studies, pp. 71–104.

Breuilly, John, 1982, *Nationalism and the State*. Manchester: Manchester University Press.

Brewin, Christopher, 1991, "The Duties of Liberal States," in Cornelia Navari, ed., *The Condition of States*. Milton Keynes: Open University Press, pp. 197–215.

Brown, Michael, 1993, "Causes and Implications of Ethnic Conflict," in Michael E. Brown, ed., *Ethnic Conflict and International Security*. Princeton: Princeton University Press, pp. 3–26.

Brownlie, Ian, 1979, *African Boundaries: A Legal and Diplomatic Encyclopedia*. Berkeley, CA: University of California Press.

Brubaker, Rogers, 1992, *Citizenship and Nationhood in France and Germany*. Cambridge, MA: Harvard University Press.

Buckheit, Lee, 1978, *Secession: The Legitimacy of Self-Determination*. New Haven: Yale University Press.

Bull, Hedley, 1977, *The Anarchical Society: A Study of Order in World Politics*. London: Macmillan.

Burr, Robert N., 1965, *By Reason or Force: Chile and the Balancing of Power in South America, 1830–1905*. Berkeley: University of California Press.

References

Busia, K. W., 1979, "Extracts from Africa in Search of Democracy," in J. Ayo Langley, ed., *Ideologies of Liberation in Black Africa 1856–1970*. London: Rex Collings, pp. 447–57.

Bustamente, Ferando, 1993, "La proyeccion Estratégica de Brasil: Vision de sus Problemas de Defensa Presente y Futura," in Va Rigoberto Cruz Johnson and Augusto Varas Fernandes, eds., *Percepciones de Amenaza y Politicas de Defensa en America Latina*. Santiago, Chile: FLACSO/Centro de Estudios Estratégicos de la Armada de Chile (CEEA), pp. 117–91.

Butterworth, Charles E, 1987, "State and Authority in Arabic Political Thought," in Ghassan Salamé, ed., *The Foundations of the Arab State*. London: Croom Helm, pp. 91–111.

Buzan, Barry, 1983, *People, States and Fear: The National Security Problem in International Relations*. Aldershot, Hants.: Wheatsheaf Books.

1988, "The Southeast Asian Security Complex." *Contemporary Southeast Asia* 10, 1, pp. 1–16.

1989, "The Concept of National Security for Developing Countries," in Mohammed Ayoob and Chai-Anan Samudavanija (eds.), *Leadership Perceptions and National Security*. Singapore: Institute of Southeast Asian Studies, pp. 1–28.

1991, *People, States and Fear: An Agenda for International Security Studies in the Post-Cold War Era*. London: Harvester Wheatsheaf.

Cabral, Amilcar, 1979, "The Weapon of Theory," in J. Ayo Langley, ed., *Ideologies of Liberation in Black Africa 1856–1970*. London: Rex Collings, pp. 682–702.

Callaghy, Thomas, 1987, "The State as Lame Leviathan: The Patrimonial Administrative State in Africa," in Zaki Ergas, ed., *The African State in Transition*. London: Macmillan Press, pp. 87–115.

1991, "Africa in the World Economy," in John W. Harbeson and Donald Rothchild, eds., *Africa in World Politics*. Boulder, CO: Westview Press, pp. 39–68.

Calvert, Peter, 1983, *Boundary Disputes in Latin America*. London: Institute for the Study of Conflict.

Camilleri, Joseph and Jim Falk, 1992, *The End of Sovereignty? The Politics of a Shrinking and Fragmented World*. Aldershot, Hants.: Edward Edgar Publishing Ltd.

Centre Québécois de Relations Internationales, 1995, "Essor ou Déclin de l'Humanitaire?" *Le Maintien de la Paix*, Bulletin No. 13.

Chaliand, Gerard, 1969, *Armed Struggle in Africa: With the Guerrillas in "Portuguese" Guinea*. New York: Martin Robertson.

1989, "Minority Peoples in the Age of Nation-States," in Gerard Chaliand, ed., *Minority Peoples in the Age of Nation-States*. London: Pluto Press, pp. 1–11.

Chamorro, Wilson, 1994, "Seguridad an las Fronteras." *El Telegrafo* (Guayaquil), June 14, section C.

Chand, Attar, 1989, *Jawaharlal Nehru and his Social Philosophy*. Delhi: Amar Prakashan.

Chatelus, Michel, 1990, "Policies for Development: Attitude Toward Industry and Services," in Giacomo Luciani, ed., *The Arab State*. London: Routledge, pp. 99–128.

Chazan, Naomi, ed., 1991, *Irredentism and International Politics*. Boulder, CO: Lynne Rienner, pp. 1–8 and 139–52.

Chazan, Naomi and Victor LeVine, 1991, "Africa and the Middle East: Patterns of Convergence and Divergence," in John W. Harbeson and Donald Rothchild, eds., *Africa in World Politics*. Boulder, CO: Westview Press, pp. 202–27.

Child, Jack, 1985, *Geopolitics and Conflict in South America*. New York: Praeger.
    1990, "The Status of South American Geopolitical Thinking," in G. Pope Atkins, ed., *South America into the 1990s*. Boulder, CO: Westview Press, pp. 53–86.

Childs, John, 1982, *Armies and Warfare in Europe, 1648–1789*. Manchester: Manchester University Press.

Chipman, John, 1993, "Managing the Politics of Parochialism," in Michael E. Brown, ed., *Ethnic Conflict and International Security*. Princeton: Princeton University Press, pp. 237–64.

Chisiza, D., 1979, "Political Problems," in J. Ayo Langley, ed., *Ideologies of Liberation in Black Africa 1856–1970*. London: Rex Collings, pp. 572–81.

Chubin, Shahram, 1991, "Third World Conflicts: Trends and Prospects." *International Social Science Journal* 31, 1, pp. 147–61.

Clapham, Christopher, 1991, "State, Society and Political Institutions in Revolutionary Ethiopia," in James Manor, ed., *Rethinking Third World Politics*. New York: Longman, pp. 242–66.

Claude, Inis, 1955, *National Minorities: An International Problem*. Cambridge, MA: Harvard University Press.

Clough, Michael, 1991, "US Policy Towards the Third World in the Twenty First Century," in Thomas Weiss and Meryl Kessler, eds., *Third World Security in the Post Cold War Era*. Boulder, CO: Lynne Rienner, 1991, pp. 67–84.

Coakley, John, 1994, "Approaches to the Resolution of Ethnic Conflicts: the Strategy of Non-territorial Autonomy," *International Political Science Review* 15, pp. 297–314.

Cohen, Lenard, 1993, *Broken Bonds: The Disintegration of Yugoslavia*. Boulder, CO: Westview Press.

Cohen, Youssef, Brian R. Brown, and A. F. K. Organski, 1981, "The Paradoxical Nature of State Making: The Violent Creation of Order." *American Political Science Review* 75, 4, pp. 901–10.

Coleman, Kenneth, 1984, "On Comparing Foreign Policies: Comments on van Klaveren," in Heraldo Munoz and Joseph S. Tulchin, eds., *Latin American Nations in World Politics*. Boulder, CO: Westview Press, pp. 22–9.

Connor, Walker, 1978, "A Nation is a Nation, is a State, is an Ethnic Group, is a . . ." *Ethnic and Racial Studies* 1, 4, pp. 441–72.
    1990, "When is a Nation?" *Ethnic and Racial Studies* 13, 1, pp. 92–104.

References

Cooper, Robert and Mats Berdal, 1993, "Outside Intervention in Ethnic Conflicts," in Michael E. Brown, ed., *Ethnic Conflict and International Security*. Princeton: Princeton University Press, pp. 181–206.

Copson, Raymond, 1991, "Peace in Africa? The Influence of Regional and International Change," in Francis Deng and William Zartman, eds., *Conflict Resolution in Africa*. Washington, DC: The Brookings Institution, pp. 19–41.

1994, *Africa's Wars and Prospects for Peace*. Armonk, NY: M. E. Sharp.

Corm, Georges G., 1988, *Fragmentation of the Middle East: The Last Thirty Years*. London: Hutchinson.

Crenshaw, Martha, 1993, "Explaining Third World Military Intervention: India and Sri Lanka, 1987." Paper prepared for the 34th Annual Convention of the International Studies Association, Acapulco, Mexico, March 23–7.

Crook, Richard, 1991, "State, Society and Political Institutions in Côte d'Ivoire and Ghana," in James Manor, ed., *Rethinking Third World Politics*. New York: Longman, pp. 213–41.

David, Steven R., 1991, "Explaining Third World Alignment." *World Politics* 40, pp. 233–56.

Davidson, Basil, 1992, *The Black Man's Burden: Africa and the Curse of the Nation-State*. London: James Curry.

Dawisha, Adeed, 1988, "Conclusion: Reasons for Resilience," in Adeed Dawisha and William Zartman, eds., *Beyond Coercion. The Durability of the Arab State*. London: Croom Helm, pp. 276–83.

1990, "Arab Regimes: Legitimacy and Foreign Policy," in Giacomo Luciani, ed., *The Arab State*. London: Routledge, pp. 284–99.

de Silva, K., 1991, "Indo-Sri Lankan Relations, 1975–89: A Study in the Internationalization of Ethnic Conflict," in K. de Silva and R. May, eds., *Internationalization of Ethnic Conflict*. London: Pinter Publishers, pp. 76–106.

Deng, Francis and William Zartman, 1991, "Introduction," in Francis M. Deng and I. William Zartman, eds., *Conflict Resolution in Africa*. Washington, DC: The Brookings Institution, pp. 1–18.

Deutsch, Karl W., 1954, *Political Community at the International Level: Problems of Definition and Measurement*. Garden City, NY: Doubleday.

Deutsch, Karl, et al., 1957, *Political Community and the North Atlantic Area*. Princeton, NJ: Princeton University Press.

Deyo, Fredric, ed., 1987, *The Political Economy of the New Asian Industrialism*. Cornell: Cornell University Press.

Dix, Robert H., 1994, "Military Coups and Military Rule in Latin America." *Armed Forces and Society* 20, 3, pp. 439–56.

Djalili, Mohammad-Reza, 1991, "Analysis of Third World Conflicts: Outline of a Typology." *International Social Science Journal* 43, February, pp. 163–71.

Douglass, William, 1988, "A Critique of Recent Trends in the Analysis of Ethnonationalism." *Ethnic and Racial Studies* 11, 2, pp. 192–206.

Doyle, Michael, 1986, "Liberalism and World Politics." *The American Political Science Review* 80, pp. 1151–69.

Dubois, Colette, 1994, "L'ONU et la décolonization de la Corne d'Afrique 1948–1977." *Relations Internationales* 77, Spring, pp. 81–98.

Dyer, Gwynne, 1985, *War*. Toronto: Stoddart.

The Economist, 1990, "The State of the Nation State." December 22, pp. 43–6.

Ecuador, Ministerio de Relaciones Exteriores, 1992, *Contrapropuesta Peruana*. Quito: Dirección General de Communicación y Prensa.

Ekwe-Ekwe, Herbert, 1990, *Conflict and Intervention in Africa: Nigeria, Angola, Zaire*. London: Macmillan.

Elaigwu, Isawa and Victor Olorunsola, 1983, "Federalism and Politics of Compromise," in Donald Rothchild and Victor A. Olorunsola, eds., *State Versus Ethnic Claims: African Policy Dilemmas*. Boulder, CO: Westview Press, pp. 281–303.

Enloe, Cynthia, 1981, *Ethnic Conflict and Political Development*. Boston: Little, Brown and Company.

Ergas, Zaki, ed., 1987, *The African State in Transition*. London: Macmillan Press, pp. 1–24, 295–330.

Eriksen, Thomas, 1992, "Linguistic Hegemony and Minority Resistance." *Journal of Peace Research* 29, 3, pp. 313–32.

Espiell, Hector Gros, 1980, *The Right to Self-Determination: Implementation of United Nations Resolutions*. New York: United Nations.

Evans, B. Peter, Dietrich Rueschemeyer, and Theda Skocpol, eds., 1985, *Bringing the State Back In*. Cambridge: Cambridge University Press.

Fenet, Alain, 1989, "The Question of Minorities in the Order of Law," in Gerard Chaliand, ed., *Minority Peoples in the Age of Nation-States*. London: Pluto Press, pp. 12–54.

Fitch, Samuel, 1986, "Armies and Politics in Latin America: 1975–1985," and "The Military Coup d'État as Political Process: a General Framework and the Ecuadorian Case," in Abraham Lowenthal and J. Samuel Fitch, eds., *Armies and Politics in Latin America*. New York and London: Holmes and Meier, pp. 26–55, 151–64.

Fitzsimmons, Michael P., 1993, "The National Assembly and the Invention of Citizenship," in Renée Waldinger, Philip Dawson and Isser Woloch, eds., *The French Revolution and the Meaning of Citizenship*. Westport, CT: Greenwood, pp. 29–42.

Foltz, William, 1990, "Dynamics of Revolutionary Change: External Causes," in Barry Schutz and Robert Slater, eds., *Revolution and Political Change in the Third World*. Boulder, CO: Lynne Rienner, 1990, pp. 54–68.

1991, "The Organization of African Unity and the Resolution of Africa's Conflicts," in Francis Deng and William Zartman, eds., *Conflict Resolution in Africa*. Washington, DC: The Brookings Institution, pp. 347–66.

Friedrich, Carl Joachim, 1963, *Man and his Government: An Empirical Theory of Politics*. New York: McGraw-Hill.

Frost, Mervyn, 1991, "What Ought to be Done about the Condition of States?" in Cornelia Navari, ed., *The Condition of States: A Study in International Political Theory*. Milton Keynes: Open University Press, pp. 183–96.

231

References

Fukuyama, Francis, 1989, "The End of History?" *National Interest*, Summer, pp. 3–18.

Galtung, Johan, 1971, "A Structural Theory of Imperialism." *Journal of Conflict Resolution* 8, pp. 387–417.

Garrett, James, 1985, "The Beagle Channel Dispute: Confrontation and Negotiation in the Southern Cone." *Journal of Interamerican Studies and World Affairs* 27, Fall, pp. 81–109.

Gelb, Leslie, 1994, "Quelling the Teacup Wars." *Foreign Affairs* 73, 6, pp. 2–6.

George, Jim, 1994, *Discourses of Global Politics: A Critical (Re)Introduction to International Relations*. Boulder, CO: Lynne Rienner.

Giddens, Anthony, 1987, *The Nation State and Violence*. Berkeley: University of California Press.

Glenny, Misha, 1993, *The Fall of Yugoslavia*. London: Penguin.

Glickman, Harvey, 1987, "Reflections on State-Centrism as Ideology in Africa," in Zaki Ergas, ed., *The African State in Transition*. London: Macmillan, pp. 25–44.

Goertz, Gary and Paul Diehl, 1992, *Territorial Changes and International Conflict*. London: Routledge.

Goldgeier, James and Michael McFaul, 1992, "A Tale of Two Worlds: Core and Periphery in the Post-Cold War Era." *International Organization* 46, 2, Spring, pp. 467–91.

Goldstein, Erik, 1992, *Wars and Peace Treaties, 1816–1991*. London: Routledge.

Goose, Stephen D. and Frank Smyth, 1994, "Arming Genocide in Rwanda." *Foreign Affairs*, September/October, pp. 86–96.

Gopinath, Aruna, 1991, "International Aspects of the Thai Muslim and Philippine Moro Issues: A Comparative Study," in K. de Silva and R. May, eds., *Internationalization of Ethnic Conflict*. London: Pinter Publishers, pp. 125–47.

Gottlieb, Gidon, 1993, *Nation Against State: New Approaches to Ethnic Conflicts and the Decline of Sovereignty*. New York: Council on Foreign Relations Press.

Granier, Jorge Gumucio, 1988, *United States and the Bolivian Seacoast*. La Paz: Ministerio de Relaciones Exteriores y Culto.

Greenfeld, Liah, 1993, "Transcending the Nation's Worth," in Claudio Véliz, ed., *The Worth of Nations: The Boston, Melbourne, Oxford Conversazioni on Culture and Society*. Boston: Boston University, pp. 43–56.

Grimmet, Richard F., 1993, *Conventional Arms Transfers to the Third World, 1985–1992*. Washington, DC: Congressional Research Service, Library of Congress, July 19.

Guazzone, Laura, 1988, "Gulf Cooperation Council: The Security Policies." *Survival* 30, 2, pp. 134–48.

Gupta, Bhabani Sen, 1991, "Internationalization of Ethnic Conflict: The Punjab Crisis of the 1980s," in K. de Silva and R. May, eds., *Internationalization of Ethnic Conflict*. London: Pinter Publishers, pp. 51–7.

Gurdon, Charles, 1989, "Instability and the State: Sudan," in Caroline Thomas and Paikiasothy Saravanamuttu, eds., *The State and Instability in the South*. New York: St. Martin's Press, pp. 61–80.

Gurr, Ted, 1988, "War, Revolution, and the Growth of the Coercive State." *Comparative Political Studies* 21, 1, pp. 45–65.

1991a "Minorities at Risk: The Dynamics of Ethnopolitical Mobilization and Conflict, 1945–1990." Paper presented at the Annual Meetings, International Studies Association, Vancouver, Canada, April.

1991b, "Theories of Political Violence and Revolution in the Third World," in Francis Deng and William Zartman, eds., *Conflict Resolution in Africa*. Washington, DC: The Brookings Institution, pp. 153–89.

1993, *Minorities at Risk: a Global View of Ethnopolitical Conflicts*. Washington, DC: United States Institute of Peace Press.

Gurr, Ted, and Barbara Harff, 1994, *Ethnic Conflict and World Politics*. Boulder, CO: Westview Press.

Gurr, Ted and James Scarritt, 1989, "Minorities Rights at Risk: A Global Survey." *Human Rights Quarterly* 11, pp. 375–405.

Haass, Richard, 1990, *Conflicts Unending. The United States and Regional Disputes*. New Haven: Yale University Press.

Hahm, Chaibong, 1994, "Democracy and Authority in the Post-Confucian Context." Paper presented at the International Conference on "The 21st Century and Democracy: Theory, Reality, Tasks." Seoul: the Korean Association of International Studies, October 28–9.

Hall, John, ed., 1986, *States in History*. New York: Basil Blackwell, pp. 1–21, 154–76.

Halliday, Fred, 1989, "States and Revolution in the South," in Caroline Thomas and Paikiasothy Saravanamuttu, eds., *The State and Instability in the South*. New York: St. Martin's Press, pp. 99–111.

Hannum, Hurst, 1990, *Autonomy, Sovereignty, and Self-Determination: The Accommodation of Conflicting Rights*, Philadelphia: University of Pennsylvania Press.

Harbeson, John, 1991, "The International Politics of Identity in the Horn of Africa," in John Harbeson and Donald Rothchild, eds., *Africa in World Politics*. Boulder, CO: Westview Press, pp. 119–43.

Harik, Iliya, 1990, "The Origins of the Arab State System," in Giacomo Luciani, ed., *The Arab State*. London: Routledge, pp. 1–28.

Hassner, Pierre, 1993, "Beyond Nationalism and Internationalism: Ethnicity and World Order," in Michael Brown, ed., *Ethnic Conflict and International Security*. Princeton: Princeton University Press, pp. 125–42.

Hawthorn, Geoffrey, 1991, "Waiting for a Text? Comparing Third World Politics," in James Manor, ed., *Rethinking Third World Politics*. New York: Longman, pp. 24–50.

Hensel, Paul R., 1994, "One Thing Leads to Another: Recurrent Militarized Disputes in Latin America, 1816–1986." *Journal of Peace Research* 31, 3, pp. 281–97.

Heraclides, Alexis, 1990, "Secessionist Minorities and External Involvement." *International Organization* 44, 3, pp. 341–78.

1991, *The Self-determination of Minorities in International Politics*. London: Frank Cass.

References

1994, "Secessionist Conflagration: What is to Be Done?" *Security Dialogue* 25, 3, pp. 293–93.

Herbst, Jeffrey, 1989, "The Creation and Maintenance of National Boundaries in Africa." *International Organization* 43, Autumn, pp. 673–92.

1990, "War and the State in Africa," *International Security* 14, 4, pp. 177–239.

1991, "The United States and Africa: Issues for the Future," in John Harbeson and Donald Rothchild, eds., *Africa in World Politics*. Boulder, CO: Westview Press, pp. 161–78.

1993, "The Potential for Conflict in Africa," in Patricia Cronin, ed., *From Globalism to Regionalism: New Perspectives on U.S. Foreign and Defense Policies*. Washington, DC: National Defense University Press, pp. 111–24.

Hermassi, Elbaki, 1987, "State-building and Regime Performance in the Greater Maghreb," in Ghassan Salamé, ed., *The Foundations of the Arab State*. London: Croom Helm, pp. 75–90.

Hersch, Seymour M., 1994, "The Wild East." *Atlantic Monthly* 273, June, pp. 61–86.

Hill, Christopher, 1991, "Diplomacy and the Modern State," in Cornelia Navari, ed., *The Condition of States. A Study in International Political Theory*. Milton Keynes: Open University Press, pp. 85–101.

Hirst, Monica, and Carlos Rico, 1993, "Latin America's Security Agenda," in Jayantha Dhanapala, ed., *Regional Approaches to Disarmament: Security and Stability*. Aldershot, Hants.: Dartmouth Press for the United Nations Institute for Disarmament Research, pp. 241–69.

Hobsbawm, Eric, 1990, *Nations and Nationalism since 1780. Programme, Myth, Reality*. Cambridge: Cambridge University Press.

Hoffmann, Stanley, 1981, *Duties Beyond Borders: On the Limits and Possibilities of Ethical International Politics*. Syracuse, NY: Syracuse University Press.

Holm, John and Patrick Molutsi, 1992, "State-Society Relations in Botswana: Beginning Liberalization," in Göran Hydén and Michael Bratton, eds., *Governance and Politics in Africa*. Boulder, CO: Lynne Rienner, pp. 75–106.

Holsti, Kalevi J., 1966, "Resolving International Conflicts: A Taxonomy of Behavior and Some Figures on Procedures." *Journal of Conflict Resolution* 10, pp. 277–96.

1980, "Change in the International System: Interdependence, Integration, and Fragmentation," in Ole R. Holsti, Randolph M. Siverson, and Alexander L. George, eds., *Change in the International System*. Boulder CO: Westview Press, pp. 23–53.

1991, *Peace and War: Armed Conflicts and Internationial Order, 1648–1989*. Cambridge: Cambridge University Press.

1992a, "International Theory and War in the Third World," in Brian Job, ed., *The Insecurity Dilemma: National Security of Third World States*. Boulder CO: Lynne Rienner, pp. 37–60.

1992b, "Polyarchy in Nineteenth-Century Europe," in James N. Rosenau and Ernst-Otto Czempiel, eds., *Governance Without Government: Order and Change in World Politics*. Cambridge: Cambridge University Press, pp. 30–57.

234

1994, "The Post-Cold War 'Settlement' in Comparative Perspective," in Douglas T. Stuart and Stephen F. Szabo, eds., *Discord and Collaboration in New Europe: Essays in Honor of Arnold Wolfers*. Washington, DC: The Foreign Policy Institute, The Paul H. Nitze School of Advanced International Studies, pp. 37–70.

Horowitz, Donald L., 1985, *Ethnic Groups in Conflict*. Berkeley, CA: University of California Press.

Horowitz, Donald., 1991, "Irredentas and Secessions: Adjacent Phenomena, Neglected Connections," in Naomi Chazan, ed., *Irredentism and International Politics*. Boulder, CO: Lynne Rienner, pp. 9–22.

Howard, Michael, 1976, *War in European History*. London: Oxford University Press.

Huntington, Samuel P., 1968, *Political Order in Changing Societies*. New Haven: Yale University Press.

1993, "The Coming Clash of Civilizations." *Foreign Affairs* 72, Summer, pp. 22–49.

1994, "Balancing Power in Asia." Article adapted from a paper delivered at the Pacific Rim Forum, Beijing, reprinted in *The Japan Times*, November 12, p. 18.

Hydén, Göran, 1983, "Problems and Prospects of State Coherence," in Donald Rothchild and Victor Olorunsola, eds., *State Versus Ethnic Claims: African Policy Dilemmas*. Boulder, CO: Westview Press, pp. 67–84.

Hydén, Göran, and Michael Bratton, eds., 1992, *Governance and Politics in Africa*. Boulder and London: Lynne Rienner.

Infante, Maria Teresa, 1984, "Argentina y Chile: Percepciones del conflicto de la Zone del Beagle," *Estudios Internacionales* 67, July–September, pp. 337–58.

Jackson, Robert H., 1990, *Quasi-states: Sovereignty, International Relations and the Third World*. Cambridge: Cambridge University Press.

Jackson, Robert H, and Alan James, eds., 1993, *States in a Changing World: A Contemporary Analysis*. Oxford: Clarendon Press.

Jackson, Robert and Carl Rosberg, 1982, "Africa's Weak States Persist: The Empirical and the Juridical in Statehood," *World Politics* 35, October, pp. 1–24.

Janowski, Oscar, 1945, *Nationalities and National Minorities*. New York: Macmillan.

Jarrin, Edgardo Mercado, 1989, *Un Sistema de Seguridad y Defensa Sudamericano*. Lima: Centro Peruano de Estudios Internacionales (CEPEI).

Jedaane, Fahmi, 1990, "Notions of the State in Contemporary Arab-Islamic Writings," in Giacomo Luciani, ed., *The Arab State*. London: Routledge, pp. 247–83.

Jervis, Robert, 1982, "Security Regimes," *International Organization* 36, 2, pp. 357–78.

Johnson, Rigoberto Cruz, and Augusto Varas Fernandez, eds., 1993, *Percepciones de Amenaza y Politicas de Defensa en America Latina*. Santiago: FLACSO/Centro de Estudios Estrategicos de la Armada de Chile (CEEA).

References

Jones, Adam, 1994, "Wired World: Communications Technology, Governance and the Democratic Uprising," in Edward A. Comor, ed., *The Global Political Economy of Communication*. London and New York: Macmillan and St. Martin's Press, pp. 145–64.

Jones, Colin, 1988, *The Longman Companion to the French Revolution*. London: Longman.

Juergensmeyer, Mark, 1993, *The New Cold War? Religious Nationalism Confronts the Secular State*. Berkeley: University of California Press.

Kacowicz, Arie, 1994, "Zones of Peace in the International System." Jerusalem: Department of International Relations, The Hebrew University of Jerusalem, (mimeo).

Kangas, Roger D., 1994, "Problems of State-Building in the Central Asian Republics." *World Affairs* 157, 1, Summer, pp. 29–37.

Kant, Immanuel, [1795] 1963, "Perpetual Peace," *Immanuel Kant: On History*, ed. and trans. Lewis White Beck. Indianapolis: Bobbs-Merrill.

Kaplan, Robert, 1994, "The Coming Anarchy." *Atlantic Monthly* 273, February, pp. 44–76.

Kapuscinski, Ryszard, 1990, *The Soccer War*, trans. William Brand. London: Granta Books.

Kedourie, Elie, 1966, *Nationalism*. London: Hutchinson and Co.

Keegan, John, 1993, *A History of Warfare*. New York: Alfred A. Knopf.

Keesing's Contemporary Archives. London: Keesing's Ltd., monthly.

Keller, Edmond, 1990, "Revolution and the Collapse of Traditional Monarchies," in Barry Schutz and Robert Slater, eds., *Revolution and Political Change in the Third World*. Boulder, CO: Lynne Rienner Publishers, pp. 81–98.

Kelsen, Hans, 1952, *Principles of International Law*. New York: Rinehart.

Kick, E. and D. Kiefer, 1987, "The Influence of the World System on War in the Third World." *International Journal of Sociology and Social Policy* 7, pp. 34–48.

Kinzer, Stephen, 1993, "Croatia's Founding Chief is Seen as 'Mixed Story,'" *New York Times*, August 5, p. A10.

Kodikara, Shelton, 1991, "Internationalization of Sri Lanka's Ethnic Conflict: The Tamilnadu Factor," in K. de Silva and R. May, eds., *Internationalization of Ethnic Conflict*. London: Pinter Publishers, pp. 107–14.

Korany, Bahgat, 1986, "Strategic Studies and the Third World: A Critical Evaluation," *International Social Science Journal* 38, 4, pp. 547–62.

1987, "Alien and Besieged, Yet Here to Stay: the Contradictions of the Arab Territorial State," in Ghassan Salamé, ed., *The Foundations of the Arab State*. London: Croom Helm, pp. 47–74.

Kuye, J., 1979, "Right of the People to Self-Determination (with a special reference to British West Africa)," in Ayo Langley, ed., *Ideologies of Liberation in Black Africa 1856–1970*. London: Rex Collings, pp. 213–19.

Laitin, David, 1983, "The Ogaden Question and Changes in Somali Identity," in Donald Rothchild and Victor Olorunsola, eds., *State Versus Ethnic Claims: African Policy Dilemmas*. Boulder, CO: Westview Press, pp. 331–49.

236

Lancaster, Carol, 1991, "The Lagos Three: Economic Regionalism in Sub-Saharan Africa," in John Harbeson and Donald Rothchild, eds., *Africa in World Politics*. Boulder, CO: Westview Press, pp. 249–67.

Langley, Ayo, ed., 1979, *Ideologies of Liberation in Black Africa 1856–1970*. London: Rex Collings, pp. 2–71.

Laponce, Jean, 1960, *The Protection of Minorities*. Berkeley: University of California Press.

Lawson, Stephanie, 1992, *The Politics of Authenticity: Ethnonationalist Conflict and the State*. Canberra: The Australian National University Peace Research Centre, Working Paper No. 125.

Lee, Shin-wha, 1994, "No Hope for Democracy?: Emerging Threats to Democratization Processes in Africa." Paper prepared for the International Conference on "The 21st Century and Democracy: Theory, Reality and Tasks," Seoul: the Korean Association of International Studies, October 28–9.

Lemaitre, Pierre, Kristian Gerner and Torben Hansen, 1993, "The Crisis of Societal Security in the Former Soviet Union," in Ole Waever *et al.*, *Identity, Migration and the New Security Agenda in Europe*. London: Pinter Publishers, Ltd., pp. 110–30.

Lemarchand, René, 1983, "The State and Society in Africa: Ethnic Stratification and Restratification in Historical and Comparative Perspective," in Donald Rothchild and Victor Olorunsola, eds., *State Versus Ethnic Claims: African Policy Dilemmas*. Boulder, CO: Westview Press, pp. 44–66.

1987, "The Dynamics of Factionalism in Contemporary Africa," in Zaki Ergas, ed., *The African State in Transition*. London: Macmillan Press, pp. 149–68.

1991, "Libyan Adventurism," in John Harbeson and Donald Rothchild, eds., *Africa in World Politics*. Boulder, CO: Westview Press, pp. 144–61.

LeoGrande, William, 1990, "Regime Illegitimacy and Revolutionary Movements: Central America," in Barry Schutz and Robert Slater, eds., *Revolution and Political Change in the Third World*. Boulder, CO: Lynne Rienner, pp. 142–59.

Levy, Jack, 1983, *War in the Modern Great Power System, 1495–1975*. Lexington: University of Kentucky Press.

1989, "The Causes of War: A Review of Theories and Evidence," in Philip E. Tetlock *et al.*, eds., *Behavior, Society, and Nuclear War*, vol. I, New York: Oxford University Press, pp. 209–333.

1994, "Learning and Foreign Policy: Sweeping a Conceptual Minefield." *International Organization* 48, 2, pp. 279–312.

Lewis, I. M., 1988, *A Modern History of Somalia: Nation and State in the Horn of Africa*. Boulder: Westview Press.

Lewis, I. M., 1989, "The Ogaaden and the Fragility of Somali Segmentary Nationalism." *African Affairs* 88, October, pp. 573–81.

Little, Richard, 1975, *Intervention*. London: M. Robertson.

Loveman Brian and Thomas Davies Jr., 1985, "Introduction," in Ernesto Che

References

ionGuevara. *Guerrilla Warfare*. Lincoln: University of Nebraska Press, pp. 1–36.

Lowenthal, Abraham, 1986, "Introduction," in Abraham Lowenthal and Samuel Fitch, eds., *Armies and Politics in Latin America*. New York and London: Holmes and Meier, pp. 3–25.

Luciani, Giacomo, ed., 1990, *The Arab State*. London: Routledge, pp. xvii–xxxii, 65–84.

Luciani, Giacomo and Ghassan Salamé, 1990, "The Politics of Arab Integration," in Giacomo Luciani, ed., *The Arab State*. London: Routledge, pp. 394–420.

MacCartney, C. A., 1934, *National States and National Minorities*. London: Oxford University Press.

Macfarlane, Neil, 1991, "The Impact of Superpower Collaboration in the Third World," in Thomas Weiss and Meryl Kessler, eds., *Third World Security in the Post Cold War Era*. Boulder, CO: Lynne Rienner, pp. 125–45.

Machel, Samora, 1982, "White Mozambicans," in Aquino de Bragança and Immanuel Wallerstein, eds., *The African Liberation Reader*. vol. II: *The National Liberation Movements*. London: Zed Press, p. 177.

Mair, Lucy, 1928, *The Protection of Minorities*. London: Christophers.

Mann, Michael, 1986, "The Autonomous Power of the State: Its Origins, Mechanisms and Results," in John Hall, ed., *States in History*. New York: Basil Blackwell, pp. 109–36.

Maoz, Zeev and N. Abdolali, 1989, "Regime Types and International Conflict." *Journal of Conflict Resolution*, 33, 1, pp. 3–35.

Maoz, Zeev and Bruce Russett, 1990, "Alliances, Contiguity, Wealth, and Political Stability: Is the Lack of Conflict Among Democracies a Statistical Artifact?" Paper prepared for the Annual Meetings of the American Political Science Association.

Marenin, Otwin, 1987, "The Managerial State," in Zaki Ergas, ed., *The African State in Transition*. London: Macmillan, pp. 61–82.

Markotich, Stan, 1993a, "Ethnic Serbs in Tudjman's Croatia." *RFE/RL Research Report*, 24 September, pp. 28–33.

1993b, "Croatia's Krajina Serbs." *RFE/RL Research Report*, 15 October, pp. 5–10.

Marti, Serge, 1995, "L'argent sale quitte massivement la Russie." *Le Monde*, March 26/27, p. 3.

Mason, David, 1990, "Dynamics of Revolutionary Change: Indigenous Factors," in Barry Schutz and Robert Slater, eds., *Revolution and Political Change in the Third World*. Boulder, CO: Lynne Rienner, pp. 30–53.

Maugué, Pierre, 1979, *Contre l'Etat-nation*. Paris: Editions Denoel.

Mayall, James, 1991, "The Variety of States," in Cornelia Navari, ed., *The Condition of States. A Study in International Political Theory*. Milton Keynes: Open University Press, pp. 44–60.

Mazrui, Ali, 1983, "Francophone Nations and English-Speaking States: Imperial Ethnicity and African Political Formations," in Donald Rothchild

238

and Victor Olorunsola, eds., *State Versus Ethnic Claims: African Policy Dilemmas*. Boulder, CO: Westview Press, pp. 25–43.

Mazrui, Ali and Michael Tidy, 1984, *Nationalism and New States in Africa*. London: Heinemann.

Mbembe, Achille, 1991, "Power and Obscenity in the Post-Colonial Period: The Case of Cameroon," in James Manor, ed., *Rethinking Third World Politics*. New York: Longman, pp. 166–82.

McKinlay, R., 1989, *Third World Military Expenditure. Determinants and Implications*. London: Pinter Publishers.

McNeill, William, 1986, *Polyethnicity and National Unity in World History*. Toronto: University of Toronto Press.

Meneses, Emilio, 1991, "Maintaining a Regional Navy with Very Limited Resources: The Chilean Case, 1900–1990," *Defense Analysis* 7, pp. 345–62.

1993, "Percepciones de Amenazas Militares y Agenda para la Politica de Defensa," in Rigoberto Cruz Johnson and Augusto Varas Fernandez, eds., *Percepciones de Amenaza y Politicas de Defensa en America Latina*. Santiago: FLACSO/CEEA, pp. 364–441.

Midlarsky, Manus, ed., 1992, *The Internationalization of Communal Strife*. London and New York: Routledge.

Migdal, Joel, 1988, *Strong States and Weak Societies: State-Society Relations and State Capabilities in the Third World*. Princeton: Princeton University Press.

Milenky, Edward, 1977, "Latin America's Multilateral Diplomacy: Integration, Disintegration and Interdependence," *International Affairs* 53, January, pp. 73–96.

Miles, William and David Rochefort, 1991, "Nationalism versus Ethnic Identity in Sub-Saharan Africa." *American Political Science Review* 85, 2, pp. 393–403.

Millán, Victor, 1983, "Regional Conflict-Building in the Military Field: The Case of Latin America," in Michael Morris and Victor Millán, eds., *Controlling Latin Amerian Conflicts: Ten Approaches*. Boulder, CO: Westview Press, pp. 89–97.

Minogue, Kenneth, 1993, "Olympianism and the Denigration of Nationality," in Claudio Véliz, ed., *The Worth of Nations: The Boston, Melbourne, Oxford Conversazioni on Culture and Society*. Boston: Boston University, pp. 71–81.

Mintz, Alex and N. Geva, 1993, "Why Don't Democracies Fight Each Other? An Experimental Study," *Journal of Conflict Resolution*, 37, 3, pp. 484–503.

Mobutu, S., 1979, "Address to the Conseil Nationale Extraordinaire, Dakar," in Ayo Langley, ed., *Ideologies of Liberation in Black Africa 1856–1970*. London: Rex Collings, pp. 722–37.

Mondlane, Eduardo, 1982, "Development of Nationalism in Mozambique," in Aquino de Bragança and Immanuel Wallerstein, eds., *The African Liberation Reader*. vol. II: *The National Liberation Movements*. London: Zed Press, pp. 15–20.

Morales, Waltraud Queiser, 1984, "Bolivian Foreign Policy: The Struggle for Sovereignty," in Jennie Lincoln and Elizabeth Ferris, eds., *The Dynamics of*

References

Latin American Foreign Policies: Challenges for the 1980s. Boulder, CO: Westview Press, pp. 171–94.

Moran, Theodore, 1974, *Multinational Corporations and the Politics of Dependence: Copper in Chile.* Princeton: Princeton Univesity Press.

Morgenthau, Hans J., 1948, *Politics Among Nations.* New York: Alfred A. Knopf.

Moynihan, Daniel, 1993, *Pandemonium. Ethnicity in International Politics.* Oxford: Oxford University Press.

Mueller, John, 1989, *Retreat from Doomsday: The Obsolescence of Major War.* New York: Basic Books.

Nafziger, Wayne and William Richter, 1976, "Biafra and Bangladesh: The Political Economy of Secessionist Conflict." *Journal of Peace Research* 13, 2, pp. 91–109.

National Congress of British West Africa, 1979, Resolution adopted in Accra, March 1920, in Ayo Langley, ed., *Ideologies of Liberation in Black Africa 1856–1970.* London: Rex Collings, pp. 741–7.

Navari, Cornelia, 1991, "Introduction: The State as a Contested Concept in International Relations," in Cornelia Navari, ed., *The Condition of States. A Study in International Political Theory.* Milton Keynes: Open University Press, pp. 1–18.

Neto, Agostinho, 1982, "Not an Isolated Struggle," in Aquino de Bragança and Immanuel Wallerstein, eds., *The African Liberation Reader.* vol. II: *The National Liberation Movements.* London: Zed Press, pp. 171–3.

Neuberger, Benyamin, 1986, *National Self-Determination in Postcolonial Africa.* Boulder, CO: Lynne Rienner.

1991, "Irredentism and Politics in Africa," in Naomi Chazan, ed., *Irredentism and International Politics.* Boulder, CO: Lynne Rienner, pp. 97–110.

Newbury, Catharine, 1992, "Rwanda: Recent Debates over Governance and Rural Development," in Göran Hydén and Michael Bratton, eds., *Governance and Politics in Africa.* Boulder, CO: Lynne Rienner, pp. 193–220.

Newland, Kathleen, 1993, "Ethnic Conflict and Refugees," in Michael Brown, ed., *Ethnic Conflict and International Security.* Princeton: Princeton University Press, pp. 143–64.

Newman, Saul, 1991, "Does Modernization Breed Ethnic Political Conflict?" *World Politics* 43, April, pp. 451–70.

Nielebock, Thomas, 1992, "Once Again: Peace Through Democracy – but Which Kind of Peace and How to Explain It?" Paper prepared for the 33rd Annual Convention of the International Studies Association, Atlanta, Georgia, 31 March-4 April.

Nietschmann, Bernard, 1987, "The Third World War." *Cultural Survival Quarterly* 11, 3, pp. 1–16.

Nohlen, Dieter, and Mario Fernandez B., 1990, "Economy, State and Social Policy in Latin America," in *Law and the State: A Biannual Collection of Recent German Contributions to these Fields.* Tübingen: Institut für Wissenschaftliche Zusammenarbeit, pp. 73–98.

1991, "Democración y Política Exterior. Análisis Comparado en Torno a tres Casos: Argentina, Brasil y Uruguay," *Estudios Internacionales*, 24, pp. 229–59.

Norbu, Dawa, 1992, *Culture and the Politics of Third World Nationalism*. London and New York: Routledge.

Nordstrom, Carolyn, 1994, "Warzones: Cultures of Violence, Militarization and Peace." Canberra: Peace Research Centre, the Australian National University, Working Paper No. 145.

North, Liisa, 1986, "The Military and Chilean Politics," in Abraham Lowenthal and Samuel Fitch, eds., *Armies and Politics in Latin America*. New York and London: Holmes and Meier, pp. 167–98.

Norton, Augustus, 1991, "The Security Legacy of the 1980s in the Third World," in Thomas Weiss and Meryl Kessler, eds., *Third World Security in the Post Cold War Era*. Boulder, CO: Lynne Rienner, pp. 19–33.

Nun, José, 1986, "The Middle-Class Military Coup Revisited," in Abraham Lowenthal and Samuel Fitch, eds., *Armies and Politics in Latin America*. New York: Holmes and Meier, pp. 59–95.

Nussbaum, Arthur, 1954, *A Concise History of the Law of Nations*. New York: Macmillan.

Nyerere, Julius, 1979, "The Dilemma of the Pan-Africanist," in Ayo Langley, ed., *Ideologies of Liberation in Black Africa 1856–1970*. London: Rex Collings, pp. 341–55.

Nyong'o, Peter Anyang, 1991, "The Implications of Crises and Conflicts in the Upper Nile Valley," in Francis Deng and William Zartman, eds., *Conflict Resolution in Africa*. Washington, DC: The Brookings Institution, pp. 95–114.

Nzo, Alfred, 1982, "Our Anti-Imperialist Commitment," in Aquino de Bragança and Immanuel Wallerstein, eds., *The African Liberation Reader*. vol. II: *The National Liberation Movements*. London: Zed Press, pp. 2–5.

Obasanjo, Olusegun, 1991, "Preface," in Francis Deng and William Zartman, eds., *Conflict Resolution in Africa*. Washington, DC: The Brookings Institution, pp. xiii–xx.

O'Brien, Donal Cruise, 1991, "The Show of State in a Neo-Colonial Twilight: Francophone Africa," in James Manor, ed., *Rethinking Third World Politics*. New York: Longman, pp. 145–66.

Odhiambo, Atieno, 1991, "The Economics of Conflict among Marginalized Peoples of Eastern Africa," in Francis Deng and William Zartman, eds., *Conflict Resolution in Africa*. Washington, DC: The Brookings Institution, pp. 292–8.

O'Donnell, Guillermo, 1986, "Modernization and Military Coups: Theory, Comparisons, and the Argentine Case," in Abraham Lowenthal and Samuel Fitch, eds., *Armies and Politics in Latin America*. New York and London: Holmes and Meier, pp. 96–133.

Omoniyi, Bandele, 1979, "Manifesto," in Ayo Langley (ed.). *Ideologies of Liberation in Black Africa 1856–1970*. London: Rex Collings, pp. 180–8.

Ottaway, Marina, 1987, "The Crisis of the Socialist States," in Zaki Ergas, ed., *The African State in Transition*. London: Macmillan, pp. 169–90.

1990, "Anti-Marxist Insurgencies: Angola's UNITA," in Barry Schutz and Robert Slater, eds., *Revolution and Political Change in the Third World.* Boulder, CO: Lynne Rienner, pp. 229–46.

Pan African Congress, 1979, "Resolution Adopted in Paris, 1919," in Ayo Langley, ed., *Ideologies of Liberation in Black Africa 1856–1970.* London: Rex Collings, pp. 740–1.

Peace Research Centre, Australian National University, 1993, *Pacific Research,* 6, 4, pp. 13–16.

Pfaff, William, 1993, *The Wrath of Nations: Civilization and the Furies of Nationalism.* New York: Simon and Schuster.

Picard, Elizabeth, 1990, "Arab Military in Politics: From Revolutionary Plot to Authoritarian Regime," in Giacomo Luciani, ed., *The Arab State.* London: Routledge, pp. 189–219.

Posen, Barry, 1993, "The Security Dilemma and Ethnic Conflict," in Michael E. Brown, ed., *Ethnic Conflict and International Security.* Princeton: Princeton University Press, pp. 103–24.

Premdas, Ralph, 1991, "The Internationalization of Ethnic Conflict: Some Theoretical Explorations," in K. de Silva and R. May, eds., *Internationalization of Ethnic Conflict.* London: Pinter Publishers, pp. 10–25.

Puchala, Donald J., 1993, "Western Europe," in Robert H. Jackson and Alan James, eds., *States in a Changing World: A Contemporary Analysis.* London: Clarendon Press, pp. 69–92.

Puig, Juan Carlos, 1983, "Controlling Latin American Conflicts: Current Judicial Trends and Perspectives for the Future," in Michael A. Morris and Victor Millán, eds., *Controlling Latin American Conflicts: Ten Approaches.* Boulder, CO: Westview Press, pp. 11–39.

1985, "Solucion Pacifica de Conflictos en America Latina y Critica de los Procedimientos Existentes." Santiago de Chile: Seminar Internacional, FLACSO, June 5–7.

Quimby, Robert, 1957, *The Background of Napoleonic Warfare.* New York: Columbia University Press.

Rasler, Karen A., 1992, "International Influences on the Origins and Outcomes of Internal War: A Comparative Analysis of the 1958 and 1975–6 Lebanese Civil Wars," in Manus Midlarsky, ed., *The Internationalization of Communal Strife.* London and New York: Routledge, pp. 93–117.

Rasler, Karen A. and William R. Thompson, 1989, *War and Statemaking: The Shaping of the Global Powers.* Boston: Unwin Hyman.

Ravenhill, John, 1991, "Africa and Europe: The Dilution of a Special Relationship," in John Harbeson and Donald Rothchild, eds., *Africa in World Politics.* Boulder, CO: Westview Press, pp. 179–201.

Retat, Pierre, 1993, "The Evolution of the Citizen from the Ancien Régime to the Revolution," in Renée Waldinger *et al.*, eds., *The French Revolution and the Meaning of Citizenship.* Westport, CT: Greenwood, pp. 3–16.

Reuters, 1990, "Roads Sealed as Yugoslav Unrest Mounts." *New York Times.* August 19, p. I(3).

Rice, Carol, 1994, "Beyond the Security Dilemma: Structure, Agency and Strategic Thought in the Post-Cold War Era." Paper presented at the 1994 Learned Societies Conference, Calgary, Alberta, (mimeo.).

Rice, Edward, 1988, *Wars of the Third Kind: Conflict in Underdeveloped Countries.* Berkeley: University of California Press.

Rieff, David, 1993, "Croatia: A Crisis of Meaning." *World Policy Journal,* Summer, pp. 41–5.

Rodinson, Maxime, 1989, "The Notion of Minority and Islam," in Gerard Chaliand, ed., *Minority Peoples in the Age of Nation-States.* London: Pluto Press, pp. 119–25.

Roberts, Adam, 1993, "The United Nations and International Security," in Michael Brown, ed., *Ethnic Conflict and International Security.* Princeton: Princeton University Press, pp. 207–36.

Rothchild, Donald, 1986, "Interethnic Conflict and Policy Analysis in Africa." *Ethnic and Racial Studies* 9, 1, pp. 66–86.

1991, "An Interactive Model for State-Ethnic Relations," in Francis Deng and William Zartman, eds., *Conflict Resolution in Africa.* Washington, DC: The Brookings Institution, pp. 190–218.

Rothchild, Donald and Victor Olorunsola, eds., 1983, *State Versus Ethnic Claims: African Policy Dilemmas.* Boulder, CO: Westview Press, pp. 1–24, 233–50.

Rothenberg, Gunther, 1978, *The Art of War in the Age of Napoleon.* Bloomington, IN: Indiana University Press.

Rouquié, Alain, 1986, "Demilitarization and Institutionalization of Military-Dominated Polities in Latin America," in Abraham Lowenthal and Samuel Fitch, eds., *Armies and Politics in Latin America.* New York: Holmes and Meier, pp. 444–77.

Ruggie, John, 1993, "Territoriality and Beyond: Problematizing Modernity in International Relations." *International Organization* 47,Winter, pp. 139–74.

Russell, Roberto, 1990, *Politica Exterior y Toma de Decisiones en America Latina.* Buenos Aires: Grupo Editor Latinoamericano S. R. L.

Russell, Sharon Stanton, 1990, "Migration and Political Integration in the Arab World," in Giacomo Luciani, ed., *The Arab State.* London: Routledge pp. 373–94.

Russett, Bruce, 1990, *Controlling the Sword.* Cambridge, MA: Harvard University Press.

1993, *Grasping the Democratic Peace: Principles for a Post-Cold War World.* Princeton: Princeton University Press.

Russett, Bruce and Harvey Starr, 1989, *World Politics: The Menu for Choice.* 3rd edn. San Francisco: Freeman.

Ryan, Stephen, 1990, *Ethnic Conflict and International Relations.* Aldershot, Hants.: Dartmouth.

Sa'adah, Anne, 1990, *The Shaping of Liberal Politics in Revolutionary France.* Princeton, NJ: Princeton University Press.

Sabagh, Georges, 1990, "Immigrants in the Gulf Countries: Sojourners or

Settlers?" in Giacomo Luciani, ed., *The Arab State*. London: Routledge, pp. 349–72.

Sadeniemi, Pentti, 1995, "Principles of Legitimacy and International Relations." Helsinki: Ph.D. Dissertation, Department of Political Science, University of Helsinki.

Salamé, Ghassan, 1990, "Strong and Weak States: A Qualified Return to the Muqaddimah," in Giacomo Luciani, ed., *The Arab State*. London: Routledge, pp. 29–64.

Samarasinghe, S, 1990, "Introduction," in Ralph Premdas, S. Samarasinghe, and Alan Anderson, eds., *Secessionist Movements in Comparative Perspective*. London: Pinter Publishers, pp, 1–9.

Samatar, Said and David D. Laitin, 1987, *Somalia: Nation in Search of a State*. Boulder CO: Westview Press.

Sampat-Mehta, R., 1973, *Minority Rights and Obligations*. Ottawa: Harpell's Press.

Samudavanija, Chai-Anan, 1991, "The Three Dimensional State," in James Manor, ed., *Rethinking World Politics*. New York: Longman, pp. 15–23.

Schopflin, George, 1991, "Nationalism and National Minorities in East and Central Europe." *Journal of International Affairs* 45, 1, pp. 51–64.

Schutz, Barry and Robert Slater, eds., 1990, *Revolution and Political Change in the Third World*. Boulder, CO: Lynne Rienner, pp. 3–18, 247–50.

Scruton, Roger, 1993, "The First Person Plural," in Claudio Véliz, ed., *The Worth of Nations: The Boston, Melbourne, Oxford Conversazioni on Culture and Society*. Boston: Boston University, pp. 82–96.

Selcher, Wayne, 1985, "Brazilian–Argentine Relations in the 1980s: From Wary Rivalry to Friendly Competition." *Journal of Interamerican Studies and World Affairs* 27, Summer, pp. 25–53.

1986, "Current Dynamics and Future Prospects of Brazil's Relations with Latin America: Toward a Pattern of Bilateral Cooperation." *Journal of Interamerican Studies and World Affairs* 28, Summer, pp. 67–99.

1990, "Brazil and the Southern Cone Subsystem," in G. Pope Atkins, ed., *South America into the 1990s. Evolving International Relationships in a New Era*. Boulder, CO: Westview Press, pp. 87–120.

Senghor, Leopold Sedar, 1979, "Nationhood: Report on the Doctrine and Program of the Party of African Federation," in Ayo Langley, ed., *Ideologies of Liberation in Black Africa 1856–1970*. London: Rex Collings, pp. 528–45.

Sewell, William H. Jr., 1988, "Le Citoyen/La Citoyenne: Activity, Passivity, and the Revolutionary Concept of Citizenship," in Colin Lucas, ed., *The French Revolution and the Creation of Modern Political Culture*, vol. II: *The Political Culture of the French Revolution*. Oxford: Pergamon Press, pp. 105–24.

Sharp, Walter R. and Grayson Kirk, 1941, *Contemporary International Politics*. New York: Rinehard and Co.

Sherman, Richard, 1980, *Eritrea: the Unfinished Revolution*. New York: Praeger.

Shiels, Frederick, 1984, "Introduction," in Frederick Shiels, ed., *Ethnic Separatism and World Politics*. Lanham: University Press of America, pp. 1–15.

Simango, Uria T., 1982, "Gloomy Situation in FRELIMO," in Aquino de Bragança and Immanuel Wallerstein, eds., *The African Liberation Reader*, vol. II: *The National Liberation Movements*. London: Zed Press, pp. 125–7.

Small, Melvin and J. David Singer, 1982, *Resort to Arms: International and Civil Wars 1816–1980*. Beverly Hills, CA: Sage.

Smith, Anthony, 1979, "Towards a Theory of Ethnic Separatism." *Ethnic and Racial Studies* 2, 1, pp. 21–37.

   1981, "War and Ethnicity: The Role of Warfare in the Formation, Self-Images and Cohesion of Ethnic Communities." *Ethnic and Racial Studies* 4, 4, pp. 373–96.

   1983, *State and Nation in the Third World*. Wheatsheaf Books Ltd.

   1984, Review Article: "Ethnic Persistence and National Transformation." *The British Journal of Sociology* 35, September, pp. 452–61.

   1986, "State-Making and Nation-Building," in John Hall, ed., *States in History*. New York: Basil Blackwell, pp. 229–62.

   1988, "The Myth of the Modern Nation and the Myths of Nations." *Ethnic and Racial Studies* 11, 1, pp. 1–26.

   1989, "The Origins of Nations." *Ethnic and Racial Studies* 12, 3, pp. 341–67.

   1990, "The Supersession of Nationalism?" *International Journal of Comparative Sociology*, 31, pp. 1–30.

   1991, *National Identity*. Reno: University of Nevada Press.

   1992, "Chosen Peoples: Why Ethnic Groups Survive." in *Ethnic and Racial Studies*, 15, 3, pp. 436–56.

   1993, "The Ethnic Sources of Nationalism," in Michael Brown, ed., *Ethnic Conflict and International Security*. Princeton: Princeton University Press, pp. 27–42.

Snyder, Jack, 1993, "Nationalism and the Crisis of the Post-Soviet State," in Michael Brown, ed., *Ethnic Conflict and International Security*. Princeton: Princeton University Press, pp. 79–102.

Sorenson, Georg, 1994, "International Relations After the Cold War: What has Changed? Toward a Theory of Units." La Jolla, CA: School of International Relations and Pacific Studies, University of California, San Diego, (pamphlet).

Spruyt, Hendrik, 1994, "Institutional Selection in International Relations: State Anarchy as Order." *International Organization* 48, Autumn, pp. 527–57.

Stavenhagen, Rodolfo, 1991, "Ethnic Conflicts and their Impact on International Society." *International Social Science Journal* 127, February, pp. 117–31.

Stedman, Stephen, 1991, "Conflict and Conflict Resolution in Africa: A Conceptual Framework," in Francis Deng and William Zartman, eds., *Conflict Resolution in Africa*. Washington, DC: The Brookings Institution, pp. 367–99.

Stepan, Alfred, 1986, "The New Professionalism of Internal Warfare and Military Role Expansion," in Abraham Lowenthal and Samuel Fitch, eds., *Armies and Politics in Latin America*. New York and London: Holmes and Meier, pp. 134–50.

References

Sterling, Richard, 1979, "Ethnic Separatism in the International System," in Raymond Hall, ed., *Ethnic Autonomy – Comparative Dynamics: The Americas, Europe and the Developing World*. New York: Pergamon Press, pp. 413–25.

Stone, John, 1983, "Ethnicity Versus the State: The Dual Claims of State Coherence and Ethnic Self-Determination," in Donald Rothchild and Victor Olorunsola, eds., *State Versus Ethnic Claims: African Policy Dilemmas*. Boulder, CO: Westview Press, pp. 85–99.

Sudetic, Chuck, 1990, "Serb Minority Seeks Role in Separate Croatia." *New York Times*, August 7, p. A7.

Ternon, Yves, 1989, "Reflections on Genocide," in Gerard Chaliand, ed., *Minority Peoples in the Age of Nation-States*. London: Pluto Press, pp. 126–48.

Thakur, Ramesh, 1994, "From Peacekeeping to Peace Enforcement: The UN Operation in Somalia." *The Journal of Modern African Studies* 32, 3, pp. 387–410.

Thomas, Caroline, 1989, "Conclusion: Southern Instability, Security and Western Concepts – On an Unhappy Marriage and the Need for a Divorce," in Caroline Thomas and Paikiasothy Saravanamuttu, eds., *The State and Instability in the South*. New York: St. Martin's Press, pp. 174–92.

Thompson, Mark, 1992, *A Paper House: The Ending of Yugoslavia*. London: Hutchinson Radius.

Thompson, Robert and Joseph Rudolph Jr., 1989, "The Ebb and Flow of Ethnoterritorial Politics in the Western World," in Joseph Rudolph Jr. and Robert Thompson, eds., *Ethnoterritorial Politics, Policy, and the Western World*. Boulder, CO: Lynne Rienner, pp. 1–14.

Thorndike, Tony, 1989, "Representational Democracy in the South: The Case of the Commonwealth Caribbean," in Caroline Thomas and Paikiasothy Saravanamuttu, eds., *The State and Instability in the South*. New York: St. Martin's Press, pp. 13–40.

Tilly, Charles, 1990, *Coercion, Capital, and European States, A.D. 990–1990*. Cambridge, MA: Basil Blackwell.

Touval, Saadia, 1972, *The Boundary Politics of Independent Africa*. Cambridge, MA: Harvard University Press.

Tow, William, 1990, *Subregional Security Cooperation in the Third World*. Boulder, CO: Lynne Rienner.

Trent, John, 1974, "The Politics of Nationalist Movements – A Reconsideration," *Canadian Review of Studies in Nationalism* 2, 1, pp. 157–69.

Treverton, Gregory F, 1983, "Interstate Conflict in Latin America." Paper prepared for the Security and Peacekeeping Working Group of the Inter-American Dialogue, Harvard University, January (mimeo).

UNAR, 1982, "Rumbezia, Not Mozambique," in Aquino de Bragança and Immanuel Wallerstein, eds., *The African Liberation Reader*, vol. II: *The National Liberation Movements*. London: Zed Press, pp. 174–7.

UPA, 1982, "Colonization and Africa," in Aquino de Bragança and Immanuel Wallerstein, eds., *The African Liberation Reader*, vol. II: *The National Liberation Movements*. London: Zed Press, pp. 75–6.

246

Van Creveld, Martin, 1991, *The Transformation of War*. New York: The Free Press.

van den Berghe, Pierre, 1983, "Class, Race and Ethnicity in Africa." *Ethnic and Racial Studies* 6, 2, pp. 221–36.

van Klaveren, Alberto, 1984, "The Analysis of Latin American Foreign Policies: Theoretical Perspectives," in Heraldo Munoz and Joseph Tulchin, eds., *Latin American Nations in World Politics*. Boulder, CO: Westview Press, pp. 1–21.

Varas, Augusto, 1983, "Controlling Conflict in South America: National Approaches," in Michael Morris and Victor Millán, eds., *Controlling Latin American Conflicts: Ten Approaches*. Boulder, CO: Westivew Press, pp. 71–87.

1987, "De la competencia a la cooperación militar en America Latina," *Estudios Internacionales*, January–March, p. 7.

1993, "La Post-Guerra Fria, la Seguridad Hemisferica y la Defensa Nacional," in Rigoberto Cruz Johnson and Augusto Varas, eds., *Percepciones de Amenaza y Politicas de Defensa en America Latina*. Santiago: FLACSO/CEEA, pp. 3–69.

Vasquez, John, 1993, *The War Puzzle*. Cambridge: Cambridge University Press.

Väyrynen, Raimo, 1984, "Regional Conflict Formations: An Intractable Problem of International Relations." *Journal of Peace Research*, 21, 4, pp. 337–59.

1994, "Towards a Theory of Ethnic Conflicts and their Resolution." Occasional Paper 6:OP:4, Joan B. Kroc Institute for International Peace Studies, University of Notre Dame, South Bend, IN.

Veatch, Richard, 1983, "Minorities and the League of Nations," in The United Nations Library, *The League of Nations in Retrospect: Proceedings of the Symposium*. Berlin: Walter de Gruyter.

Velit, Juan, 1993, "El Contexto Politico-Estrategico del Peru," in Rigoberto Cruz Johnson and Augusto Varas, eds., *Percepciones de Amenaza y Politicas de Defensa en America Latina*. Santiago: FLACSO/CEEA, pp. 213–48.

Voll, John and Fred von der Mehden, 1990, "Religious Resurgence and Revolution: Islam," in Barry Schutz and Robert Slater, eds., *Revolution and Political Change in the Third World*. Boulder, CO: Lynne Rienner, pp. 99–116.

Waever, Ole, Barry Buzan, Morten Kelstrup, Pierre Lemaitre, *et al.*, 1993, *Identity, Migration and the New Security Agenda in Europe*. London: Pinter Publishers.

Wai, Dunstan, 1983, "Geoethnicity and the Margin of Autonomy in the Sudan," in Donald Rothchild and Victor Olorunsola, eds., *State Versus Ethnic Claims: African Policy Dilemmas*. Boulder, CO: Westview Press, pp. 304–30.

Wallensteen, Peter and Karin Axell, 1994, "Conflict Resolution and the End of the Cold War, 1989–1993." *Journal of Conflict Resolution* 31, 3, pp. 333–49.

Walt, Stephen, 1992, "Revolutions and War." *World Politics* 44, April, pp. 321–68.

Waltz, Kenneth, 1979, *Theory of International Politics*. Reading, MA: Addison-Wesley.

Weber, Eugene, 1976, *Peasants into Frenchmen: The Modernization of Rural France, 1870–1914*. Stanford, CA: Stanford University Press.

Weber, Max, 1978, *Economy and Society: An Outline of Interpretive Sociology*. Berkeley, CA: University of California Press.

Weiner, Myron, 1992, "Peoples and States in a New Ethnic Order?" *Third World Quarterly* 13, 2, pp. 317–33.

Welsh, David, 1993, "Domestic Politics and Ethnic Conflict," in Michael Brown, ed., *Ethnic Conflict and International Security*. Princeton: Princeton University Press, pp. 43–60.

Wiarda, Howard, 1990, "South American Domestic Politics and Foreign Policy," in G. Pope Atkins, ed., *South America into the 1990s. Evolving International Relationships in a New Era*. Boulder, CO: Westview Press, pp. 27–52.

Wilson, Woodrow, 1889, *The State: Elements of Historical and Practical Politics*. Boston: Heath.

Windsor, Philip, 1991, "The State and War," in Cornelia Navari, ed., *The Condition of States. A Study in International Political Theory*. Milton Keynes: Open University Press, pp. 125–42.

Young, Crawford, 1983, "Comparative Claims to Political Sovereignty: Biafra, Katanga, Eritrea," in Donald Rothchild and Victor Olorunsola, eds., *State Versus Ethnic Claims: African Policy Dilemmas*. Boulder, CO: Westview Press, pp. 199–232.

1985, "Ethnicity and the Colonial and Post-Colonial State in Africa," in Paul Brass, ed., *Ethnic Groups and the State*. London: Croom Helm, pp. 57–93.

1991a, "The Heritage of Colonialism," in John Harbeson and Donald Rothchild, eds., *Africa in World Politics*. Boulder, CO: Westview Press, pp. 19–38.

1991b, "Self-Determination, Territorial Integrity and the African State System," in Francis Deng and William Zartman, eds., *Conflict Resolution in Africa*. Washington, DC: The Brookings Institution, pp. 320–46.

Young, Robert A., 1994, "How Do Peaceful Secessions Happen?" *Canadian Journal of Political Science*, 27, 4, pp. 773–92.

Young, Tom, 1989, "The State and Instability in Southern Africa," in Caroline Thomas and Paikiasothy Saravanamuttu, eds., *The State and Instability in the South*. New York: St. Martin's Press, pp. 112–26.

Zartman, William, 1988, "Introduction," in Adeed Dawisha and William Zartman, eds., *Beyond Coercion. The Durability of the Arab State*. London: Croom Helm, pp. 1–13.

1989, *Ripe for Resolution. Conflict and Intervention in Africa*. Oxford: Oxford University Press.

1990, "Opposition as Support of the State," in Giacomo Luciani, ed., *The Arab State*. London: Routledge, pp. 220–46.

1991a, "Conflict Reduction: Prevention, Management and Resolution," in Francis Deng and William Zartman, eds., *Conflict Resolution in Africa*. Washington, DC: The Brookings Institution, pp. 299–319.

1991b, "Inter-African Negotiations," in John Harbeson and Donald Rothchild, eds., *Africa in World Politics*. Boulder, CO: Westview Press, pp. 268–83.

Zartman, William, ed., 1995, *Collapsed States: The Disintegration and Restoration of Legitimate Authority*. Boulder, CO: Westview Press.

Index

Africa, 69, 102, 109, 127
Amin, Idi, 127
anarchy, 7
Anderson, Charles, 93
Angola, civil war in, 133
Arab League, 143
Arab nationalism, 111–12
Argentina, Beagle Channel problem, 160, 170; Brazilian relations, 175; Chilean naval exercises, 178; diplomatic relations of, 160–1; Malvinas War, 167, 170, 176; nineteenth century, 152; Plan Rosario, 160; Treaty of Tlatelolco, 176; United States arms sales to, 162
Aron, Raymond, 35
Association of Southeast Asian Nations (ASEAN), 128
atomic bomb, 11, 188 (*see also* deterrence)
Ayoob, Mohammed, 125, 128, 129, 134

Baker, James, 208
Bangladesh, 126, 194
Baron do Rio Branco, 151–2
Barre, Siad, 120–1, 203
Bismarck, Otto von, 50
Bogotá Pact (1948), 156
Bolivia, 151, 152,154, 173; *coup d'état* in, 155; diplomatic relations with Chile, 161–2; territorial losses, 156, 159; threat perceptions, 160; as weak state, 152; withdrawal from OAS, 163
Bosnia, 194, 196; constitution of, 200; "ethnic cleansing" in, 88; Muslims, 199; Owen–Stoltenberg peace formula, 202; peace proposals, 200; plebiscite (spring, 1992), 199
Braudel, Fernand, 28, 48, 49, 58
Brazil, 162–3; Brazil–Argentine relations,

175; as empire, 151–2; military regime in, 161, 174; as regional hegemon, 151, 157, 162; relations with South America, 162
Breuilly, John, 58
Brewin, Christopher, 146
Bull, Hedley, 141
Butros-Ghali, Butros, 193
Buzan, Barry, 83, 92, 97, 102, 108, 143, 149n,151
Canada, 85, 91, 93, 184; Canadian-Chinese, 4; Quebec, 85, 18
Catholic Church, 17
causes of wars of the "third kind", 127–8, 129; arms transfers, 131–2; contagion phenomenon, 133; domestic sources of, 129–30, 131, 136, 141; external sources of, 129–30, 131; great powers, 133, 134; role of weaponry in, 132; sources of funding for, 133
Chad, 133, 184
Charter of the Organization of American States (OAS), 156, 163, 171
Child, Jack, 164
Chile, 90, 91, 147, 152; Allende regime, 155, 180; Argentine naval exercises, 178; Beagle Channel crisis, 158–9, 170, 176; deterrence of Bolivia/Peru, 162; military intervention in Peru, 151; Peruvian crisis, 159; Pinochet, Augusto, 158, 164; United States arms sales to, 162; War of the Pacific (1879–84), 166–7; war plans, 160
China, 144; Soviet relations, 144
citizenship, concept of, 46, 48–9, 80 (*see also* political community; France, citizenship in)
Clausewitz, Karl von, 12; conception of

Index

League of Nations, 5, 56, 59, 66, 194;
Covenant of, 5, 13; Leticia dispute,
arbitration of, 171
Lebanon, 93, 94, 119–120, 121, 130
legitimacy of states, 84, 87, 90, 91, 95–7,
108; erosion of, 109, 110, 113, 119, 139;
horizontal, 84, 85, 87, 88, 90, 91, 93–7,
102, 103, 106, 107, 202; international
aspect of, 95; vertical, 84, 87, 88, 89–97,
102, 103, 104, 202
Lenin, Valdimir Ilyich, 9, 42, 142, 144;
solution to problem of war, 11
liberal-institutionalist theory, as
explanation of South American peace,
161, 171
Locke, John, 46, 99
Louis XIV, 7, 27, 105, 157

MacCartney, C.A., 57
Macfarlane, Neil, 128, 134
Malaysia, 90
Mao Tse-tung, 119, 144
Marcos, Ferdinand, 114
Marenin, Otwin, 121–2
Middle East, 102, 120, 121
Mobutu, Joseph, 69, 104, 109
Morgenthau, Hans. J, 10
Munich, 166

Nagasaki (Japan), *see* atomic bomb
Napoleon Bonaparte, 3, 4, 33, 50, 157
Napoleonic Wars, 4, 33, 50
nationalism, 48, 50, 58, 65, 70, 106;
cultural, 52; and de-colonization, 65, 67,
68, 70
nationalists, Hindu, 112, 186; Sikh, 112–13;
Sinhalese, 113
Nauru, 121
Nazi Germany, as strong state, 142
Nehru, Jawaharlal, 80, 185, 186
neo-realism, 8, 10, 25, 82, 151, 152, 155,
156, 157, 206, 207; explanation of South
American peace, 161, 166 (*see also* Waltz,
Kenneth)
new world order, 41, 123
Nietschmann, Bernard, 107
no-war zones, 147, 157–8; militarized
conflicts in, 148
non-aligned movement, 143
Norbu, Dawa, 67–8
North Atlantic Treaty Organization
(NATO), 6, 14, 46, 206; Bosnia, 200, 201,
207
Northern Ireland, 88
Nyerere, Julius, 69, 203 (*see also* Tanzania)

Organization of African Unity, 143
Organization of Islamic Conference, 127
Organization on Security and Cooperation
in Europe (OSCE), 6, 141, 178; Charter of
Paris (1990), 10, 141
Owen, David, 200 (*see also* Bosnia; United
Nations)

Pakistan, 109
Palestine Liberation Organization (PLO),
73, 119
Paraguay, 154
peace, as condition *within* states, 190
peace movements, 4
peace-through-democracy theory, 180
peace treaties, character of, 20
Peru, 152; crisis with Chile, 158, 159;
Ecuador border incident, 160, 181;
intervention in Ecuador, 151; Rio de
Janeiro Treaty (1942), 163; Sendero
Luminoso rebellion in, 140, 179; Soviet
arms sales to, 162; weak governments
in, 153
Peter the Great, 3, 7, 43, 44
Philippines, Moro insurrection, 127, 135
Pinochet, Augusto, 158, 164 (*see also* Chile)
pluralistic security communities, 147, 158,
160; militarized conflicts in, 148
political community, citizenship in, 46 (*see
also* state); conception of, 17, 45;
definition of, 45, 84, 87; ethnicity, 88–9,
106, 123, 124, 198; language in, 50–2, 55,
56, 57, 81, 107, 124, 198; minorities in, 55,
57, 89, 106, 111, 118, 124; minorities,
exclusion of, 88–9, 111; self-
determination, 56, 58
Pope John Paul II, 159
post-Cold War era, 123
post-colonial state, 72

Quadaffi, Muammar, 103, 112

Rasler, Karen, 130
Rawls, John, 99
Reagan, Ronald, 13; administration, 38–9
refugees, 204
regions, defined, 142–3
rentier states, 103, 118, 121
Rio de Janeiro Treaty (1942), 163
Romania, 114
Rousseau, Jean-Jacques, 6, 7, 10, 11, 14, 25,
44, 188; security dilemma, 9, 44; stag
hunt parable, 7–9, 205
Russia, 118, 121, 126; corruption in, 118
Rwanda, 100, 121; weaponry used in, 132

CAMBRIDGE STUDIES IN INTERNATIONAL RELATIONS